African Americans and the Presidency

Barack Obama's successful run for the presidency has certainly changed the way Americans view race and leadership. However, his campaign was not the first attempt by an African American to gain the White House.

African Americans and the Presidency explores the long history of African American candidates for president and vice president, examining the impact of each candidate on the American public, as well as the contribution they all made toward advancing racial equality in America. Each chapter takes the story one step further in time, through original essays written by top experts, giving depth to these inspiring candidates, some of whom are familiar to everyone, and some whose stories may be new.

Presented with illustrations and a detailed timeline, *African Americans and the Presidency* provides anyone interested in African American history and politics with a unique perspective on the path carved by the predecessors of Barack Obama, and the meaning their efforts had for the United States.

Contributors: Omar H. Ali, Josephine A. V. Allen, Charles Orson Cook, David Cullen, Donald R. Deskins, Jr., Paul Finkelman, Bruce A. Glasrud, Dwonna Naomi Goldstone, Maxine D. Jones, Sherman C. Puckett, James M. Smallwood, Jean Van Delinder, Hanes Walton, Jr., Carolyn Wedin, Kyle G. Wilkison, Cary D. Wintz.

Bruce A. Glasrud is Professor Emeritus of History at California State University, East Bay and retired Dean of the School of Arts and Sciences at Sul Ross State University. Among his co-edited publications are *Black Women in Texas History* and *Buffalo Soldiers in the West: A Black Soldiers Anthology*.

Cary D. Wintz is Professor of History at Texas Southern University. His most recent works include serving as co-editor of *The Encyclopedia of African American History, 1896 to the Present: From the Age of Segregation to the Twenty-first Century*, and authoring *Harlem Speaks: A Living History of the Harlem Renaissance*.

African Americans and the Presidency

The Road to the White House

Edited by
Bruce A. Glasrud
and
Cary D. Wintz

Routledge
Taylor & Francis Group

NEW YORK AND LONDON

First published 2010
by Routledge
270 Madison Avenue New York, NY 10016

Simultaneously published in the UK
by Routledge
2 Park Square, Milton Park, Abingdon, Oxon OX14 4RN

Routledge is an imprint of the Taylor & Francis Group, an informa business

© 2010 Taylor & Francis

Typeset in Minion by
Swales & Willis Ltd, Exeter, Devon
Printed and bound in the United States of America on acid-free paper by
Edwards Brothers, Inc.

Library of Congress Cataloging-in-Publication Data
African Americans and the presidency : the road to the White House / edited by
Bruce A. Glasrud and Cary D. Wintz. — 1st ed.
p. cm.
Includes bibliographical references and index.
1. African American presidential candidates—History. 2. African American
vice-presidential candidates—History. 3. Presidents—United States—Election—History.
4. United States—Politics and government. 5. African Americans—Politics and government.
6. United States—Race relations. I. Glasrud, Bruce A. II. Wintz, Cary D., 1943–
E185.96.A455 2009
324.973—dc22
2009022696

ISBN10: 0–415–80391–8 (hbk)
ISBN10: 0–415–80392–6 (pbk)
ISBN10: 0–203–86433–6 (ebk)

ISBN13: 978–0–415–80391–5 (hbk)
ISBN13: 978–0–415–80392–2 (pbk)
ISBN13: 978–0–203–86433–3 (ebk)

Contents

Timeline

BRUCE A. GLASRUD AND CARY D. WINTZ

1830	National Negro Convention held in Philadelphia, first of numerous—united to protect and enhance their rights
1835	Alexander Twilight elected to Vermont legislature
1839	Blacks involved in formation and convention of the Liberty Party
1855	Early elected black official, John Langston in Ohio
	Frederick Douglass nominated by the Liberty Party as candidate for secretary of state in New York
1856	Frederick Douglass—Political Abolition Party, vice presidential candidate, nomination soon refused and rescinded
1864	National Convention of Colored Citizens met in Syracuse, New York
1865	Thirteenth Amendment
1866	Second elected black to northern state assembly, Massachusetts
1868	Fourteenth Amendment
1870	Fifteenth Amendment
1870–1900	Twenty-two blacks serve in U.S. Congress, two are senators
1872	Equal Rights Party, Frederick Douglass, vice presidential candidate, turned opportunity down
1880	Blanche K. Bruce—Republican Party, received eight votes for vice presidential nomination
1888	Former senator Blanche K. Bruce received votes for vice president at the Republican Party convention

	Frederick Douglass received votes for vice president at the Republican Party convention
1904	George Edwin Taylor—National Liberty Party, first black to be nominated to be president
1916	W. E. B. Du Bois issued call for all-black independent political party
	Robert Church, Jr. organized Lincoln League in Memphis, Tennessee to oppose "lily white" Republicans
1920	No candidates were elected—Texas Black and Tan Party nominated electors for presidency, on ballot 27,247 votes
	Lincoln League held national meeting in Chicago, 400 representatives
1921	Lincoln Independent Political Party, organized in Louisville to counteract "lily white" Republicans
1928	First black congressman elected from north, in Chicago—Republican Oscar De Priest
1932	James W. Ford—Communist Party, vice presidential candidate
1936	National Negro Congress met in Chicago—although accused of being a communist agent, it was devoted to a united movement for racial progress, essentially ended in 1940, though lasted to 1948
	James W. Ford—Communist Party, candidate for vice presidency
1940	James W. Ford—Communist Party, candidate for vice presidency
1948	A. Philip Randolph offered vice presidential nomination of Socialist Party; he turned it down
1952	Charlotta A. Bass—Progressive Party, vice presidential candidate
1960	Reverend Clennon Washington King, Jr.—Independent Afro-American Party (votes only from Alabama), 1,485 votes Afro-American Party; objectives: black equality and social justice, presidential candidate
	Reginald Carter—Independent Afro-American Party, vice president
1964	Clifton DeBerry—Socialist Workers Party, presidential candidate
	Civil Rights Act
1965	Voting Rights Act
1968	Eldridge Cleaver—Peace and Freedom Party presidential nominee, coalition party, black militants and liberal whites, nineteen states, 195,000 votes

Paul Boutelle—Socialist Workers Party, vice presidential candidate

Channing E. Phillips nominated as favorite son for president at Democratic convention, D.C.

Julian Bond nominated for vice presidency at Democratic convention (stepped down, too young)

Dick Gregory—Independent, ran for president

Charlene Mitchell—Communist Party, presidential nominee, first black woman to be party nominee for president—racism the "number one issue in the United States"

Coretta Scott King—Freedom and Peace Party, offered King vice president, she refused the offer

Senator Edward Brooke—Republican, received votes from Republican convention

1969   Congressional Black Caucus organized

1972   Walter E. Fauntroy campaigned, won D.C. primary, toward Democratic nomination

Shirley Chisholm campaigned for Democratic Party nomination, received over 400,000 votes, at the Democratic convention she received votes also for vice president

Andrew Pulley—Socialist Workers Party vice presidential candidate

Julius Hobson—People's Party, vice presidential candidate (Benjamin Spock pres.)

Jarvis Tyner—Communist Party, vice presidential candidate

National Black Political Convention, Gary, Indiana

1976   Barbara Jordan—Democratic Party convention, not a candidate, but did receive delegate votes for president and for vice president

Willie Mae Reid—1976, 1992, Socialist Workers Party vice presidential candidate

Margaret Wright—People's Party, presidential nominee

Ron Dellums turned down nomination for the presidency from the National Black Political Assembly, Dellums also nominated for vice president at Democratic convention

Julian Bond turned down nomination for the presidency from the National Black Political Assembly, the party had not been able to get on any state ballots

Reverend Frederick Douglass Kirkpatrick nominated by NBPA as presidential candidate

Jarvis Tyner—Communist Party, vice presidential candidate

1996 Alan Keyes campaigned for Republican nomination, also sought third-party nominations

Colin Powell in 1995 had a committee to determine his chances of victory if he ran in 1996 for the presidency, Powell eventually chose not to run

James Harris—candidate of Socialist Workers Party for president

Monica Moorehead—Workers World Party, presidential candidate

Joan Jett Blakk—Queer Nation Party, presidential candidate

Isabell Masters—Looking Back Party, presidential candidate

2000 Ezola Broussard Foster—Reform Party (Pat Buchanan, pres.) vice presidential nominee

James Harris—candidate of Socialist Workers Party for president

Monica Moorehead—Workers World Party, presidential candidate

Alan Keyes campaigned for Republican nomination, also sought third-party nominations

Isabell Masters—Looking Back Party, presidential candidate

2004 Al Sharpton campaigned for Democratic nomination for president

John Parker—Workers World Party, also received a few votes from Liberty Union Party of Vermont

Arrin Hawkins—Socialist Workers Party, vice presidential candidate (did not meet age requirement)

Carol Moseley-Braun made brief campaign for Democratic nomination to president—raised nearly $630,000

Mildred Glover campaigned for Democratic nomination for presidency

Isabell Masters—Looking Back Party, presidential candidate

2008 Stewart A. Alexander—Socialist Party, vice presidential candidate

Cynthia McKinney—Green Party, presidential candidate, also endorsed by Workers World Party

Elaine Brown sought Green Party nomination, resigned from party in Dec. 2007

Eugene Puryear—Party for Socialism and Liberalism, vice presidential nominee (not old enough)

Alan Keyes campaigned briefly for Republican nomination; also sought third-party nominations; was selected by America's Independent Party as its presidential candidate

Condoleeza Rice—Republican Party, draft movement for vice presidency

Alyson Kennedy—Socialist Workers Party, vice presidential nominee

Barack Obama—Democratic presidential nominee, Democratic president-elect

2009   Barack Obama—Democrat, President of the United States

Preface

From the first beginning of the United States the vote was often denied to two classes of citizens—African Americans and women. African Americans received citizenship and civil rights protection with the Fourteenth Amendment to the Constitution in 1868; the second section of that amendment included a male-only proviso that resulted in most states denying women the vote. With the Fifteenth Amendment to the Constitution in 1870 black men no longer could be barred from voting due to race but not until passage of the Nineteenth Amendment to the Constitution in 1920 was denial of the vote to women prohibited. Over the years the Supreme Court, state laws, and white racism united to curtail black voting despite constitutional guarantees.

African Americans responded by challenging discriminatory voting restrictions, notably in Texas, and in 1944 the U.S. Supreme Court declared the white primary unconstitutional in *Smith vs. Allwright*. In 1965 the Voting Rights Act protected and enhanced the black vote in southern states by providing federal marshals and registrars to oversee voting in that region of the nation.

With that historically negative picture, imagine the thrill and sense of history we (and a huge number of other Americans) felt during the spring of 2008 when it became obvious that a white woman or a black man could triumph over the obstacles and become a major party candidate for the presidency of the United States. As specialists in the history of African Americans in the United States, the editors were excited spectators when as the days progressed it appeared that the junior senator from Illinois, Senator Barack Obama, would become the Democratic Party's nominee for the presidency, poised to win the November election. It was an astounding time for historians as for other scholars and citizens. Pundits, guest speakers, and election analysts discussed the history of African American candidates in commentary that failed to recognize the significant, albeit forgotten, historic contributions of black candidates to the political process in the United States. Glasrud e-mailed Wintz and suggested preparing a book to fill that gap; Wintz responded positively with "count me in." At the time, we assumed that twenty to twenty-five black presidential and vice presidential candidates had sought their respective offices on the long road to the White House.

Thus began the process of putting together a study that became *African Americans and the Presidency: The Road to the White House.* The editors researched for black candidates, prepared an outline, developed a timeline, and discussed the project with Kimberly Guinta of Routledge publishers. She provided support and encouragement as well as a contract. Glasrud and Wintz then solicited writers for the individual chapters. We were able to induce well-known and distinguished scholars to join the project. It was a diverse lot. Some were well-established senior colleagues; some were up-and-coming junior scholars. Some were black, some white, some were female, some male. The disciplines were varied; some were political scientists, at least one a sociologist, one a constitutional legal scholar, one an urban geographer, one in urban planning and management, another in policy analysis and management, two in English and literature, and some were historians. All were astute observers of the African American experience.

The list of candidates grew. The authors located black candidates the editors overlooked; the number reached forty, forty-five, and, at present, we can say that over fifty African Americans have in some form or another been candidates for the presidency or vice-presidency of the United States. The process started in 1856, when Frederick Douglass was offered the opportunity to run as vice president for the Political Abolitionist Party. In 1872 Douglass once more gained the vice presidential nomination of a political party, this time the Equal Rights Party. Douglass, a Republican, turned both nominations down. In 1904, the first African American candidate for president, George Edwin Taylor, received the nomination of the all-black National Liberty Party. The twentieth century witnessed an increasing number of black office seekers, especially in the years after 1968. Forty years after that date, Barack Obama gained the Democratic Party's nomination for president of the United States and in November was elected the forty-fourth president of this nation. As we all know, in January of 2009 Obama assumed the presidency and became the first black president of the United States. *African Americans and the Presidency* describes this long and courageous road to the White House.

The completed book consists of an Introduction written by the editors, "The African American Quest for the Presidency," and twelve chapters, arranged in essentially a chronological order. Six of the chapters cover individual candidates, ranging from Charlotta Bass to Barack Obama. The other six chapters cover multiple candidates such as a chapter on the Socialist Workers Party and one on black politicians. The remaining pages of the book include a timeline, a selected bibliography, a list of contributors, and an index. There are no comparable studies that investigate the long line that marched toward the election of Obama. Although some authors have addressed black politics in the United States, most notably Ronald W. Walters, *Freedom Is Not Enough: Black Voters, Black Candidates, and American Presidential Politics*, as well as Hanes Walton, Jr. in books such as *Black Political Parties: An Historical and Political Analysis* and his edited *Black Politics and Political Behavior: A Linkage Analysis*, no one has traced the background and emergence of black presidential (and vice-presidential) candidates.

African Americans and the Presidency is intended for a wide audience. For academics certainly; the authors have academic backgrounds and we trust the book will be read and used by faculty, students, and others connected with the academic endeavor. It is designed for course use; potential disciplines include history, political science, law, sociology, and black studies. However, this book is not limited to scholars and students. We encouraged our authors to prepare interesting, readable, and thought-provoking articles. We hope the book, *African Americans and the Presidency*, is of interest to the general public; those interested in the political process, speakers, political analysts, politicians, commentators and newscasters, civil and political rights activists, and the African American community.

We incurred numerous debts during the process of putting this book together. Bill Stein, a friend and colleague always, encouraged us, asked questions, and offered the hospitality of Nesbitt Memorial Library in Columbus, Texas to us before his sudden and early death. Ron Walters, professor of political science at the University of Maryland, answered questions, made recommendations, and otherwise aided the study. Most importantly, we owe a tremendous obligation to the authors of the chapters in this book. You have contributed mightily to a matter of historical importance. We hope you are as pleased with the result as we are. Kimberly Guinta, you listened, you promoted, and you brought your expertise as well as that of the staff at Routledge to bear on our project. Thank you, and thank everyone at Routledge.

Bruce A. Glasrud, Seguin, Texas
Cary D. Wintz, Houston, Texas

Introduction

The African American Quest for the Presidency

BRUCE A. GLASRUD AND CARY D. WINTZ

Forty years ago (1968), the African American political scene began to change dramatically, the culmination of Supreme Court decisions such as *Smith vs. Allwright, Baker vs. Carr*, and *Terry vs. Adams*; amendments to the United States Constitution including the fourteenth, fifteenth, nineteenth, and twenty-fourth; federal legislation, especially the Civil Rights Act (1964) and Voting Rights Act (1965); and determined black leaders and voters. African Americans as never before voted and contended for national office. Some white liberals abetted and encouraged the metamorphoses. All was not well, however. Civil rights leader and black activist Martin Luther King, Jr. was assassinated while leading a reform effort in Memphis, Tennessee. Two months later, while completing a primary election victory in California, Democratic senator Robert F. Kennedy, a white proponent of black rights, was assassinated. Perhaps propelled by these losses on the national scene, African American men and women participated in the national political process as delegates and voters, both vital steps, and also as nominees and candidates.

A few years before, while serving as Attorney General of the United States for his brother, John F. Kennedy, Robert Kennedy asserted that the United States could have a black president within forty years. As Kennedy phrased it, "in the next forty years a Negro can achieve the same position that my brother has." From the perspective of 2008 Kennedy's prescience is remarkable. Forty years after the assassinations of King and Kennedy, an African American, Senator Barack Obama, was the Democratic Party's nominee for

1

the presidency. By mid-September most polls suggested that he was the front-runner to be elected president of the United States, and in November Obama was elected the forty-fourth president of the United States. President Obama was not the first African American to seriously pursue the presidency. In fact, more than forty black men and women candidates paved the way for a black president; Obama stands on the shoulders of those other black leaders and politicians.

Even in 2008 Obama was not the only black candidate in the quest for the presidency; the presidential candidate for the Green Party as well as being endorsed by the Worker's World Party, former Georgia congresswoman Cynthia McKinney, was a black woman. Conservative Alan Keyes acquired the nomination of America's Independent Party as its candidate for the presidency. Three African Americans received vice presidential nominations from their respective parties; some Republicans started a draft movement to make Secretary of State Condoleeza Rice that party's vice presidential candidate. How has this development transpired?

The year 1968 was pivotal. At the Democratic convention, a black man and civil rights activist, Channing E. Phillips, was nominated by a "black caucus" gathering as a favorite son for president of the United States, the first time that an African American had been nominated to be president at a major party political convention. Phillips received sixty-seven votes from eighteen states. Georgia leader and black civil rights activist Julian Bond was nominated for vice president at the Democratic convention in 1968, the first time since Blanche K. Bruce and Frederick Douglass that an African American had been so nominated by a major party convention. In one other momentous development of that historic Democratic convention, delegates of the Loyal Democratic Party of Mississippi (mainly black), were seated in place of the regular "white" Mississippi delegates at the convention. The Democratic candidate for the presidency was Hubert H. Humphrey, a white liberal from Minnesota whose persistence on behalf of black civil rights traced to the Democratic convention of 1948. On the other hand, the party of Abraham Lincoln and numerous former black leaders, the Republican Party, nominated a "law and order" presidential candidate, Richard M. Nixon, who perfected his "southern strategy" for the election.

Other political parties went beyond the two major parties and actually nominated African Americans as candidates in 1968. In one selection, Charlene Mitchell became the first black woman to be a presidential candidate when the Communist Party chose her as standard bearer. Mitchell, who joined the party when she was sixteen, argued that racism was the "number one issue in the United States." That year, former Black Panther leader Eldridge Cleaver carried the banner of the Peace and Freedom Party as the presidential candidate. A coalition group, the Peace and Freedom Party comprised both black militants and liberal whites. Cleaver managed to be on the ballot in nineteen states and garnered over 195,000 votes. Receiving endorsements from the Peace and Freedom as well as the Freedom and Peace Parties, and running as an Independent, the comedian and reformer, Dick Gregory, added to the list of black presidential candidates in 1968. All together, three black men and women ran for the presidency that year. In addition, the Socialist Workers' vice-presidential candidate in 1968 was a black man from New Jersey, Paul Boutelle. The Freedom and Peace Party, a merger of disgruntled communists and the New Politics Party, offered its vice presidential candidacy to Coretta Scott King, who turned it down.

What made 1968 so special for African Americans? The changes in black voting and legal status, the overturning via the civil and political rights struggle of the white southern way of life, the energies of Vietnam War opponents, student activists, the increasing role of women in politics, the successes of liberalism, and responsible and courageous leadership all promoted an unprecedented level of black political activity. To a certain extent it was also a reflection of the political theater of the times—doing the audacious, no matter how hopeless or impractical the idea or goal. One later, and somewhat extreme, example of opportunity and audacity emerged in the candidacy of Joan Jett Blakk. Blakk was the drag persona of Terence Smith, a performer running for president in 1992 and 1996 who documented the campaigns with videos. Likely Barack Obama knew well the history and challenges behind his grueling race for the presidency; his book *The Audacity of Hope: Thoughts on Reclaiming the American Dream* certainly considers the topic of audacity.

Overall, however, the black efforts in 1968 were insignificant in terms of their political results. The Republican candidate Richard Nixon became president. However, even though dispirited, a political base grew from the 1968 election that precipitated an expanded political involvement by African Americans in the United States political process. Three new black Democratic representatives, including Shirley Chisholm, were elected to Congress in 1968 thereby bringing the total to nine. Four years later, black Texan Barbara Jordan and black Georgian Andrew Young became the first African Americans elected to Congress from southern states in the twentieth century.

The election of 1968 reflected the changing nature of black politics. Rather than extremist figures like Eldridge Cleaver (who loved frightening whites) or professional race leaders like Jesse Jackson or Al Sharpton, we began to see the rise of mainstream black politicians, first elected in majority black districts (often specifically gerrymandered for the purpose of electing a black candidate) and black majority cities, then prevailing in cities and states where blacks were not the majority, such as David Dinkins in New York, Lee

P. Brown in Houston, Tom Bradley in Los Angeles, or Douglas Wilder in Virginia.

By 2008 the road to the White House on behalf of black Americans had been laid over a period of a century and a half; it proved to be a long, unpredictable, and arduous journey. This book, *African Americans and the Presidency: The Road to the White House*, offers various aspects of black political history in order to depict this journey: individuals, groups, leadership, mainstream parties, behavior, the political system, black consciousness, candidates, third parties, elections, black women, all-black parties, black politicians, voters, and black power. Barack Obama's successful 2008 campaign for the Democratic nomination and his subsequent campaign for the presidency was certainly an altering political event in U.S. history. People are excited about Obama. However, Obama was far from the first African American to present himself (or herself) as a potential presidential candidate. *African Americans and the Presidency* will examine the long history of African American candidates for the presidency and vice presidency in the United States. The book will help sort out the facts and misinformation that are floating around about the history of blacks and the presidency. The book contains twelve chapters, plus an introduction. Each chapter examines a different candidate or set of candidates, beginning with third party and all-black party efforts and culminating with the Obama campaign. We point out that dozens of African Americans participated in the race for the presidency, but we argue that only relatively recently did serious African American politicians become involved, and that only two really had a chance of being elected. Although authors/scholars have addressed black politics in the United States, no one has traced the background and emergence of black presidential (and vice presidential) candidates.

There is an extensive literature about black politics and history upon which this book is based. First, and foremost, one must look at the works of Hanes Walton, Jr.; among his valuable studies are *Black Political Parties*, *Black Republicans*, *The Negro in Third Party Politics*, *Black Politics*, *Invisible Politics: Black Political Behavior*, *African American Power and Politics: The Political Context Variable*, and an edited work, *Black Politics and Black Political Behavior: A Linkage Analysis* that ties many of these issues together. An author whose works also impacted this study is Ronald W. Walters: three of his studies especially proved significant, *Black Presidential Politics in America*, *Freedom Is Not Enough: Black Voters, Black Candidates, and American Presidential Politics*, and *White Nationalism, Black Interests*. Most recently Omar H. Ali published his instructional *In the Balance of Power: Independent Black Politics and Third-Party Movements in the United States*. PBS moderator and correspondent Gwen Ifill took a look at the features that allowed Barack Obama to ascend to the presidency in *The Breakthrough:*

Politics and Race in the Age of Obama. We have placed a much more complete list of references at the end of the book.

The first national recognition of black voters and their support derived from the Liberty Party. That Party, organized in 1839 with the help of at least two black abolitionists, encouraged African Americans to attend their national convention in 1840, likely the first national political convention that catered to the black electorate. The Liberty Party was a political party dedicated to the abolition of slavery and to broadening the black electorate. Its appeal was to African Americans but it encouraged white Libertarians to seek black support as well. The Liberty Party failed. Black leaders such as Frederick Douglass turned to the fledgling Free Soil Party in 1852, but it was the Republican Party, established in 1854, that promised the most benefits for black Americans, even though it was not opposed to the institution of slavery, just to its spread into the territories. Douglass maintained ties to the political abolitionists, and in 1856 the Political Abolitionist Party nominated Douglass as its vice presidential candidate; however, for various reasons Douglass refused the offer and the PAP rescinded its nomination of Douglass. The Republican Party, with the Union victory in the Civil War, was given credit for ending slavery and known as the party of Abraham Lincoln (the Great Emancipator) and of African Americans. The Republican Party also included other opponents of the Democratic Party; it could and did win presidential elections.

It was during the era of Reconstruction that African Americans (in the South at least) achieved a semblance of political power, and were victorious in elections. Two United States senators, both from Mississippi (Hiram Revels and Blanche K. Bruce) were elected. One African American governor (P. B. S. Pinchback), three lieutenant governors, and twenty congressmen also held office between 1868 and 1901. One electoral opportunity was turned down. In 1872 Frederick Douglass, a leading black Republican, was nominated to be the vice presidential candidate of the Equal Rights Party, to run with its presidential candidate, Victoria Woodhull. Upon consideration he declined the offer. Eight years later, at the Republican convention of 1880, Senator Blanche K. Bruce received eight votes as a nominee for vice president. Both Senator Bruce and Frederick Douglass received votes for vice president at the 1888 Republican Party convention.

Not until the twentieth century were African Americans chosen to be presidential or vice presidential candidates of a political party, and for such a selection to come from a major political party, it took eight years into the twenty-first century. Following their political successes during Reconstruction, black Americans and the Republican Party in the South were removed from office by white racists and Democrats. By the beginning of the twentieth century white Democrats had eliminated most black southerners from the voting process, assuring that blacks would not be elected to a political office, and certainly not the office of president of the United States.

As a result, as in so many other endeavors, blacks turned to themselves. Although during the nineteenth century black leaders worked through the National Negro Convention movement, the Republican Party, and third parties such as the Populists, in 1904 African Americans created the first political party exclusively for and by blacks, the National Liberty Party. To a certain extent based upon the concepts of self-help, struggle, and separation the NLP was reflective of an awareness of black-nationalist efforts, including that of Bishop Henry M. Turner. The National Liberty Party, with delegates from thirty-six states at its convention in St. Louis, chose George Edwin Taylor from Ottumwa, Iowa to be its candidate for the president of the United States in 1904; Taylor thus became the first African American nominated by a political party for president. Born in Arkansas, formerly the editor of a radical labor newspaper in LaCrosse, Wisconsin, the *Wisconsin Labor Advocate*, then editor of *The Negro Solicitor* in Oskaloosa, and in 1900 president of the Negro National Democratic League, Taylor's disillusionment by 1904 with the two major parties led him to accept the nomination.

White political behavior did not change during the ensuing years. By 1920, Texas black and tan Republican Party members were refused seating at the Republican National Convention. Furthermore, when the Republican candidate (Warren G. Harding) visited the Lone Star state, he reached over the hands and heads of black school children to shake the hands of white children. White Texas Democrats were no better; as a result Texas black Republicans created the Black and Tan Republican Party, and ran a slate of electors for the presidency. The Black and Tans came in third with a total of 27,247 votes, in front of American and Socialist Party candidates.

Forty years later, 1960, the Independent Afro-American Party, with a purpose and rationale similar to the two previous all-black political parties, and with the specific objectives of black equality and social justice, selected the Reverend Clennon Washington King, Jr., a civil rights activist, to be its nominee for president and Reginald Carter for vice president. On the ballot only in Alabama, the party totaled 1,485 votes. In 1958 King, with his daughter, tried to integrate an all-white elementary school in Mississippi, and the same year he applied for admission to the University of Mississippi. For his efforts he was placed in an asylum from which C. B. King, his brother, helped release him. One vital organization, the Mississippi Freedom Democrats, challenged the white Democrats of that state, and in 1968 by merging with other groups, received the conservative white Democratic seats of Mississippi at the national convention.

Interest in all-black parties continued. In 1976 the National Black Political Assembly, though turned down by California representative Ron Dellums and by Georgian Julian Bond, selected a candidate from New York City for president, the Reverend Frederick Douglass Kirkpatrick. However, the NBPA had been unable to get on the ballot in any state. In 1980 a new organization, the National Black Independent Political party was established, but ran no candidates. The NBIPP was a mix of black leaders disappointed in both major parties, and influenced by the thoughts and rhetoric of the black power movement. Despite their efforts the NBIPP was not able to create a black political party that could serve as an alternative to the Republican or Democratic Parties.

The difficulties black Americans encountered in their efforts to acquire political office can be observed in state and local as well as in national elections. The first African Americans elected to political positions were Alexander Twilight, elected to Vermont's legislature in 1835 and John Mercer Langston, who was elected to a local office in Ohio in 1855. It remained unlikely for blacks to be elected to state legislatures; the second such election took place in Massachusetts in 1866. During Reconstruction black southerners were elected to state legislatures, both the lower and upper houses. Election to the U.S. House of Representatives for African Americans took a momentous turn of events during and after Reconstruction, when twenty blacks served in the House of Representatives. The last one left Congress in 1901. A black Republican from Chicago, Oscar De Priest, was the first to reach Congress in the twentieth century when he took office in 1929. De Priest was replaced by black Democrat Arthur W. Mitchell in 1935. By 1968, six northern congressmen (none from the South) serving major metropolitan, black majority districts participated in Congress. With the 1968 election results, the number of black representatives increased to nine. Black congressional office-holders decided that they should work together on behalf of their constituencies and race interests, and formed the Congressional Black Caucus in 1969. The number of black representatives by 2008 was in the mid-forties.

The predicament of African Americans in public office is even more apparent in the sparse number of black officials in two elected positions that often lead to consideration for president or vice president of the United States, the United States Senate and state governors. To date, six African Americans have served as United States senators; the office of a seventh, P. B. S. Pinchback, although elected from Louisiana, was instead determined by the U.S. Senate to belong to a white from that state. In 1870, Hiram Revels of Mississippi became the first African American senator. Five years later, Blanche K. Bruce of Mississippi took the oath of office where he served from 1875 to 1881. It would be nearly another century, 1967, before Republican Edward Brooke of Massachusetts followed in their historic footsteps. The first African American elected to the Senate by popular vote, Brooke served two full terms, from 1967 to 1979. In 1993, Democrat Carol Moseley-Braun of Illinois broke new ground again, becoming the first African American female to serve as U.S. senator. During her Senate career, Moseley-Braun sponsored progressive education bills and campaigned for gun control. A recent African American senator, Barack Obama of Illinois, took office in 2005; however, Obama moved from the United States Senate to the White House in January, 2009. Among potential Senate replacements for Obama was Jesse Jackson's son, Jesse Jackson, Jr., a Democratic Illinois politician and Obama supporter. Obama's eventual replacement, appointed by the governor of Illinois, was Roland W. Burris, a Democrat, and the third black senator from the state of Illinois—one half the total of African American United States senators.

The number of African American governors also is paltry. At most one can record five, with extenuating circumstances for two. Such a list of black governors includes the last governor of Mexican California, Pio de Jesus Pico, who served briefly in 1831 and then again in 1845 and 1846. Pico's background consisted of African, Indian, and Spanish ancestry. The next African American governor, Republican P. B. S. Pinchback, served as acting governor of Louisiana for thirty-six days in 1872–73 while the sitting governor was being impeached. For over a century there was not another black governor of a state; then in 1990 Democrat L. Douglas Wilder of Virginia became the nation's first popularly elected black governor. Deval Patrick, the current Democratic governor of Massachusetts, and David A. Paterson, who recently became governor of New York when the elected governor resigned, are the only black governors at the current time (2009). Wilder briefly sought the presidency during the Democratic primary in 1992; his quest can be followed in Dwayne Yancey, *When Hell Froze Over: The Untold Story of Doug Wilder, A Black Politician's Rise to Power in the South.* As indicated by Yancey's title, the few African American governors had little opportunity for national election.

Unable to consistently ascend to political positions of influence and unable to turn black political party candidacies to victory, some African Americans, beginning in the 1930s, turned to left-wing political parties. These parties, despite their often doctrinaire ideological stances, actively sought black voters and members. To help accomplish that task, in 1932 the Communist Party nominated James W. Ford, a black WWI army veteran from Alabama and 1920 Fisk University graduate, as its vice presidential candidate. During the twenties Ford resided in Chicago, and late in the decade moved to New York City after joining the Communist Party in 1926. Technically, since apparently the National Liberty Party did not name a vice presidential candidate, nor did the Texas Black and Tans, Ford was the first black candidate to run for vice president. However, African Americans did not move in substantial numbers to the Communist Party, despite Ford. Many who voted for the Communists did so as a race protest, not as part of the grand scheme of class struggle pushed by the communists and socialists. The Party ran Ford again in 1936 and in 1940, but the vote for the party declined each year. The Communists did not run candidates for the 1944 election, and supported the Progressives in 1948. Government pressure precluded the Communists from running candidates for the next twenty years. On the other hand, prominent black labor and civil rights leader A. Philip Randolph was offered the vice presidential nomination of the Socialist Party in 1948. Norman Thomas was the presidential nominee, but Randolph did not accept the nomination.

Despite the fact that the Communist Party did not run candidates in 1952, African Americans on the left had an option, the Progressive Party, which that year nominated as its vice president a black woman from California who had been prominent from the beginning in the organizational efforts of the Progressive Party, Charlotta Bass. Bass, a former newspaper editor and publisher (*California Eagle*) from Los Angeles previously supported the Republican Party. However, as did so many other African Americans, she looked for alternatives when the Republican Party increasingly became the party of "lily whites." Bass, the first African American woman to be selected as a candidate for vice president, campaigned diligently but with, to her, disappointing results.

The left in the United States continued, albeit sporadically, to select African American candidates for president and vice president. Twelve years later, in 1964, the Socialist Workers Party nominated Clifton DeBerry as its presidential candidate. A civil rights activist, DeBerry, the third African American presidential candidate (Clennon Washington King was the second), supported African liberation movements and U.S. withdrawal from Vietnam. A Trotskyite party, the Socialist Workers strove in the remaining years of the twentieth century to attract black voters and black members. In 1980, when the Socialist Workers Party ran three candidates for the presidency, depending on the state, two—Clifton DeBerry and Andrew Pulley, the 1972 Socialist Workers Party vice president candidate—were black.

The 1968 elections, nominating processes, candidates, and conventions tipped the scale. From that point forward African Americans began to play much more significant and active roles in presidential politics. Some thought maybe they could win, others that their positions and presence would provide a message of hope to the black community, or enhance their position within the black political community. Participants often involved themselves in the politics of the presidency as a means of protest, some to provide support for causes, whether for workers, for labor unions, for the environment, for women's rights, and especially for black rights. After 1968 many more African Americans sought the office of president of the United States, and a considerable number actually ran as candidates from political parties for either the post of president or vice president. Most achieved their nominations and support from third party organizations; a few challenged the two major parties (primarily the Democratic) for nomination.

Shirley Chisholm's 1972 campaign for the Democratic Party's nomination for president signaled this new effort; her campaign also signaled the introduction of a new political process—the primary and the caucus—that enabled black candidates to have more opportunities. A congresswoman from New York City, Chisholm, unlike many other black and female candidates, was not ignored. She averred that she was the candidate of the people, but she lacked financing, professional staffing, and endured campaign squabbling. Still, she entered fourteen Democratic primaries and received over 430,000 votes. Chisholm was both the first black woman elected to the United States Congress and the first black woman to challenge for a major party's presidential nomination. She entered the race to bring hope to people by helping them realize that politics could make a difference. Not only did Chisholm receive votes for the presidency, she was nominated for vice-president as well. Chisholm was not the only black politician in the 1972 spotlight; the Reverend Walter E. Fauntroy campaigned and won the District of Columbia primary for the Democratic nomination. Andrew Pulley received the Socialist Workers vice presidential nomination, labor organizer Jarvis Tyner the same from the Communist Party (he also received its nomination in 1976), and Julius Hobson was the People's Party choice for vice president; the People's Party presidential nominee was Dr. Benjamin Spock.

Shirley Chisholm, Charlotta Bass, and Charlene Mitchell were not the only black women entering the national political scene by the late 1970s and early 1980s; the names of Barbara Jordan, Willie Mae Reid, Margaret Wright, and Angela Davis also became notable in connection with the presidential races. A valuable article by the preeminent scholar of African American politics, Hanes Walton, Jr., focuses on black women candidates. The article, "Black Female Presidential Candidates: Bass, Mitchell, Chisholm, Wright, Reid, Davis, and Fulani," can be found in his *Black Politics and Black Political Behavior: A Linkage Analysis*. Overall, these black women candidates raised important issues, developed new techniques, but essentially were ignored. Texas African American politician, Barbara Jordan, noted for her starring role in the impeachment proceedings of Richard Nixon in 1974, was not a candidate in 1976, but at the Democratic Party Convention did receive delegate votes both for president and for vice president. That same year the Socialist Workers Party named Willie Mae Reid its vice presidential candidate; she ran for that post again in 1992. Reid, as other black female candidates, had difficulty gaining attention. She spoke principally to small groups, and received little recognition, support, or votes.

Margaret Wright, the 1976 People's Party presidential nominee, was the second African American woman to be chosen to run as a presidential candidate by a political party. Wright too faced limited exposure. She was on the ballot in only six states but she, as did many of the other black women candidates, brought energy and knowledge to their respective campaigns. The People's Party, according to Wright, was a socialist feminist democratic party that sought to run their communities from the bottom up rather than from the top down. Small finances and the difficulty in getting on state ballots also hindered Angela Davis, undoubtedly the most well-known of the black female candidates of the seventies and eighties. Davis, selected as the vice presidential candidate by the Communist Party in both 1980 and 1984, struggled to put together a campaign message that would be heard.

The African American candidate who was not obscured, and who was heard, was a black male, the Reverend Jesse Jackson. In 1984 and again in 1988 Jackson campaigned for the Democratic Party nomination for president. Jackson's campaigns were arresting and important for the black community and beyond. Although not a professional politician, Jackson had the skills, the recognition, the professional staff, and the ability to run an aggressive campaign. Although Jackson definitely set out to win the nominations, at the same time he was just as cognizant of raising issues faced by black Americans in the 1980s United States. Jackson also worked diligently to elect state and local officials, both white and black progressives. For that purpose he created the Rainbow Coalition. He lost in 1984, and arrived with the second largest number of delegates in 1988, but was unable to parlay that number into either the nomination or selection as vice president. His campaigns caught the spirit of the times, and he captured the imagination of the African American community. They wanted to see a black president.

In Jackson's two campaigns, 1984 and 1988, other African American candidates appeared. Shirley Chisholm received votes at the Democratic convention for vice president. The Socialist Equality Party ran two black candidates in both 1984 and 1988, Edward Winn for the presidency, and Helen Halyard for the vice presidency. As already noted, in 1984 Angela Davis ran for vice president on the Communist Party ticket, and that year the New Alliance Party ran a black man, Dennis L. Serrette, for its presidential candidate. In 1988, also in 1992, the New Alliance Party presidential candidate was Lenora Fulani. Fulani was the third black female presidential candidate, and was also the first woman and first black to be placed on the ballot in all fifty states. Fulani's 1992 campaign is depicted in her book, *The Making of a Fringe Candidate, 1992*. There was one other African American candidate in both 1988, Jackson's final campaign, and 1992; the presidential candidate from the Socialist Workers in those years was James "Mac" Warren, a politician, author, and long-time member of that party. Warren's book, *Independent Black Political Action: The Struggle to Break with the Democratic and Republican Parties,* is a poignant account of the failures of the major parties and the problems of the third parties for African Americans.

The two presidents of the United States between 1981 and 1992 were conservative Republicans, Ronald Reagan and George Bush. As Hanes Walton, Jr. asserts in *African American Power and Politics,* during these years the conservative movement refused to push for a black agenda, and in many instances took away from African Americans. A key result was that black voters even more attached themselves to the Democratic Party, and conservative African Americans joined the Republicans.

For the twenty-year period from 1988 to 2008, black voters and politicians continued to expand their contributions to black candidates, parties, political behavior, and causes. Though the struggle is sometimes incidental to getting their messages out, and to supporting the black community, they seek to become president of the United States. Sometimes an empathetic white can gain some of the race stature. Elected in 1992, former Arkansas governor, Democrat William "Bill" Clinton was so supportive and committed to black Americans that he was referred to as "the black President" by famed African American novelist Tony Morrison. In 2001 the congressional Black Caucus recognized Clinton as the "First Black President," the one who bridged the racial divide. It is significant that only eight years before Obama's sweeping victory, in the absence of a black president, President Bill Clinton earned and eagerly wore the mantle of black president. On the other hand, perhaps President Clinton as black surrogate aided in making Obama's election more feasible.

Clinton as black president also leads us to consideration of the myths of the black president. In 1965, J. A. Rogers published *The Five Negro Presidents.* In essence, this eighteen-page booklet, with scant evidence, asserted that Presidents Jackson, Jefferson, Harding, Lincoln, and one unnamed were of black heritage. Even if that were true, it does not negate the fact that Obama is the first African American president. He considers himself black, is considered to be black, and voters assumed he was black. The others, on the other hand, considered themselves white, were assumed to be white, and voters supported them since they were white. It is interesting that the little evidence cited by Rogers generally derived from campaign accusations of opposition politicians.

In addition to Clinton, and to the aforementioned Fulani and Warren, other black Americans sought, or at least campaigned for the presidency during the 1990s. Virginia governor Douglas Wilder briefly pursued the

Democratic nomination for the presidency in 1992 but he lacked the necessary financing. Ohio congressman Louis Stokes garnered "favorite son" votes for president. That year the Socialist Equality Party selected Helen Halyard as its presidential nominee, and Larry Holmes was chosen by the Workers World Party to be the vice president. Ronald Daniels, formerly Jesse Jackson's campaign advisor for Jackson's 1984 and 1988 presidential campaigns, received the nomination of the Peace and Freedom Party, the Campaign for a New Tomorrow Party, and the New Jersey Independent Party as their nominee for president. That same year, 1992 (she also ran in 1996), Joan Jett Blakk campaigned for the presidency on the Queer Nation Party ticket. In 1992 Isabell Masters received one of at least five nominations for the presidency from the Looking Back Party.

Masters, born in Topeka, Kansas, also ran as a candidate for the Looking Back Party in 1984, 1996, 2000, and 2004; she unsuccessfully entered Republican primaries during the 1990s. One other black politician also entered the Republican presidential sweepstakes in 1996, again in 2000, and briefly in 2008, Alan L. Keyes, former radio talk show host and perennial conservative black candidate. In addition to Masters, third party African American 1996 presidential aspirants included James Harris for the Socialist Workers Party and Monica Moorehead for the Workers World Party. Both also ran in 2000. One additional black American became a candidate in 2000; Ezola Broussard Foster was the Reform Party's vice presidential candidate that year (the party's presidential candidate was the outspoken conservative, Patrick Buchanan). Foster, born in Louisiana, received a Master's degree from Texas Southern University, and moved to Los Angeles. A conservative, she published *What's Right for All Americans.*

Perhaps the most telling political development in the black quest for the presidency occurred in the last decade of the twentieth century when a movement surfaced to nominate Colin Powell as the Republican Party candidate in 1996. While Powell ultimately disassociated himself from the effort, for a moment it seemed possible that an African American candidate of national stature and broad appeal would enter the race, and, perhaps win.

The number of African Americans seeking the presidency continued to grow in the twenty-first century, although the parties and the issues did not always seem to change. There are important reasons for this expansion; increased opportunity was present, the Democratic Party nomination seemed open to black seekers, and President George W. Bush showed little sympathy for the problems and needs of the masses of lower-income black Americans. Five black individuals sought the nomination of their respective parties in 2004; only two were successful in becoming candidates. Selected by the Workers World Party as its presidential candidate, Californian John Parker, who also received a few votes from the Liberty Union Party of

Vermont, was a former school teacher and communist political organizer. The Socialist Workers Party selected Arrin Hawkins as their vice presidential aspirant even though she was not old enough.

Setting the stage for Obama's challenge four years later, three African American aspirants in 2004 pursued the Democratic Party nomination— Carol Moseley-Braun, Mildred Glover, and Al Sharpton. Each came from slightly different backgrounds, but emphasized race issues as well as tackling critical issues of the day. Former Democratic Senator Moseley-Braun of Illinois brought a wealth of support and recognition from her experiences as a U.S. senator; she continued in her presidential campaign to stress racial, social, and economic justice. Moseley-Braun, an African American first-term, junior senator from Illinois, helped pave the way for Obama. Although she did not catch on as did Obama, her ability to raise funds via the internet, her poise at the debates and in interviews, her audacity, signaled the arrival of the new black politician. Mildred Glover, a former Georgia politician who moved to Maryland, while in Georgia challenged for the gubernatorial election. In 2004 she campaigned to end the war in Iraq and to locate jobs for the unemployed. Race activist and black Baptist minister, Alfred Charles "Al" Sharpton brought his ability to excite (and occasionally exasperate) his audience to political campaigns; Sharpton was able to focus publicity on the issues, help black Americans, and defy those in power.

In 2008 opportunity and audacity combined, and the list of African American presidential/vice presidential candidates also was lengthy, including the aforementioned Alan Keyes who became the presidential nominee of America's Independent Party. A short-lived Republican draft movement to select Secretary of State Condoleeza Rice as the party's vice president emerged. Some became candidates for their respective third parties. Howard University student Eugene Puryear received the Party for Socialism and Liberalism's vice presidential nomination. Stewart A. Alexander received the nomination of the Socialist Party USA as its vice presidential candidate; Elaine Brown, former Black Panther leader, considered the Green Party for its presidential nomination, but resigned from the party in December, 2007; the eventual Green Party nominee for the presidency was former Georgia congresswoman Cynthia McKinney. McKinney also received the endorsement/nomination of the Workers World Party. A former coal miner and garment worker, political activist Alyson Kennedy was chosen by the Socialist Workers Party as its vice presidential nominee.

The 2008 Democratic Party nominee for the president of the United States, Illinois senator Barack Obama, followed a lengthy and arduous but successful primary struggle with an overpowering victory in the general election. An African American presidency, Barack Obama made it. The years, the efforts, the struggles, and the challenges have been numerous and seemingly insurmountable. More than fifty individuals, African Americans all, have considered, been voted for, been selected by political parties, and have pursued that elusive quest. Why? Obviously the answers vary widely, and yet are surprisingly similar—for ego, for pride, for the race, to help African Americans achieve recognition, to bring about change, for reform, to overturn a white way of life. The key challenge for Obama, the African American community, and for fair-minded white Americans in 2008 was, would white supremacy be defeated, or at least overturned? The answer is murky; although the election of Barack Obama as the forty-fourth president of the United States challenged previous assumptions, the fact is that with the exception of North Carolina and Virginia, the Solid South, the historic home of white supremacy, remained solid and voted against Obama. Whites in the rest of the United States voted for Obama, sometimes in spite of his race, and for some liberals, because of his race. The complete answer awaits the decision of history. Other questions await the verdict of history: was the wait and struggle worth it? What will blacks gain from the Obama presidency? What will the nation gain?

Frederick Douglass, the most significant African American abolitionist and political leader, was also the first black candidate involved in presidential politics. He was briefly a vice presidential nominee of the Political Abolitionist Party in 1856, and was offered a spot on the Equal Rights Party ticket in 1872. (Courtesy of the Library of Congress, LC-USZ62-15887.)

CHAPTER 1

Beginning the Trek

Douglass, Bruce, Black Conventions, Independent Political Parties

BRUCE A. GLASRUD

On January 20, 2009, a former Democratic United States senator from Illinois, African American Barack Obama, was sworn in as the forty-fourth president of the United States; he thus became the first black president of this nation. One hundred and forty-two years earlier, in 1856, an escaped slave from Maryland and then current race and abolitionist leader, Frederick Douglass, began the long African American road to the White House when he was nominated by the Political Abolition Party as its candidate for vice president of the United States. The nomination was short-lived. Likely Douglass refused the position; before adjourning, the PAP rescinded its nomination and instead gave the spot on the ticket to Samuel McFarland, a little-known white abolitionist from Pennsylvania. The path to the White House for blacks was not only lengthy; it proved to be filled with pot holes.

Frederick Douglass' political path was itself long and tortuous. He was the first black American to receive even a modicum of political recognition and encouragement as well as to be mentioned as a possible candidate for high office. Born a slave in Maryland in 1817, Douglass was sent to Baltimore in 1825 to work as a houseboy. He not only worked but received educational instruction. Douglass wanted to be free. One effort to escape failed but in 1838 Douglass successfully escaped from slavery. Upon escaping he married, settled in Massachusetts, and worked at varying jobs. After attending an abolitionist rally in 1841, where he spoke, Douglass accepted an invitation from the Massachusetts Anti-Slavery Society to be an agent. He became a prominent abolitionist speaker (among the finest of nineteenth-century orators), an ardent abolitionist, and later a newspaper editor. Douglass' newspaper, the *North Star*, was started over the objections of some white abolitionists, who thought one major abolitionist newspaper, William Lloyd Garrison's *The Liberator*, to be enough.

At first a "moral suasionist," that is someone who believed that slavery could best be overturned by example and telling arguments, Douglass eventually broke with that group (led by William Lloyd Garrison) and began to participate in politics as a way to rid the nation of slavery, America's "peculiar institution." He began with the Liberty Party, then turned to the Free Soil Party, and in 1854, after initial hesitation, he joined with the Republicans. Douglass was among the group who met together in 1848 at the inaugural meeting of the "Free Soilers" although he remained connected to the Liberty Party. In fact, in 1855 the Liberty Party nominated Douglass to be secretary of state in New York, the highest office for a black candidate at that time. The following year Douglass received his short-lived nomination as vice presidential candidate. He welcomed the Civil War as an opportunity both to free those African Americans yet enslaved (approximately four million) and to obtain basic rights and privileges of citizenship for free blacks.

After the War Douglass spoke for the right to vote, for civil rights, and for equality for women. A steadfast supporter of the Republican Party, during the latter years of his life (he died in 1895, the same year that Booker T. Washington gave his famous speech at Atlanta) Douglass received patronage appointments from his party. His loyalty to the Republicans even overcame political opportunity; in 1872 the Equal Rights Party offered him its candidacy for vice president to run along with Victoria Woodhull but he turned it down. Later his own party recognized him; in 1888 Douglass received a few delegate votes for vice president at the Republican Party convention. Douglass viewed the Republican Party as the party of Lincoln; the party that freed the black slaves. Unfortunately, by the time of his death, the Republican Party had begun its retreat from support of black rights and from encouragement of black votes and increasingly was influenced by its "lily white" faction. Nevertheless, through the 1920s it was Republicans who continued to retain a civil rights plank in its platform, led the unsuccessful effort in Congress to make lynching a federal crime, and elected the first black congressman of the twentieth century.

A United States senator from Mississippi, Blanche K. Bruce, also received early consideration and support in the black quest for the presidency. Bruce was rewarded by a major party, the Republicans, when in 1880 he received eight delegate votes for the position of vice president of the United States, the first time that a major party had so recognized a black political leader. He also received votes for the vice presidential nomination in 1888 at the Republican convention. Bruce, a Mississippian and the second African American United States senator (Hiram Revels of Mississippi was the first), was born a slave in Virginia. Transported by his owner to Missouri, Bruce escaped to Kansas and when slaves were freed in Missouri he returned to that state and set up a school, having been tutored while a slave.

In 1869 Bruce moved to Mississippi, correctly judging that opportunities for black leadership would be available in that state. In 1874 the Mississippi state legislature selected Bruce as a Republican United States senator. Bruce previously had purchased a plantation, and from that base worked diligently in a variety of political positions in the state. By 1880 Bruce had served six years as a senator but white Democrats, who earlier gained control of state politics, prevented Bruce's reelection. However, Bruce, as Douglass, received national patronage appointments from Republican presidents over the succeeding years. He died in 1898, two years after Jim Crow segregation was legitimatized in *Plessy v. Ferguson* and the same year that black voting elimination was sanctioned by the Supreme Court in *Williams v. Mississippi.*

Frederick Douglass and Blanche K. Bruce were not alone in their roles and efforts toward political respectability and responsibility for black Americans but serious obstacles to black success existed: slavery, right to vote, economic independence, education, segregation, and white supremacy all militated against black officeholders. Prior to the Civil War many black individuals organized, agitated, worked, and met in the National Negro Convention movement in order to improve their status. The early nineteenth-century National Negro Convention movement lasted from 1830 to 1864 and included all the major political factions in the black community: conservatives, radicals, integrationists, nationalists, political party adherents, nonviolent "moral sua-sionists," and revolutionists. It attracted leading blacks of the day including Richard Allen, Bishop of the black Methodist church, who became conference president for the first meeting, James Forten, a leading black abolitionist, and Frederick Douglass. The participants of the National Negro Conventions focused on three aspects of African American life—black unity, abolition of slavery, and the right to vote. Their goals were problematic; the vast majority of African Americans were enslaved, there was a limited number of free blacks, restrictions upon black suffrage, and prior to the Convention movement, little political or pressure group activity from blacks or whites.

In September, 1830, the first National Negro Convention took place in Philadelphia. Forty blacks from seven states attended the meeting. From that meeting emerged a new organization, the American Society of Free Persons of Color. The participants encouraged migration to Canada but acknowl-edged the need to improve the lives of those who remained in the United States. This convention, and the next five, followed the basic views and tenets of the "moral suasionists," led by the Garrisonians and New Englanders. They opposed participating in the political arena since the Constitution, and hence political involvement, was a covenant with hell. This first meeting also developed a plan that called for interim state and local conventions to be held and they were. By 1859 one newspaper glibly reported that the Negro conventions were almost as frequent as church meetings.

Three national conventions were held in the 1840s when proponents of political action slowly gained ascendancy. A key aspect of the 1840s was that fewer whites attended the meetings, and mostly African Americans attended, led, and determined the organizations strategy and positions. The 1843 convention, held in Buffalo, New York, for example, called for support of the Liberty Party and the right to vote for all people. The 1848 convention elected Frederick Douglass its president, even though a serious rift emerged between moderates and militants. Douglass himself did not support political activism over "moral suasion" until the early 1850s. The concluding National Convention of Colored Citizens through the Civil War occurred in 1864 in Syracuse, New York when Douglass once more was elected president. Members pushed for political equality, especially the right to vote. To some extent the successful passage of the Fifteenth Amendment can be traced to this meeting's effort. The Convention movement continued after the Civil War, on local, state, and national levels. The 1872 national meeting took place in New Orleans with Frederick Douglass presiding—a primary issue before the membership was whether to support the Liberal Republicans or U. S. Grant. The convention gave its endorsement to U. S. Grant and the regular Republicans. Although not so esteemed as Lincoln, Grant too garnered favorable support as a result of his role in freeing the slaves.

During the nineteenth century free black Americans worked through the Negro Convention movement, the Republican Party, and third parties in order to improve their status and to secure voting and other political rights and privileges. The first national recognition of black voters and their support derived from the Liberty Party. That party, organized in 1839 with the help of at least two black abolitionists, encouraged African Americans to attend the national convention in 1840, likely the first national political convention that catered to the black electorate. The Liberty Party was a political party dedicated to the abolition of slavery and to broadening the black electorate. Its appeal was to African Americans but it encouraged whites in the party to seek black support as well. Ultimately the single-issue Liberty Party failed. Black leaders such as Frederick Douglass turned to the fledgling Free Soil Party in 1852 but it was the Republican Party, established in 1854, that promised the most benefits for black Americans, even though (as was the Free Soil Party) it was not opposed to the institution of slavery, but only to its spread into the territories.

After the Civil War opportunities for political participation, especially for the recently freed slaves, blossomed. In the South, African American freedom and the Fourteenth and Fifteenth Amendments to the Constitution meant that black males were eligible to vote and during the late 1860s and into the 1870s vote they did, almost always on behalf of the Republican Party. But white Democratic control of the southern states by the mid-1870s left blacks without a viable political option in those states. Freed blacks certainly could not work with the racist southern Democrats, which included most white Southerners and, increasingly, not with Republicans who reduced their pressure for black rights and for the black vote after 1877. Frequently those white Southerners who remained in the Republican fold sought control of the party, and the new white leadership was referred to by blacks (the name was given by black Texas leader Norris Wright Cuney) as "lily whites." Blacks organized themselves into the "Black and Tan" wing of the Republican Party, while focusing their efforts on federal patronage. However, in some states blacks served in Congress until the end of the century, held leadership posts in state parties, and were successful in local politics. Limited third-party involvement by black Southerners included support for the Greenback and Prohibition Parties but it was the Populists who appeared to offer a chance for political success and the downfall of white hegemony.

The black Populists emerged from the tangled economic plight facing African American farmers and laborers in the South by the 1880s. The southern sharecropping system particularly was deleterious since control of crops, mortgages, and day-to-day survival was in the hands of white plantation owners, storekeepers, and bankers. Black Texans began the movement. In 1886 black Texas farmers formed the Colored Farmers' Alliance that soon grew into a statewide organization. Three years later a national alliance, chartered by the corresponding white alliance, emerged at a meeting in Lovelady, Texas—the Colored Farmers' National Alliance and Cooperative Union. The Colored Farmers' Alliance grew rapidly. By 1891 interest in setting up a biracial third party grew and discussions were held. Finally in 1892 agreement was reached and a political party, the People's Party (nicknamed the Populists), was established. Large numbers of black farmers and laborers supported the People's Party as in their best interests politically, racially, and economically. The party had varied electoral successes in 1892, depending frequently on the black vote and on the relationship to the major parties in a given state or locale.

For Southern blacks the primary obstacle to political achievement was the racist, white-dominated Democratic Party. Black Populists looked forward to 1896 and the defeat of that party. However, on the national level the People's Party merged with the Democratic Party; nationally the result was a ready Republican victory and the defeat of the Populists locally and statewide. In the South, white supremacy proved too difficult to overturn. White Populists and Democrats defeated alliances of Black Populists and Republicans. The Populist movement promised an opportunity for African Americans; its defeat crushed that possibility. By 1900 black efforts to work with white-dominated parties, whether major or third parties, had proved to be unsuccessful.

Limited black success toward the end of the nineteenth century came from establishing and supporting all-black political parties, a strategy that would be pursued frequently in the twentieth century. As early as 1883 African Americans in Pennsylvania set up an all-black political party, the Colored Independent Party. Although it perhaps protested more than engaged in politics, the party did emphasize major issues facing the Pennsylvania black community and dramatized the need for black independence as well as a black political party. In Ohio in 1897, an all-black political party, the Negro Protective Party, selected S. J. Lewis as its gubernatorial candidate. The party fielded a full set of candidates opposing the Republicans after the governor, a Republican, failed to investigate and otherwise condemn the lynching of a black man in that state. Lewis ran on a platform of equal rights and promised to protect black rights. Although Lewis received nearly five thousand votes, he and the Negro Protective Party lost and the party soon declined.

For African Americans by the end of the century the choices seemed dismal. The two-party system by 1900 provided minimal access or support for black Americans. More and more blacks turned to independent political movements such as statewide all-black political parties. They pushed that independence increasingly in the twentieth century. Partially that meant, in the North, forming relationships with the Democratic Party rather than the Republican Party, once the party of African American freedom. The African American quandary was even more pronounced in the South where few blacks could vote.

The prospect of a switch by African Americans to the Democratic Party took a potentially positive turn in 1900 when an alliance of alienated Republicans, independent blacks, and black Democrats formed the Negro National Democratic League. A Midwesterner, George E. Taylor, became president of the Democratic League and asserted that a large percentage of black voters of the country supported the principles of the Democratic Party as well as that party's presidential candidate, William Jennings Bryan. During these years Northern Democrats in fact treated blacks better than the reactionary Republicans or the Southern Democrats. However, a Democratic victory twelve years later had little positive effect for black Americans. Woodrow Wilson's election brought scant benefit to black Americans even though a goodly number of black Democrats did support him. Wilson's administration increased segregation in the nation's capital and brought it to federal offices; it also reduced the number of African Americans holding office.

Without aid or support from the two major political parties and only limited third-party success, independent-minded African Americans in 1904 created the first national political party exclusively for and by blacks, the National Liberty Party. Based upon the concepts of self-help, struggle, and to some extent separation the NLP was reflective of an awareness of black-nationalist efforts including that of Bishop Henry M. Turner. The National Liberty Party, with delegates from thirty-six states at its convention in St. Louis, chose George Edwin Taylor from Ottumwa, Iowa as its candidate for president of the United States in 1904. Taylor thus became the first African American nominated by a political party for president.

Born in Arkansas in 1857, formerly the editor of a radical labor newspaper in La Crosse, Wisconsin, the *Wisconsin Labor Advocate*, then editor of *The Negro Solicitor* in Oskaloosa, Iowa, and in 1900 president of the Negro National Democratic League, Taylor's disillusionment by 1904 with the two major parties led him to accept the nomination. Taylor arrived in Iowa from Wisconsin in 1891, and for a few years early in the twentieth century served as justice of the peace in Hilton, Iowa; he died in Florida in 1925. The NLP platform championed pensions for ex-slaves, government support and protection of civil rights, and a return of voting and other political rights to African Americans that had eroded in the latter nineteenth century.

Neither working with the Democratic Party nor establishing a separate all-black political party proved to be a successful avenue for black political progress, and it appeared to many African Americans as if the Republican Party too moved away from the black voter during the early twentieth century. But African Americans continued their political efforts in the twentieth century. In 1916 three black leaders separately stepped forward to argue that blacks must pursue an independent voice in politics and should once more form a national black political party. Two leaders, both educators and race advocates, William Pickens and R. R. Wright, called upon the "black masses" to create their own black political parties. In October of that same year prominent NAACP leader, W. E. B. Du Bois, urged forming a black independent political party. Du Bois argued that since the Republican Party was the party of wealth and big business and the Democratic Party dependent upon the Solid South, which was built on hate and fear of African Americans, blacks needed their own organization. Du Bois acknowledged that "the only effective method in the future is to organize in every congressional district as a Negro Party to endorse those candidates . . . whose promises or past performances give greatest hope for remedying the wrongs done them"

(Holmes, 15). That November Du Bois recommended either voting for the Socialist candidate or staying home in the presidential election. Nonetheless, Woodrow Wilson won with his slogan of "he kept us out of war."

That same year (1916), in Memphis, Tennessee one black man stepped forward to establish, at least in that city, an all-black party—that man was Robert R. Church, Jr. Church, a prominent black businessman in Memphis, was born in 1885 and died in 1952. In 1916 he formed, and then financed, the Lincoln League, an all-black political party in Memphis. Essentially it operated as the black wing of the Republican Party. The league increased voter registration, held voter schools, ran candidates for public office, and eventually expanded into a successful statewide organization. The league soon registered 10,000 voters, and the black votes made the difference for winning candidates in numerous races. Church soon became one of the more important black leaders in national Republican circles as the Lincoln League movement expanded beyond Tennessee. In 1920 a Lincoln League convention was held in Chicago with over four hundred black attendees representing thirty-three states. In Tennessee, and elsewhere, racial solidarity in politics seemed to work via the Lincoln Leagues.

Such efforts, however, did not change white political behavior in the ensuing years. In Texas white Democrats, who gained control of the state in 1874, removed black voters as well as poor whites with a poll tax and the exclusive Democratic white primary. Republican "lily whites" fought successfully for control of the Republican Party in the Lone Star state. By 1920, Texas black and tan Republican Party members were refused seating at the Republican National Convention. When the Republican candidate (Warren G. Harding) visited the Lone Star state, he reached over the hands and heads of black school children to shake the hands of white children. White Texas Democrats were no alternative; as a result black Republicans created the Black and Tan Republican Party and ran a slate of electors for the presidency. Even though the Black and Tan Republican Party did not run a specific candidate, they came in third with a total of 27,247 votes, ahead of James Ferguson's American Party, as well as the Socialist Party candidate. Although this early effort to forge an electoral base failed, effort in other states continued, including movements in Virginia and Kentucky the following year (1921).

For blacks in 1921 Virginia, the political situation was similar to that in Texas: white Democrats placed voting restrictions on African Americans and used the issue of race in the 1920 election. Republicans were dominated by a "lily white" group who expressed no desire for the black vote. Approximately 20,000 black voters would likely vote in the election but neither Democrat nor Republican sought their support. As a result black Republicans ran a slate of black candidates, referred to as the "lily blacks," for the state elections in 1921. The gubernatorial candidate of the Virginia African

Americans, John Mitchell, Jr., editor of the Richmond *Planet*, had been a constant critic of white racial policies in Virginia over the years. However, the black candidates faced two significant obstacles, a lack of voting strength and a lack of unity, as not all blacks agreed with either the all-black party or with the candidacy of Mitchell. In the election Mitchell received only 5,000 votes, not even enough to make a significant statement and particularly not enough to win the election. However, Virginia blacks, even if not united and if not enough African Americans had been able to register and vote, did show that they were not to be ignored.

The same year (1921) as the "lily black" party emerged in Virginia an all-black political party cropped up in Louisville, Kentucky. Since the local Republican Party ignored African American civil rights issues, blacks in Louisville formed their own party, the Lincoln Independent Party. The LIP likely was modeled after the Lincoln League established by Robert Church in Memphis, Tennessee, five years earlier. African Americans in Louisville found themselves increasingly marginalized within the Republican Party. The white Republicans also supported white Democratic over black Republican candidates and endorsed the growth of segregated facilities. Supported and influenced by NAACP leader, W. E. B. Du Bois, the leadership of the Lincoln Independent Party challenged the more conservative local black leadership as well as white Republicans. Although the movement was not successful, it produced a vocal and activist leadership, a greater responsiveness from white Republicans, and an increased movement away from the Republican fold by blacks in Louisville.

All-black parties would reemerge; forty years later, in 1960, the Independent Afro-American Party, with a purpose and rationale similar to the previous all-black political parties, and with the specific objectives of black equality and social justice, selected the Reverend Clennon Washington King, Jr., a civil rights activist, to be its nominee for president and Reginald Carter for vice president. King thus became the second African American chosen by a political party to be its candidate for the office of president of the United States.

On the ballot only in Alabama, the party totaled 1,485 votes. In 1958 King, with his daughter, sought to integrate an all-white elementary school in Mississippi and the same year he applied for admission to the University of Mississippi. For his efforts he was consigned in an asylum from which C. B. King, his brother, helped release him. All-black parties would continue, although after 1960 only one selected a candidate for president—the Independent Freedom Party in 1976. One vital organization, the Mississippi Freedom Democrats challenged the white Democrats of that state and in 1968, by merging with other groups, received the conservative white Democratic seats of Mississippi at the national convention.

Earlier in the 1930s black Americans borrowed a tactic from the previous century, striving for black unity among varied organizations and philosophies as a means of gaining black rights and attaining racial justice. In 1935 a conference held at Howard University issued a call for a National Negro Congress (similar in scope to the Negro Convention movement of the 1830s) to be held the following year, 1936. The National Negro Congress (NNC), established in part to argue for the rights of labor and civil rights, existed until 1948 although many writers contend that it ceased to be a player in racial matters after the 1940 national convention.

The First National Negro Congress met in Chicago and was a marked success with delegates and representatives coming from across the nation. An exceptionally diverse opening session of five thousand attendees, with widely divergent philosophies, sought a common denominator among old line Republicans, young Democrats, Communists, nationalists, civic groups, trade unions, religious bodies, political parties, and fraternal societies. They were determined not to be dominated by a particular philosophy or agenda, but rather to project a nonpartisan, united movement for racial progress. An extremely successful Second Congress met in 1937 in Philadelphia.

By the Third Congress of 1940, significant numbers of labor representatives attended the meeting and a larger than previous number of white delegates also attended; these developments as well as the Communist Party's turn from its "popular front" approach (see Chapter 2 for more on the Communist Party and the NNC), meant a lesser emphasis on racial justice. More importantly, the NNC veered from its original purpose of being nonpartisan and led race activists such as A. Philip Randolph, who served as president of the NNC, to resign from the organization. Although the NNC unsuccessfully fought for an anti-lynching law, it was successful in accomplishing a number of goals such as increased black union activism, successful support of the CIO effort to organize the steel industry, and election of liberal local and national candidates, including Maury Maverick in San Antonio, but it failed to maintain the cooperative spirit and purpose of the First Congress.

The National Negro Congresses of the 1930s and the National Negro Convention movement of a century earlier were not the only black convention efforts that surfaced. During the 1970s one more effort to forge a black agenda and movement emerged, the National Black Political Conventions. The first, held in Gary, Indiana in 1972, portrayed many of the same positives as well as negatives of prior convention actions. All started from the acknowledged and necessary premise that a unified black approach to electoral, racial, and civil rights was needed. All brought together diverse groups and began by enacting proposals of unification. At Gary, 3,000 delegates from forty-four states established a national structure, the National Black Assembly. The Gary Declaration that emerged soon ruptured due to differences in ideology, strategy, and tactics. One outcome, the National Black Political Agenda, reflected a nationalist leaning and ultimately to a loss of support from civil rights groups, such as the NAACP and from political leaders who were primarily part of the Democratic Party. Over the remainder of the decade, three more national conventions were held, at Little Rock in 1974, at Cincinnati in 1976, and at New Orleans in 1980.

A common purpose permeated each meeting, that of a separate, independent black party with a progressive black candidate to run for the position of president of the United States. That objective had been part of the National Black Political Agenda. It was a key aspect of the considerations at the Third National Political Convention in Cincinnati in 1976. Among the more likely presidential candidates at that time was Georgia congressman, Julian Bond; Bond turned down the offer shortly before the meeting began. Other potential candidates considered by members and leaders at the 1976 Black Political Convention included Michigan congressman John Conyers, California congressman Ron Dellums, Indiana leader Richard Hatcher, and reformer Dick Gregory. Dellums became the choice of the convention; nonetheless he too refused the position. Dellums' life and career is catalogued in his autobiography, *Lying Down with the Lions: A Public Life from the Streets of Oakland to the Halls of Power.* After Dellums' refusal, the Cincinnati convention turned to Frederick Douglass Kirkpatrick as presidential candidate for the Independent Freedom Party. Unfortunately, the party had not organized an effective political structure (perhaps part of the reason why Bond and Dellums declined to be the candidate), and it did not appear on the ballot in any state. Also important, African American politicians in the major political parties were unwilling to be sacrificial lambs in likely losing efforts.

The Black Political Convention movement did not completely go away; it re-emerged as an organization named the National Black Independent Political Party, giving a name and focus to an idea and a concept that loomed in the black community for the past century—that of forging an-all black political party to challenge the Democrats and the Republicans. Established in 1980 at a meeting in Philadelphia, the National Black Independent Political Party (NBIPP) existed for six years and represented an ambitious attempt by black Americans to establish an independent third-party movement. At its height the NBIPP developed chapters throughout the country and attracted to its membership young, well-educated, and professional individuals who had been influenced by the black power movement of the 1960s. The NBIPP did not nominate a presidential candidate but helped in Jesse Jackson's campaign in 1984. Leaders of the Black Political Conventions and the NBIPP became Jackson's advisors and supporters (in 1988 as well), including Ron Daniels and former Howard University political scientist (currently at the University of Maryland) Ronald Walters. Daniels would run in 1992 as the presidential candidate for the New Tomorrow Party.

Despite its effort, the NBIPP faced the formidable challenge that every all-black party, as well as most other third parties also dealt with—the entrenched political membership of the two major parties. Whether it was Frederick Douglass who said no to offers of candidacy for high office, or Julian Bond or Ron Dellums, the basic reason was the same—they were attached to their respective political parties, and could lose their positions or their prestige by running as a candidate for a third party. On the other hand, it was obvious that if they could run, it would have helped the third parties considerably although it was unlikely that they would be victorious. The three Convention movements, too, were replete with positive and negative elements. They strove for black unity and worked to further the civil, economic, and political rights of African Americans. On the other hand, they generally discovered that the Convention movements' diversity, whether of the pre-Civil War, the 1930s, or the 1970s, was also one of its biggest challenges since the diversity sometimes precluded black unity. The African American political community was not monolithic.

It would take pursuing other types of challenges and strategies for African Americans to "breakthrough," to borrow a term from Gwen Ifill, to ascend to the presidency. Dedicated black politicians, race activists, and fringe party candidates strove for the office of president or vice president. Left-wing political parties such as the Communist Party and the Socialist Workers Party, committed third-party candidates such as Charlotta Bass and Lenora Fulani, black challenges to the two major parties, especially those of Shirley Chisholm and the Reverend Jesse Jackson, and the campaign consideration by supporters of General Colin Powell would help set the stage for the victory of Barack Obama in 2008. The beginning of the trek signaled the issues and the parameters for the possibility of an African American president.

Further Reading

Ali, Omar H. *In the Balance of Power: Independent Black Politics and Third-Party Movements in the United States.* Athens: Ohio University Press, 2008.

Bell, Howard H. "National Negro Conventions of the Middle 1840s: Moral Suasion vs. Political Action." *Journal of Negro History* 42.4 (1957): 247–260.

——. *A Survey of the Negro Convention Movement, 1830–1861.* Reprint; New York: Arno Press, 1970.

Buni, Andrew. *The Negro in Virginia Politics, 1902–1965.* Charlottesville: University Press of Virginia, 1967.

Daniels, Ron. "The National Black Political Assembly: Building Independent Black Politics in the 1980s." *The Black Scholar* 11 (March/April 1980): 32–33.

Foner, Eric, "Politics and Prejudice: The Free Soil Party and the Negro, 1849–1852." *Journal of Negro History* 50 (October 1965): 239–258.

Gilmore, Glenda Elizabeth. *Defying Dixie: The Radical Roots of Civil Rights, 1919–1950*. New York: W. W. Norton, 2008.

Glasrud, Bruce A. "Blacks and Texas Politics during the Twenties." *Red River Valley Historical Review* 7 (Spring 1982): 39–53.

Gross, Bella. "The First National Negro Convention." *Journal of Negro History* 31 (1966): 435–443.

Holmes, Warren N. *The National Black Independent Party: Political Insurgency or Ideological Convergence?* New York: Routledge, 1999.

McFeely, William S. *Frederick Douglass.* New York: W. W. Norton, 1995.

Pease, Jane H., and William H. Pease. "Black Power—The Debate in 1840." *Phylon* 29 (1968): 19–26.

———. "The Negro Convention Movement." In *Key Issues in the Afro-American Experience*, ed. Nathan I. Huggins, Martin Kilson, and Daniel M. Fox, 191–205. New York: Harcourt Brace Jovanovich, 1971.

Taylor, George E. "The National Liberty Party." *Voice of the Negro* 1 (October 1904): 479–481.

Walters, Ronald W. "Black Presidential Politics in 1980: Bargaining or Begging?" *The Black Scholar* 11 (March/April 1980): 22–31.

———. *Freedom Is Not Enough: Black Voters, Black Candidates, and American Presidential Politics.* Lanham, MD: Rowman & Littlefield, 2005.

Walton, Hanes Jr. "The Negro in the Early Third Party Movements." *Negro Educational Review* 19 (April 1968): 73–82.

———. *Black Political Parties: A Historical and Political Analysis.* New York: The Free Press, 1972.

———. *Black Republicans: The Politics of the Black and Tans.* Metuchen, NJ: Scarecrow Press, 1975.

———. *The Negro in Third Party Politics.* Philadelphia: Dorrance, 1969.

———, ed. *Black Politics and Black Political Behavior: A Linkage Analysis.* Westport, CT: Praeger, 1994.

Walton, Hanes Jr., and Ronald Clark. "Black Presidential Candidates: Past and Present." *New South* (Spring 1970): 6–10.

Wesley, Charles H. "The Participation of Negroes in Anti-Slavery Political Parties." *Journal of Negro History* 29.1 (January 1941): 32–76.

Wittner, Lawrence S. "The National Negro Congress: A Reassessment." *American Quarterly* 22 (1968): 883–901.

Wright, George C. "Black Political Insurgency in Louisville, Kentucky: The Lincoln Independent Party of 1921." *Journal of Negro History* 50 (October 1965): 239–258.

Angela Davis was an African American professor and political activist. She was a candidate for vice president on the Communist Party ticket in 1980 and 1984. (Courtesy of the Library of Congress, LC-USZC4–7998.)

CHAPTER 2

The Communist Party of the United States and African American Political Candidates

DAVID CULLEN AND KYLE G. WILKISON

Between 1932 and 1984, the Communist Party of the United States (CPUSA) nominated four African Americans as presidential or vice-presidential candidates over the course of eight elections. These candidates and the strategy they embodied of CPUSA outreach to blacks reflect important facets of the changing twentieth-century experiences of African Americans. Born in Alabama in 1893, James William Ford's personal and family history—his grandfather died at the hands of a white mob and he was part of the Great Migration—epitomized the existential struggle of black people in a white supremacist society. Ford ran as the party's vice presidential nominee in 1932, 1936 and 1940. After a long underground period of persecution, the party emerged in 1968 to nominate Charlene Mitchell for president. Mitchell, born in Ohio in 1930, grew up in a family who saw the fight for African American equality as part and parcel of the communist struggle. In the 1970s the CPUSA chose Philadelphian Jarvis Tyner (b. 1941), a youthful activist in the labor and civil rights movements of the 1960s, to run as vice presidential candidate. The final twentieth-century Communist Party vice presidential nominee was Angela Davis, born into a black middle-class family in Alabama in 1944. Davis had wide vistas and obtained a world-class education from a private high school in New York City, a baccalaureate from Brandeis, study abroad at Frankfurt and the Sorbonne, and a graduate degree with Herbert Marcuse at the University of California-San Diego.

The origins of the relationship between the party and the black community began in 1928 when Communists took up the "Negro Question" at the Sixth Congress of the Communist International in Moscow. The Comintern Congress declared that the African American community suffered both economic and racial persecution as a result of the exploitive nature of the modern industrial capitalistic state. Further, the congress recognized that blacks living in the former Confederacy existed in an oppressed nation, separate from the rest of American society. These statements and the perception by some within the black community that the Soviet Union was a state free of racial prejudice attracted a small but active group of African American intellectuals and activists to the CPUSA.

Among the first to join was James William Ford. Born in 1893 in Pratt City, Alabama, the son of Lyman and Nancy Reynolds Foursche, his family surname became Ford when a police officer, citing difficulty spelling "Foursche," declared that his father's name was now "Ford." His father worked in the steel mills of Birmingham while his mother cleaned and cooked in the homes of the white upper class of the city. Ford began his working career at the age of thirteen as a railroad gang waterboy, working his way up to steamhammer operator for the Tennessee Coal, Iron and Railroad Company. With his parents' encouragement, Ford continued his education while working. In 1913 he enrolled in Fisk University where his play as tailback on the football team gained him regional recognition. He also ran track and played baseball, briefly playing semipro ball in Chicago. Although close to graduation, Ford accepted the challenge by black activist W. E. B. Du Bois who called for African Americans to demonstrate their physical courage and their loyalty to the nation by enlisting in the military and serving in World War I. Ford joined the Army Signal Corps, serving in France as a radio engineer with the 86th Brigade of the 92nd Division. Within a year of his enlistment he was made a non-commissioned officer. His first formal effort to challenge racism occurred in France. Following slanderous remarks by a white officer to a group of black soldiers, Ford organized a protest and filed an official complaint. The army removed the officer from his command. After the war, Ford returned to Fisk and completed his degree. He then traveled to Chicago in search of work, arriving in time to witness the attacks on the black community in the bloody summer of 1919.

Thus Ford's experience in Chicago was not unlike what other African American veterans encountered upon their return, evidence that their acts of patriotism abroad had little if any effect on lessening American racism at home. In addition to the violence in Chicago, a number of white mob attacks against black communities erupted throughout the country in 1919 and the number of lynchings increased after declining in the previous few years. These events could not have failed to stir the painful memory of the lynching of Ford's own grandfather years earlier in Georgia. His frustration and anger grew when the federal government turned down—without explanation—his application for a job in Chicago utilizing both his Signal Corps training and his work in radio. Ford was convinced this rejection was because of his race. He managed to get a job with the post office as a dispatcher and soon joined the postal workers' union. During this time he supported the first organizing efforts by A. Philip Randolph to establish the Brotherhood of Sleeping Car Porters. His increasing political activism, however, resulted in his dismissal from his job. Ford claimed that the department framed him because of his militant trade union efforts.

By the mid-1920s, Ford's political temperament and experience resulted in his rejection of the Booker T. Washington philosophy of accommodation to segregation and support of the capitalist system. After reading the works of Eugene V. Debs, examining the labor question, and holding conversations with black critics of American society such as Randolph, Ford concluded that only the uniting of poor black and white workers through class solidarity into an alternative economic system would serve the interests of the majority of African Americans. So, by the mid-1920s, Ford was primed for recruitment by someone or something that promised a better world for the black community. Lovett Fort-Whiteman was that someone; Communism was that something.

Nicknamed the "Reddest of the Blacks," Fort-Whiteman was born in Dallas in 1889. Following his graduation from Tuskegee Institute, he traveled to Harlem and worked briefly as an actor. Interested in the Mexican Revolution, Fort-Whiteman entered Mexico and soon joined the Casa del Obrero Mundial (House of the World Worker), an anarcho-syndicalist organization. When the Mexican government attacked the group, Fort-Whiteman returned to New York, where he joined the state's Socialist Party and wrote for A. Philip Randolph's *The Messenger*. In 1919, Bolshevik leaders in the Soviet Union invited American Socialists to attend the First Congress of the new Third Communist International. Before Fort-Whiteman could leave for the conference, however, the government arrested him as part of its Red Scare campaign to break up leftist organizations. During this time he became a Communist but did not reveal his membership until 1924 when he traveled to Chicago to attend a Communist-sponsored "All Race Assembly." Following the meeting, he decided to stay in Chicago to become a full-time recruiter for the Party. Within a year and a half he met James Ford.

In 1925 Fort-Whiteman established the American Negro Labor Conference (ANLC), a communist front organization. James Ford attended the 1926 meeting where Fort-Whiteman convinced him that communism promised the best hope for ending institutional racism and the physical brutality that it allowed. That year, Ford joined the CPUSA. Although the ANLC claimed to have forty-five chapters, there were none in the South and the only two active organizations were in Harlem and Chicago. The failure to establish a foothold in the South and Fort-Whiteman's eccentric behavior led to a falling-out between the first successful black organizer and party leaders during the latter 1920s, leaving a void for Ford to fill as the leader of black communists.

In 1927, Ford traveled to Moscow as the elected delegate of the Trade Union Educational League, led in America by William Z. Foster. The relationship between the two men grew especially close during the meeting of the Fourth World Congress of the International Labor Union and would soon reward Ford with political opportunities upon his return home. The congress elected Ford to its executive committee. He returned to Moscow in 1928 to attend the Sixth World Congress of the Communist International. That year the congress called for "Self-Determination for Negroes in the Black Belt," that is the creation of a separate nation, a Soviet Black Republic. In 1929, Ford made New York his base of operations, hoping in part to take advantage of the political interest expressed by some members of the Harlem Renaissance and because the city was both the point of arrival and departure for the West Indies and Africa. Among the first to appreciate the link between the liberation of American and colonized blacks throughout the world, Ford traveled to Africa a number of times between 1930 and 1931 to organize workers. During this time, he helped organize the First International Conference of Negro Workers, attending their first meeting in Hamburg, Germany in 1931.

But events within, not outside the United States proved to be the catalyst that led to his political ascendancy within the CPUSA. As the stock market crash of October 1929 became the Great Depression of the 1930s, the CPUSA found itself in a position to attract members of the black community. The economic crisis weakened the ties that held the black community to the Republican Party and decreased the community's support of moderate organizations such as the NAACP and the Urban League. Black activists searched for an organization that held the promise of real change. The CPUSA quickly saw its opportunity and focused its energies on organizing the 1.5 million black workers in the North through various front organizations and appealing to the emotions of the 9 million who lived in the South through efforts that demonstrated the party's sympathies to the Southern black underclass.

The catalysts for the emotional appeal were the Scottsboro and Angelo Herndon cases. The International Labor Defense (ILD), a Communist Party-sponsored organization, saw that these cases provided an opportunity for the party to demonstrate its sympathies with the black community. The 1931 Scottsboro case involved nine young African Americans who were found guilty of raping two white women on a freight train traveling through Alabama. Many in the Northern press criticized the trial, arguing that it was an example of Southern bigotry. The nine defendants, ranging in age from thirteen to twenty, became national and then international symbols of racial and class oppression. The ILD successfully used their time, money, and publications to link the CPUSA and the "Scottsboro Nine" to the plight of all blacks trapped in an economic system that still considered them slaves. Following the Supreme Court's decision to overturn the convictions from their first trial, the ILD provided defense attorneys for the second trial but the verdict remained the same. Once again, however, the Supreme Court overturned the jury's decision. The State of Alabama held a third trial in 1936 during which five of the nine were found guilty. The CPUSA gained a great deal of publicity by providing both legal and emotional support to the defendants and by gaining the freedom of four of the nine young men.

The Herndon case linked the issues of race, class, and communism directly. Angelo Herndon was a black Communist arrested by Atlanta authorities for attempting to incite an insurrection in 1932. As a card-carrying Communist Herndon's offenses included receiving communist materials through the mail and publicly criticizing city officials for their handling of the poor, white and black, who sought public assistance. His attempts to organize the unemployed frightened public authorities and they arrested him under a state law that made it illegal to incite an insurrection The case quickly became a basic Freedom of Speech issue. Did a communist, a black one at that, have the right to speak his mind? Although Herndon was found guilty, the ILD worked over the next five years on his behalf. Thus, during this time the case provided a vehicle for the party to recruit new members and to publicize its policies. Herndon won on appeal in 1937 when the Supreme Court declared Georgia's insurrection statute unconstitutional in a five to four vote. CPUSA involvement in these two trials between 1931 and 1937 identified the Communist Party as one of the few organizations in the country willing to defend African American rights.

Ford benefited from these cases when the party promoted him as one of its most visible public speakers. In part this was a result of Ford's co-opting the authority of black communists Cyril Briggs and Richard Moore, leaders of the African Blood Brotherhood. The party argued that Briggs and Moore had strayed from the mandate to link race and class as a single issue. Instead, the African Blood Brotherhood emphasized a race-conscious nationalism and ignored the white working class of New York. Although stressing the need for black liberation, Ford argued that the community's freedom could not be achieved unless the economic system that enslaved both black and white workers was destroyed. Thus, he argued, the two groups must not allow themselves to be divided over the issue of color, but should be united by the issue of class. As the economic crisis worsened between 1930 and 1932, more and more black activists came to agree with Ford's arguments.

As a result of the Scottsboro and Herndon cases, Ford's work in Harlem on behalf of the party and his ability to articulate the goals of communism, the CPUSA nominated him as its vice-presidential candidate in 1932. His running mate was his friend, William Z. Foster. Ford campaigned mostly in urban areas and participated in the Bonus March of 1932, being jailed when General Douglas MacArthur forced veterans from their makeshift camps at Anacostia Flats before burning the campsite to the ground. The CPUSA received 102,785 votes in 1932 and black membership in the party rose to an estimated 1,300.

Between 1933 and 1940, however, CPUSA political strategy strained logical consistency, placing Ford in the difficult position of explaining the ever-shifting policies of the party. For example, for years the party had denounced such moderate organizations as the NAACP and the Urban League as the dupes of capitalists. Beginning in 1934, however, the party announced a call for a "United Front" arguing that the CPUSA and such reformist groups must work together in order to end discrimination in the workplace and lynchings in the South. In 1936 the party helped to organize the National Negro Congress (NNC). Over 800 representatives from 550 organizations attended the meeting at which the assembly elected A. Philip Randolph as its president. The party made sure however, that the position of Executive Secretary, which held appointive and budgetary power, would always be held by a Communist. Between 1936 and 1938, the NNC established dozens of chapters throughout the South. As a result of this success, for the first time the CPUSA finally seemed close to achieving its goal of being embraced by the black community. Ford's profile within the black community and the party was at its peak during this period. The party again chose him as their vice-presidential candidate for the 1936 election. His running mate this time was Earl Browder, a rising political star within the party. The two received 80,159 votes.

The decline by over 20,000 votes might have concerned traditional party leaders, but the CPUSA had other issues to address. The Soviet Union's show trials and the Great Purge of 1937 caused tension within and outside the party. United Front members began to question the goals and methods of Joseph Stalin. Ford found himself attempting to justify the mass convictions of many of those who had been the most loyal members of the party, including the "Reddest Black" Fort-Whiteman. In fact, Ford and Browder assisted in the defamation of Fort-Whiteman, when Ford was given the mandate to assure black Bolsheviks that their former colleague had betrayed the party. Fort-Whiteman ended up in a labor camp in Serbia where he died in January 1939.

The year of his death marked a new change in party strategy and another complication for Ford. For the previous two years the Soviet Union had denounced Hitler's Germany and called for both the United States and Great Britain to take action against the Third Reich. In September 1939, however, the USSR and Germany agreed to a Non-Aggression Pact. With the Soviets and Germans having come to terms, the U.S. and Great Britain were branded as being responsible for the war that had broken out that same month. Against this background, Ford was nominated as the party's vice-presidential candidate again, running once more with Browder. The CPUSA ticket received 46,251 votes in 1940. Black membership matched the rapid decline in votes, as the number of black party members slipped to under 200.

Less than a year after the election and shortly after Germany invaded Russia, the CPUSA announced yet another new policy position: the USSR, the USA, and Great Britain were now military partners and the party called for a united front in order to defeat Hitler. Ford now found that he had to caution against any black actions that might hinder the war effort, including Randolph's threat of a march on Washington if President Roosevelt did not open military industrial jobs to black workers. The NAACP's call for a "Double V" campaign, victory over fascism abroad and racism at home, proved far more popular with the black community than the Communist Party's call for patience. By 1944, black workers found the NAACP more radical than the CPUSA, increasing membership in the civil rights organization to over 400,000. That year, the party did not run candidates for national office but called for members to support the reelection of President Roosevelt.

In 1944, Ford turned 51. Although he remained a communist and an active member of the party, the combination of age, party politics and the Red Scare of the 1950s greatly reduced his activities. He lived in New York until his death on June 21, 1957, of natural causes. During his career he wrote one book, *The Negro and the Democratic Front* (1938), was a regular contributor to the *Daily Worker*, published a number of essays in pamphlet form, and consistently argued that his goals for the black community were those that all peoples wanted and deserved: a secure livelihood and an equal and respectable status in society. His old friend William Z. Foster wrote, in the *Daily Worker* (July 2, 1957) that, "in the death of James W. Ford, the Negro people have lost one of their most active, loyal, and farsighted leaders, and the Communist Party one its best workers and fighters."

In the year of Ford's death the modern civil rights movement was coming into being. A series of events in the 1950s combined to provide the catalysts for a community-based movement that challenged segregation and fought to secure equal rights for African Americans: these were the Supreme Court's *Brown v. Board of Education* decision (1954), the murder of Emmett

Till (1955), the Montgomery Bus Boycott (1955–56), and federal action to desegregate Central High School in Little Rock, Arkansas (1957). To discredit the civil rights movement, Southern opponents of desegregation argued that groups like the NAACP and the Southern Christian Leadership Conference were communist front organizations, or at the very least these groups had been infiltrated by Soviet agents. Increasingly sensitive to such accusations and conscious of the political atmosphere created by the Red Scare, the NAACP and civil rights leaders such as Martin Luther King, Jr. quickly moved to distance themselves from any hint of association with communism or communist front organizations. In 1950 the NAACP announced that it would expel any local chapter that the national office felt had come under communist control. King removed individuals from his inner circle of advisors because of accusations they were communist sympathizers. In a 1963 report to Director J. Edgar Hoover, FBI intelligence operatives concluded that communists had failed to infiltrate or influence the movement. That year King gave his famous, "I Have a Dream" speech, and in the following two years Congress passed the Civil Rights Act (1964) and the Voting Rights Act (1965).

Although institutional segregation and obstacles to prevent blacks from voting had been defeated, movement leaders, especially those who were young and had grown up in the inner cities of the North, realized that political power and social prestige were tied to wealth and the movement had accomplished little to close the economic gap between black and white citizens. This growing awareness that economic discrimination was perhaps more harmful than social discrimination was combined with widespread anger over the Vietnam War, which many argued was disproportionately fought by working-class blacks. These issues resulted in a consensus by many young black activists that as long as capitalism existed oppression would exist. Thus by the late 1960s, these activists argued that it was the capitalistic system that produced poverty, oppression, and war and therefore must be overturned.

One of those young activists was Charlene Mitchell. Born in Cincinnati, Ohio in 1930, she moved with her parents Naomi Taylor Alexander and Charles Alexander (Mitchell is her married name) to Chicago where her father joined the CPUSA in the late 1930s. Her first political act occurred at the age of thirteen when she joined the American Youth for Democracy, a communist front organization. In 1943 she was part of a group of demonstrators who forced the Windsor Theater in downtown Chicago to desegregate. Three years later she joined her father as a party member. As the post-World War II Red Scare developed, Mitchell went underground and hid her political sympathies, living in St. Louis between 1952 and 1954. From the late 1950s, however, she was more open about her membership and began to participate in party activities. Mitchell also had a growing interest in the liberation movements taking place in Africa. She participated in demonstrations that took place in New York in the late 1950s and the early 1960s in support of the liberation movement in Kenya. In the early 1960s she began what became a decade-long project, as she hoped to link the civil rights movement in the United States to the liberation movements of Africa. During this period, she traveled throughout the African continent, becoming very close to South Africa's African National Congress. Although she supported the American civil rights movement, Mitchell disagreed with the assumption that an exploitative economic system such as capitalism would ever tolerate the economic ambitions of the black underclass. She argued that the only true measurement of success was economic liberation and that would only occur under communism.

Thus, Mitchell was poised to take advantage of the "Black Power" movement that developed between 1966 and the early 1970s. In 1966, the leading student civil rights movement, the Student Non-Violent Coordinating Committee, voted to remove its white members, arguing that only African Americans understood the needs of the black community and that American society must recognize and accept the differences between its black and white citizens. Identity politics became the rallying cry of the movement, as, for the next decade, some within the black community celebrated their African ancestry and rejected their American heritage. With her travels throughout Africa, her rejection of capitalism, and her party membership, Mitchell held the credentials to speak to members of such groups as the Black Panthers, and the Revolutionary Action Movement and to support ambitious projects such as Amiri Baraka's Black Arts movement. The CPUSA encouraged her work and rewarded her efforts by nominating her as its 1968 presidential candidate. Her running mate was Michael "Mike" Zagarell, who was 23 and thus not legally eligible to run. Mitchell campaigned primarily in the Northeast and mostly on college campuses. The ticket received 1,075 votes and appeared on the ballot in only four states. The election proved how far the CPUSA had fallen from its zenith in the 1930s. Her campaign, however, was historic as she was the first African American woman to be nominated for the presidency by a political party.

Although she continued to support the party's efforts over the next decade and a half, Mitchell's status among party leaders declined as the younger and more celebrated Angela Davis replaced her as the highest-profile African American party member. Mitchell remained politically active, running for a New York senate seat in 1988 representing the Independent Progressive Party. At around this time, she openly complained about Communist party management and strategy. Her challenge to party leadership resulted in her "purge" from the party in 1992 by Gus Hall, leader of the CPUSA. Following her removal, Mitchell helped to establish the Committees of Correspondence for Democracy and Socialism, an organization whose goal is economic and political equality for all. She continues to live in New York.

In *Far Left of Center* Harvey Klehr writes that the party achieved its highest votes, membership and influence during the Depression era and that only a "trickle" of 1960s-era radicals from the New Left came to join the CPUSA, many of whom were children of "members or sympathizers." The party's leadership expressed frustration that more of the New Left had not come their way. As they had in the past, the Communists reached out to African Americans whom they saw as a natural constituency, arguing from the pages of the party organ *Political Affairs* in 1982 that the struggle against racism was "intertwined" with the struggle against class oppression. By then, Ronald Reagan had become a galvanizing figure for the party to oppose.

As it had in the 1930s, the 1970s and 1980s, CPUSA argued that racism and classism were the twin by-products of capitalism. For many in the party, the candidacy and presidency of Ronald Reagan seemed to open up opportunities with black voters. During his 1976 Republican primary campaigns Reagan had used the imagery of "strapping young bucks" using food stamps for T-bone steaks. Whether or not Northern white workers understood the significance of Reagan's choice to launch his campaign from notorious Neshoba County, Mississippi, with a speech endorsing "states' rights," the Communists knew that black workers, North and South, "got" that symbolism.

The Communist Party already had in place an outreach group for African Americans. After Angela Davis' acquittal in 1972 on murder, kidnapping and conspiracy charges, the organization created to agitate for her freedom transformed itself into the National Alliance Against Racist and Political Repression and became the CPUSA's principal hope for recruiting within the African American community. Although the party attracted few black voters during the years of the civil rights and black power movements, there were those who found the CPUSA's integration of appeals for racial justice and economic equality appealing. Jarvis Tyner was one of them.

Both as a trade unionist and campaigner for black equality, Jarvis Tyner (b. 1941) established himself as an activist on the Philadelphia Left while a very young man. One year out of high school, in 1960 he led sit-down protests at the lunch counters of Philadelphia's chain stores whose corporate sisters denied service to Southern blacks. Within two years he participated in a lithographers' strike, organized a Teamsters' local and brought groups from Philadelphia to participate in the 1963 "March on Washington." In 1961 he joined the Communist Party. He later moved to New York City to lead the party's national W. E. B. Du Bois clubs. On April 5, 1968, he organized an impromptu protest march on City Hall memorializing the death of

Martin Luther King, Jr. In 1971 he helped lead the party's attempt to link the widespread anti-Vietnam War movement to the party's interest in supporting North Korea through the "American-Korean Friendship and Information Center" which called for U.S. military withdrawal, not only from Vietnam, but also from South Korea. He later fended off a Nixon administration "investigation" alleging that the Young Worker's Liberation League (YWLL) was a communist front by pointing out that he had proclaimed the group's communist affiliation months earlier.

In 1972 Tyner, then chair of the party's YWLL, ran as the vice presidential candidate of the CPUSA along with presidential candidate and party general secretary Gus Hall. At its February 19, 1972, convention, the party, in an apparent overture to both the black and youth vote, named the 31-year-old Tyner as Hall's running mate in spite of the fact that he was too young to have served if elected. In further efforts to reach out to disaffected young people and blacks, the convention also featured the then-jailed Angela Davis in absentia with a large "I am a Communist" Davis poster and an impassioned plea for her release by Charlene Mitchell. After Davis' release on bail, Tyner made a point of accompanying her to her first court appearance and, later, after her acquittal that same year, he led a YWLL rally for Davis at Madison Square Garden.

Of course Gus Hall and Jarvis Tyner expected no significant showing in the general election. Indeed, their status as candidates was taken more seriously outside the country than within; perhaps this helps explain why, in the midst of their "campaign" for the presidency and vice presidency of the United States, Tyner and Hall paid a visit to Hanoi, North Vietnam, just before an American air raid on the city. Although they only appeared on the ballot in thirteen states this was a significant improvement over 1968 as was their vote total of 25,595 compared with the results of the last campaign.

In 1976 once more the party named Tyner to accompany Hall in the VP slot as the party's electoral standard-bearer. That year, 1976, marked the high-water mark in the postwar era for Communist votes with 58,992 nationwide. In the 1980s Tyner remained active in the party, serving as New York party chair, running for Mayor of New York City in 1985 on the "People Before Profits" coalition ticket and campaigning against apartheid in South Africa and for the release of Nelson Mandela. During the first decade of the twenty-first century, Jarvis Tyner continued to serve as executive vice chair of the CPUSA.

In 1979 the Central Committee of CPUSA renominated the party's general secretary Gus Hall as its standard-bearer for the 1980 presidential election. For vice president they chose iconic African American radical Angela Davis (b. 1944). By then, naming a black running mate for Hall was standard practice in the party's continued outreach to the African American population. Once more, the party hoped to broaden its sectarian appeal with a candidate who might not just arouse the interest of radical blacks, but of young people as well. For, by 1979, the 35-year-old Davis was an almost universally recognizable figure in American popular culture, the author of a best-selling autobiography, the subject of pop music tributes from the Rolling Stones ("Sweet Black Angel," 1972) and John Lennon ("Angela," 1972) and popular consciousness from the "Free Angela" posters across American campuses during her California incarceration and trial. The Communists could claim no other American with similar celebrity status.

As a bonus, the Republican Party's front-runner and soon-to-be presidential nominee was Davis' arch-nemesis Gov. Ronald Reagan of California. For it was through Reagan's 1969 efforts that she first shot to stardom on the far left when he vowed that she would never teach again in a California state college.

How a philosophy instructor at UCLA became a pop culture icon is also why she was so attractive to the leadership of the Communist Party. Born in Birmingham, Alabama, in 1944, Davis seemed slated for distinction. The daughter of college-educated teachers, Davis grew up in a postwar middle-class neighborhood. But, as the great-granddaughter of slaves she experienced another Alabama as well. She spent girlhood summers on her grandmother's farm where she slept on the floor of a four-room cabin and experienced the fullness of rural African American culture from feeding chickens to Sunday worship. In her *Autobiography,* Davis recalls with lyrical passion the bonds that grew between her, her grandmother and the ancestors she told of, and the very countryside itself: "After her burial the old country lands took on for me an ineffable awe-inspiring dimension."

A child of both Birmingham and the Southern countryside, young Angela also occasionally visited New York City where her mother earned a graduate degree during summers off from teaching. Back home, she attended the segregated public schools of Birmingham until high school. Both for educational quality and for safety, her politically active parents sought high school opportunities for their children as far away from Birmingham as possible and from the very real threat of Ku Klux Klan attacks on their racially integrated neighborhood. Thus, it was that Angela Davis graduated from private, progressive Elizabeth Irwin High School in New York City, staffed by blacklisted teachers who bought the school and ran it themselves after the public system shut it down. It was there she first fell in love with utopian communism and there where she first read Marx. She chose Brandeis as her university and graduated magna cum laude. During both undergraduate and graduate stints she also studied at the Sorbonne and the University of Frankfurt.

Hoping to re-connect with Black America and the struggle for equality, she returned to the US where, at the University of California at San Diego she earned a Master's in philosophy and completed the course work for a doctorate. By 1969 she was teaching philosophy at the University of California at Los Angeles, was deeply involved in the civil rights and black power movements, and had joined the CPUSA.

Her membership in the Communist Party gained the attention of California's anti-communist governor, Ronald Reagan. Under pressure from Reagan, the UCLA Regents ordered university president Charles Young to fire Davis. He refused, leading to the Regents' intervention to do so directly. Reagan publicly boasted he had fired her for her politics and promised his supporters she would never teach in a California state university again. But, by then, she had bigger problems.

Part of her political activism in California centered on her work on behalf of the "Soledad Brothers," a trio of state prison inmates whose cause she championed. During the summer of 1970 she traveled the state making speeches and raising money for their defense. A frequent companion was Jonathan Jackson, the seventeen-year-old brother of Soledad Brothers' leader George Jackson. On August 7, 1970, young Jonathan Jackson attempted to free three prisoners during a trial at the Marin County Courthouse. In the ensuing shoot-out, two of the prisoners, Jonathan Jackson, and the presiding judge were all killed and other hostages were seriously injured. The state alleged that some of the firearms used in the escape attempt belonged to Angela Davis. She contended that she owned the guns for her own protection and that Jackson acted without her knowledge. The State of California charged her with capital murder, kidnapping, and conspiracy; she fled the state and spent the next two months on the run. Captured and tried, Davis was found not guilty on each count. Due in part to the organizing work of party activists and in part to her identification with the Black Panthers and the black freedom struggle, during her incarceration she achieved worldwide stature on the Left as a political prisoner. "Free Angela" banners and posters, many bearing her striking likeness, became ubiquitous in youth culture across Europe and the United States

Once free, she made a triumphant world tour including the Soviet Union where she accepted the Lenin Peace Prize. She had become, amongst rebellious youth, a pop icon. She returned to teaching, in California, but remained active in CPUSA work as well. By 1979 she was the best-known Communist in the United States, and, it came as no surprise that the Communist Party named her to its national ticket for the 1980 election.

Although they made an unlikely pair—Hall, an aging Stalinist relic, and Davis, the essence of radical chic—they touched upon contemporary concerns of the Left. Their 1980 Communist platform demands ranged from free public transportation for senior citizens to the closing of all nuclear power plants until certified safe by committees of workers and scientists, as well as public ownership of "the oil monopolies and all energy production." Davis and Hall launched their campaign before the party faithful in New York City calling for a reduction in military spending, an arms reduction treaty with the Soviets, a guaranteed annual income for US households, and a freeze on plant closings by US automakers.

The Hall-Davis ticket succeeded in getting on the ballots in twenty-four states plus the District of Columbia. They received 45,023 votes nationwide, down by over a quarter from four years earlier. Undeterred, the party renominated the duo again in 1984. The party's official position was to cooperate with all anti-Reagan forces in an all-but-endorsement of Democrat Walter Mondale along with an enthusiastic lauding of the Democrats' historic nomination of Geraldine Ferraro. In the Democratic primary races the CPUSA rank-and-file were enthusiastic about Jesse Jackson and the Rainbow Coalition while the leadership remained cool to the idea, principally out of fear of diluting Mondale's potential strength. Nevertheless, rank-and-file members expressed support for Jackson as did Angela Davis who hoped Jackson's numbers would push other Democratic candidates to the Left. In fact, in an August 19, 1984, *New York Times* advertisement, Davis gave none-too-subtle permission to her supporters to vote the Democratic ticket. Admitting that some on the Left, disappointed with the Democrats' failure to adopt significant portions of the Jackson program, were planning to sit out the election, she warned that every such abstention "is a vote for Reagan." She continued: "Of course we say the most powerful vote, the vote with the biggest clout, is a vote for the Communist ticket. But the bottom line is a vote against Reaganism and Reaganomics."

Most American voters disagreed. Mondale got just under 41 percent of the vote with Reagan carrying every state but one. Hall and Davis lost ground from the previous two elections with only 35,561 votes nationwide. Gus Hall and Angela Davis would be the last Communist slate for president and vice president of the twentieth century.

Five years later the CPUSA was convulsed with diverse responses to the collapse of the Soviet Union. Disenchanted with the party leadership's inflexibility in the face of cataclysmic change, and alarmed at the support of some for the Soviet Army's attempted coup against reformer Mikhail Gorbachev, Davis and others left the party. Davis and Charlene Mitchell founded the Committees of Correspondence for Democracy and Socialism. Angela Davis never left behind her involvement with the cause of prisoners. At the end of the first decade of the twenty-first century she continues to lecture and write against what she has dubbed "the prison-industrial complex." In 2009 she continued to teach at the University of California—Santa Cruz where she is a Presidential Chair.

In the end, the CPUSA attracted few African Americans to its cause. Nevertheless, the party's early and insistent call for racial equality—as opposed to its call for a revolution in class relations—would one day be joined by a myriad of voices united in the mid-twentieth century civil rights and black power movements. The civil rights movement, especially, shook off its radical lineage and merged into the American mainstream.

Further Reading

Anderson, Carol. *Eyes Off the Prize: African Americans, the United States and the Struggle for Human Rights, 1944–1955*. New York: Cambridge University Press, 2003.

Berman, William. *The Politics of Civil Rights in the Truman Administration*. Columbus: Ohio State University Press, 1970.

Carter, Dan T. *Scottsboro: A Tragedy of the American South*. Baton Rouge: Louisiana State University Press, 1969.

Cruse, Harold. *Crisis of the Negro Intellectual*. New York: William Morrow, 1967.

Davis, Angela. *An Autobiography*. New York: International Publishers, 1988.

Douglas, Ann. "Jarvis Tyner: A Tireless Fighter for Race, Class and Socialist Revolution." *Morning Star* (UK) (October 11, 2006).

Dudziak, Mary. *Cold War Civil Rights: Race and the Image of American Democracy*. Princeton: Princeton University Press, 2000.

Foner, Philip S., and James S. Allen. *American Communism and Black Americans: A Documentary History, 1919–1929*. Philadelphia: Temple University Press, 1987.

Gilmore, Glenda Elizabeth. *Defying Dixie: The Radical Roots of Civil Rights, 1919–1950*. New York: W. W. Norton & Company, 2008.

Horton, Gerald. *Communist Front? The Civil Rights Congress, 1946–1956*. Rutherford, NJ: Fairleigh Dickinson Press, 1988.

Hutchinson, Earl Ofari. *Blacks and Reds: Race and Class in Conflict, 1919–1990*. East Lansing: Michigan State University Press, 1995.

Klehr, Harvey. *Far Left of Center: The American Radical Left Today*. New Brunswick, NJ: Transaction Books, 1988.

Klehr, Harvey, and John Earl Haynes. *The American Communist Movement: Storming Heaven Itself*. New York: Twayne Publishers, 1992.

Lewis, David Levering. *W. E. B. Du Bois: The Fight for Equality and the American Century, 1919–1963*. New York: Holt, 2000.

Maxwell, William J. *New Negro Old Left: African-American Writing and Communism Between the Wars*. New York: Columbia University Press, 1999.

Naison, Mark. *Communists in Harlem during the Depression*. Urbana: University of Illinois Press, 1983.

Record, Wilson. *Race and Radicalism: The NAACP and the Communist Party in Conflict*. Ithaca, NY: Cornell University Press, 1964.

Charlotta Bass at her desk in the editorial offices of the *California Eagle*, circa 1931/1940, Los Angeles.(Photograph courtesy of the Southern California Library for Social Studies and Research, Record ID scl-m0001.)

CHAPTER 3

Charlotta A. Bass

Win or Lose, We Win

CAROLYN WEDIN

Despite her having published an autobiography in 1960, *Forty Years: Memoirs from the Pages of a Newspaper*, and despite her having written millions of words in that paper as an adult from 1912 to 1951, the early life of Charlotta A. Bass, as she titles herself in her memoir, remains mostly a mystery. She arrived in Los Angeles, California from Rhode Island on the other side of the continent in 1910, having been sent to the sunshine, as were many people, for her health. But also as did many people, she seems to have aimed to begin anew on the West Coast, revealing little about her life before California.

Disagreement abounds in documents such as her marriage certificate, U.S. Census reports, her death certificate and burial records, as to whether Charlotta Amanda Spear Bass was born in 1874, 1879, 1880, or 1890 and even whether her name was "Spear" or "Spears." There is disagreement as to whether she hailed from Sumter, South Carolina, or from Rhode Island, or from Ohio. There is disagreement as to whether her parents were named Hiram and Kate or Joseph and Catherine. There is disagreement as to what kind of formal schooling she had.

Some of the seemingly erroneous information which is then repeated from one biographical reference to another appears to have come from census records of the nineteenth century, but the child born in Sumter, South Carolina in 1874 was not Charlotta, but Charlotte, did not have the middle name Amanda, and was born to Hiram and Kate Spears, not Spear. Most reasonable in regard to her birth date and place is the conclusion reached by

Douglas Flamming in his wonderful *Bound for Freedom: Black Los Angeles in Jim Crow America,* that we go by the document Bass herself filled out and signed, her Social Security Form from her work for the Republican National Committee in 1940. In this typed document, with hand-written information added, she said she was born on 14 February 1890, in Little Compton (Newport County), Rhode Island, and that her parents were Joseph Spear and Catherine Durant (Flamming, 385).

From the time Charlotta Spear moved from Providence, where she possibly worked on a local newspaper, the *Providence Watchman,* to California, there is no doubt whatsoever as to her achievements: That she took over a small Los Angeles newspaper upon the death of its owner in 1912, renaming it *The California Eagle;* caused it, with courage and determination and consummate writing skills, to soar; that she hired an experienced newspaperman named Joseph Bass, who arrived on the West Coast in 1911 from Kansas and Montana, to act as editor, and that she within three short years married him; that she and her husband formed an effective team as managing editor and editor for almost two decades until Joseph Bass's decline and death in the early 1930s, growing the paper to state and then national significance; that she engaged politically from the local to the national, to the international, moving ever leftward, culminating in her candidacy for vice president of the United States on the Progressive ticket in 1952. Yes, there is no doubt as to the achievements of this African American woman radiating out from the Los Angeles, California base she adopted and then developed from 1910 onward.

Finally, there is no doubt whatsoever that this skilled and concerned woman, Charlotta Spear Bass, devoted a lifetime of energy to fighting racial discrimination with writing, speaking, organizing activities, ranging from the pragmatic to the visionary. Nor is there any doubt that her disappearance from all too many histories is a loss to us all of an innovative mode, and of a wise, forward-looking activist and author. Likely she has vanished from common historical knowledge because her thinking, writing, and action moved her ever leftward, while officialdom of the United States of America bent the opposite way, particularly after the 1930s and into the 1950s. Like the Federal Bureau of Investigation (FBI) applicant outraged at a security report which labeled her "innocuous," causing her to become a flaming radical, Charlotta Bass seems to have grown increasingly outspoken as her FBI file grew and agents trailed after her. Following the 1952 election and her return to California from New York City, where she had briefly moved, possibly to be close to Progressive Party headquarters, she remained active, including publishing her 1960 book, until a debilitating stroke placed her in a nursing home three years before her death on April 12, 1969. It was only then, when she was dead and buried at Evergreen Cemetery in Los Angeles, that government officials decided she was no longer a security danger to the country and FBI agents were given other citizens to watch. Charlotta Bass, though not commonly known in American history, has nevertheless "become a larger-than-life legend for community activists and radicals of all stripes" (Flamming, 380).

Charlotta Bass's written legacy in the pages of the *California Eagle* lives on, especially in her autobiography which is so thoroughly the story of this African American newspaper. Childless, Bass had hoped that her nephew, John Kinloch, who worked at the paper as managing editor after Joseph Bass's death, would continue it when she was no longer able to do so. But he died in World War II. Some have credited Kinloch's left-leanings with Bass's leaving the Republican Party for the Democratic, and then the Progressive, during and after World War II, but that, among so many things about this remarkable woman, is not entirely clear. She wrote the last of her "On the Sidewalk" weekly columns (begun in 1927) on 26 April 1951 and soon thereafter sold the paper. In 1965, the *Eagle* ceased publication.

Since the Watts riots in 1965 and the Rodney King beatings in 1992, there has been a surge of historical interest in Los Angeles and its increasingly multi-ethnic history. From an urban area very white and Protestant from 1920 to 1961, the city became by the twenty-first century 30 percent white, 10 percent Black, 10 percent Asian, and almost half Latino, groups at times forming alliances, at times at enmity with one another. Charlotta Bass's own narration in *Forty Years . . . .* demonstrates the centrality of Los Angeles to her early activism, and her own life and writing become a major source for understanding multi-racial and multi-ethnic interactions, especially through the first half of the twentieth century. The city's early history was above all African American, she points out beginning in her Foreword, with twenty-six Negroes, sixteen Indians and only two Caucasians among the founding families. By the time the number of families had gone from eleven to ninety-one in 1816, most of the residents of the city were Negroes, she writes, and by the time of her own arrival in 1910, it had become very much a city of refuge for Black Americans, with the promise of higher wages, better working conditions, freedom from lynching terror, civil rights, and dignity.

But it was also by that time increasingly a segregated city, partly from an influx of whites, especially from Texas, who went about trying to isolate the black population in housing and in schooling, in restaurants and recreational areas, and partly from city leaders using the Southern immigrants as an excuse for increased segregation. These clashing sensations of hope and harbor on the one hand, and exclusion and violence on the other provided Bass with the deep activist motivation that would propel her through the next forty years. Why did she promise Mr. Neimore, the founder of the paper, to keep it going after his death? As she writes in 1960,

> my reason was very simple: I have always believed in the Constitution of the United States and in the Bill of Rights and all of the Amendments; I have always believed that this great charter of human rights was conceived and written by men who advocated freedom and liberty and equality for all Americans, even for those who were once slaves.

These rights must be "defended, yes, and extended," she declared (Bass 1960, 29).

Visibility beyond Los Angeles came for Bass in part through the *Eagle's* protests over D. W. Griffith's feature length film, *Birth of a Nation*, in 1915. Both Griffith and Thomas Dixon, author of the novel and play on which the film was based, came to Los Angeles to make the film. As in other locales across the county, the campaign against its showing was only partially successful, with some particularly violent scenes cut. But unusual and impressive were the efforts made by Bass and the newspaper to influence Griffith while *Birth . . .* was in the planning and filming stages, not waiting until it was finished and its showing was reaching vast audiences. Here, however, Bass ran into a difficult issue—many L. A. Negroes were employed by Griffith in making the film, and they were loath to have one of their own protest them out of their jobs.

Bass traveled to Houston, Texas in 1917, two weeks after the "Houston riots," in which, as she summarizes, the Negro soldiers arrested

> had a single thought that prompted their action, . . . a united demonstration to show that they would not continue to bleed and die for this nation and not fight back to defend their own lives and honor against mob violence.

The riots of Houston and East St. Louis and Chicago and Washington, D.C. in those war and post-World War I days should cause the American people to know, writes Bass, "that Negro citizens are determined to win complete citizenship rights and will fight and die to win them" (Bass 1960, 45, 46).

Other labor and union issues also intensified during these early years of the paper. In one of her early successes, Bass convinced the Los Angeles County Hospital to hire black women for the first time. When the hospital acquiesced, it asked her to serve as employment screener, taking applications and then selecting from among them. The Bass partnership had a perpetual problem in finding printers for the *Eagle*, a problem solved in part by setting up their own print shop. Negroes who despaired of work in the city and who sought agricultural employment were faced with the importation of Chinese laborers. It was in speaking to a laboring group in the cotton-growing area of Wasco, in the San Joaquin Valley, that Bass was introduced as "a lady next in greatness to Marcus Garvey," the "Moses of his people" who drew followers with his "Back to Africa" rallying cry. But Bass strongly contradicted the return to Africa portion of Garvey's message in her own, emphasizing instead the impact of Garvey which is so often missed in brief summaries—black empowerment in the USA Mr. Herbert C. Hoover, who owned the land, needed to be told by the Negroes of Wasco, Bass said: "'We will plant and harvest cotton if you, the great leader in the Republican Party, will demand the equal protection for us which is guaranteed every American by the Constitution.'" And, indeed, Bass realized that "the struggle for Negro rights must be carried right into the Republican Party . . ., that issues, rather than party labels, were the things to fight for" (Bass 1960, 41).

By remaining simultaneously a member of the Republican Party, the National Association for the Advancement of Colored People (NAACP), and an organizer and activist in the local Division 156 of Garvey's Universal Negro Improvement Association (UNIA), both before and after it broke from the national group to become the Pacific Coast Negro Improvement Association in 1921, Bass "covered all the bases," so to speak—center, left, and right—maintaining a pragmatic position toward progress, whatever would work best in each particular instance. Emory J. Tolbert, in *The UNIA and Black Los Angeles*, describes Bass in Sacramento in September 1921 speaking at a UNIA Art Club, and at a local chapter of the NAACP, receiving an award for civic mindedness, and says that it is hard to find examples of overlap in membership in these organizations—except for Charlotta Bass (Tolbert, 92). Charlotta and Joseph Bass also throughout their lifetimes found no contradiction, but rather synergy, between their political and civic beliefs and activities and faithful membership in the Second Baptist Church. As Bass put it, with the emphasis hers: "The early church was not only a place of worship; it was likewise the social, civic, and political headquarters where the people assembled for spiritual guidance, *and* civic analyses, political discussions, and social welfare talks and lectures" (Bass 1960, 21).

In the mid-1920s, with increasing Ku Klux Klan harassment, the *Eagle* published letters outlining the Klan's attempts to frame Bass and others and were sued for libel. The *Eagle* easily won the 1925 case, *The People of the State of California v. J. B. Bass, Charlotta A. Spear Bass and Robt. T. Anderson.* Congratulations poured in from across the country and of course Klan hassling only increased. From scurrilous phone calls morning to night, Bass said she learned "that those gentlemen who cover their heads and faces with sheets and hoods, are cowards of an indiscriminate and blasphemous type." Attempts to intimidate the paper even included Klan members appearing at the offices late at night when Bass was alone—she pulled a gun on them, and they ran. And from her later experience with surveillance she concluded that the government was certainly after the wrong people: that those who lynch and kill, who push to the back of the bus and to the slums, who deny citizens the right to vote "should be the object of the House Un-American Activities Committee's search for subversives" (Bass 1960, 58, 59).

By 1925, the *California Eagle* had a circulation of 60,000, employed twelve people and published twenty pages a week, making it the largest African American paper on the West Coast. By the time of the Great Depression, after 1929, much changed and much remained the same at the *Eagle*. Joseph Bass was ailing, and would be incapacitated as editor several years before his death in 1934, mourned by his widow as a man very unusual for the time in fully sharing authority and support with her. (Flamming tells a sadly humorous story of the couple at the height of their publishing achievements. In the 1920 census, they are first indicated to be a Negro couple, with occupational positions of editor—Joe—and managing editor—Charlotta. But someone up the line in the bureaucracy evidently concluded that such respectable and impressive work did not match the race designation, and changed the check marks to "white." The Central Avenue apartment the Basses rented near the newspaper office was in fact at that time in a very mixed area racially, with black neighbors along their side of the street, white on the other.)

With Charlotta Bass essentially moving to the editor position in Joe's illness, in the first issue of 1931, she published the platform that had previously guided and would continue to guide the editorial policies of the paper:

1. The hiring of Negroes as a matter of right, rather than as a concession, in those institutions where their patronage creates a demand for labor;
2. The increased participation of Negroes in municipal, state, and national government;
3. The abolition of enforced segregation and all other artificial barriers to the recognition of true merit;
4. The patronizing of Negroes by Negroes as a matter of principle;
5. More rapid development of those communities in which Negroes live by co-operation between citizens and those who have business investments in such communities; and
6. An enthusiastic support for a greater degree of service at the hands of all social, civic, charitable, and religious institutions (Bass 1960, 63).

Charlotta Bass seemed always to be willing to put herself on the legal line if that appeared to advance her people's cause. As early as 1918, she tried to join the all-white Typographical Union and was turned down. In the mid-1920s she sued a restaurant for refusing service to her and her companions. Then she took to pressure group organization, forming the Industrial Council in 1930, and becoming its president. This group aimed to encourage business in the Central Avenue district which was rapidly becoming Los Angeles' black district, and to combat discrimination against blacks wherever it might be found. From 1933 to 1936 she campaigned to convince the Southern California Telephone Company to hire blacks, and with the coming of World War II, from 1941 to 1945 was an organizer of and then strong participant in the Los Angeles Negro Victory Committee, challenging discrimination in the defense industry in its broadest sense, from job training centers in Watts, to locomotive drivers on the Los Angeles Railway, to the United States Employment Service, which up to 1942 placed black women in defense plants only in janitorial and service positions.

In the decade leading up to the war, and throughout its duration and beyond, Charlotta Bass and the *Eagle* also waged an unflagging campaign against segregated housing and restrictive covenants in property deeds, a practice which effectively barred blacks from certain areas of the city until it was outlawed by a United States Supreme Court ruling in 1948. And she and her paper were in the midst of early battles against police brutality, one of the harsh realities that pushed Bass during World War II toward a more sympathetic and inclusive view toward two other minority groups in Los Angeles, the Latino and the Japanese. The *Eagle* published a plan for an end to discrimination against and hiring and promotion of Spanish-speaking and Negro police officers during what were called the "Zoot suit riots" in 1943. In 1944 as a member of the Sleepy Lagoon Defense Committee, she railed against the criminal justice system in its prosecution of twelve Mexican American young men accused of the murder of Jose Diaz, comparing the Sheriff's Department urging of a "biological basis" for guilt to Adolf Hitler's theories of race. She did not speak out against the internment of Japanese Americans at the beginning of war, but by the end, she was vocal on the un-American nature of this action, too. World War II definitely caused Charlotta Bass's circle of concern to widen beyond her race, and then beyond her nationality as well.

In political party affiliation, Bass moved during World War II from semistalwart Republican, for example serving as western regional director for Wendell Wilkie, Republican candidate for president in 1940, to clear postwar radicalism, including the Progressive Party. The Republicans themselves as well as events appear to have pushed her out, for she says she voted for Al Smith, Democrat, against Herbert Hoover in 1928, based on the latter's attitude toward the Belgian Congo; for Franklin Delano Roosevelt against Hoover in 1932, and again for Roosevelt in 1944, since he "had not just advocated social, civic, and educational reforms in government, but he had started to make them real" (Bass 1960, 175). In 1952, she used Biblical allusions to depict her transformation, recalling that in thirty years in the Republican Party "I was as bewildered and as hopeless for the future as the children of Israel when they marched through the Jordan and failed to envision the other side." There were two worlds at Republican headquarters, she had discovered—"upstairs was a world for white Republicans and down below was the world for Negro Republicans.... As a member of the great elephant party, I could not see the light of hope shining in the distance...."

Then one day

> the news flashed across the nation that a new party was born. In 1948, in the Progressive Party, I found that one political world that could provide a home big enough for Negro and white, for native and foreign born, to live and work together for the same ends—as equals. (Bass 1952)

Between her disillusionment with the elephant party and the new party news flash, Charlotta Bass, particularly in war support, had warmed to FDR and the Democrats enough to be given the honor of christening the United States Liberty Ship *James Weldon Johnson*. This first American vessel to bear the name of one of her race was a sign, she said, "that slowly but surely the light of a better racial understanding and recognition is dawning, nearing the goal of true democracy" (Bass 1960, 131).

But after Roosevelt's death, by 1947 she effectively broke with the Democratic Party, too, urging in an *Eagle* editorial the formation of a new third party. In less than a half year, Henry Wallace of Iowa, former vice president, became the candidate for president on that new Progressive Party ticket. Bass helped collect the signatures required to get the party on the California ballot, was a California delegate to the Progressive Party's National Convention, and campaigned for Wallace.

It is natural to be confused by references to the Progressive Party of 1948–55 since this incarnation bears little or no continuing relation to the more famous Progressive Party of Theodore Roosevelt in 1912 nor that of Robert M. La Follette in 1924. Known in states in addition to California as the Independent Progressive Party, the 1948 group was formed as a vehicle for Wallace, who ran with vice presidential candidate U.S. senator Glen H. Taylor of Idaho, gaining the support of several other small parties, the American Labor Party of New York, for example, and, to the essential detriment of the campaign, the Communist Party, USA. As peace candidates in a time of temperatures rising in the Cold War, Wallace and Taylor in the November 1948 election drew close to 2.5 percent of the popular vote, much of that from New York State, and no electoral votes.

Wallace was not a member of the Communist Party, but the CP and sympathizers influenced the Progressive Party to the extent that by 1950, both those who believed Communist Party support should have been disavowed and the moderates who thought it hypocritical to condemn Red-baiting and yet force Communists out of the Progressive Party had left for good, so that by the time of the 1952 presidential election, the Progressives were a much smaller and more leftist group than they had been in 1948, and it proved much more difficult to get the ticket on the State ballots. The four-year difference would be clear in the votes garnered in 1952, only a tenth of what Wallace and Taylor had received, or two-hundredths of the votes cast.

Since a president Henry Wallace was not to be, after the 1948 election Bass continued her journey leftward without him. In 1950, she traveled to Europe, with the FBI turning over to the Central Intelligence Agency surveillance of this woman described as "short, elderly, negro [sic], female, gray hair, fat, wearing glasses, waddling walk" (Flamming, 368). She was headed first, via Paris and Brussels, for a meeting of the Defenders of the Peace Committee of the World Congress in Prague, Czechoslovakia in September. "The Stockholm Appeal" which was debated contained the following manifesto:

> We demand the banning of the atom bomb. We demand the establishment of strict international control to insure the implementation of this banning measure. We consider that any government which would be first to use the atom weapon against another country would be committing a crime against humanity, and should be dealt with as a war criminal. (Bass 1960, 159)

This resolution was to be brought before the Second World Peace Congress in Sheffield, England, in November 1950. But before that congress, students from seventy nations attended the Second World Student Congress in Prague, and so did Charlotta Bass. Here she was surprised and pleased with the wide racial representation, not only from African and Caribbean countries, but from places such as the Soviet Union. (Some authors, such as Jacqueline Leavitt and Gerald Gill, indicate that Bass attended W. E. B. Du Bois' Pan-African meetings in Paris after World War I. This apparent error perhaps originated in their both having been at the World Student Congress in Prague in 1950, where Du Bois was a speaker.)

It was to the Soviet Union that Bass traveled next, having learned that she could get in as an American journalist. In Moscow, she was met with flower bouquets by members of the Peace Committee whom she had met in Prague; taken to dinner; included in a celebration of Pushkin, the poet with, significantly, African ancestry; and, overall, made to conclude that "in Moscow there was absolutely no color bar or race prejudice of any kind whatsoever" (Bass 1960, 163). In Moscow, too, she found "During the ten days I spent . . ., I heard no talk of war" and "women had as many rights and opportunities as men" (Bass 1960, 167). The grand finale of her trip was the opportunity to visit Tbilisi, Georgia, which she compared climate-wise to her California, and which she contrasted, race-wise, with Georgia, USA Somehow, Bass concluded, Soviet Georgia had managed to end "the ages-old bitterness, rivalries, cruelties and general inefficiency of the old system of national, race and class hatred" (Bass 1960, 171).

En route Bass had received a cablegram asking her to become the Fourteenth Congressional District candidate for the U.S. House of Representatives on the Independent Progressive Party ticket. Despite a European doctor's orders that she do nothing but rest for three months, likely because of the arthritis she battled throughout her life, she accepted the nomination, answering in a cablegram of her own, "Start the campaign." Her platform? "World peace, world-wide neighborliness, jobs for all, civil liberties, and security" (Bass 1960, 173).

As a candidate for public office herself, she had begun locally with a run for the Los Angeles City Council from the Seventh District in 1945. Though she was unsuccessful in gaining the seat, she drew enough votes to force a run-off election. When she became a candidate in 1950 for Congress, it was for the seat previously held for three terms by actress Helen Gahagan Douglas, who would run unsuccessfully for the Senate against the man to whom she gave the enduring nickname, "Tricky Dick" Nixon. Bass's opponent and victor in the race, Liberal Democrat Sam Yorty, would eventually become one of Los Angeles' more conservative mayors.

Bass used her column in the *Eagle* as well as radio broadcasts to campaign for the Congressional seat. She grounded her appeal in, first, being thoroughly "of" the people she hoped to represent, and, second, the promise of America's founding documents, the Declaration of Independence and the Constitution, and one of the resoundingly echoing speeches of the nineteenth century, President Abraham Lincoln's Gettysburg Address.

> I have not lived on the border of this cauldron of racial mixtures known as the Eastside, and only hurled my "sympathy" at you in your pain and distress, in combating police brutality, in trying to secure jobs and find houses to live in. I have been a part of the struggle, and still am a fighting part. I feel that as your Congressional representative I can do more on the national front than on the home front to bring to fruition your desires for peace and security.... If elected to represent you in the Congress of the United States, I pledge myself and my sacred honor to aid in the task of bringing forth a new nation conceived in the hearts of the people, and really dedicated to the cause of freedom, liberty, and justice for all mankind. (Bass 1960, 174, 175)

Charlotta Bass did win the vote of the Sixty-second Assembly District, primarily Central Avenue, but not that of the other districts comprising the

Fourteenth Congressional District. After the election, she wrote in her *Eagle* column, "I shall continue my fight for decent living conditions and for all the little plain people in the city and in the United States of America" (Bass 1960, 175). But the 1950 campaign, undertaken while she was already under doctor's orders to rest, took much out of her, and it was following the election that she determined that she must sell the *Eagle.* Her final "sidewalk" column on 26 April 1951 accurately predicted something other than retirement for Charlotta Bass, however. After more than forty years of serving her people and her country as a neighbor, editor, and fighter "for Negro liberation," she said,

> I feel that I must now take time out to regain my health, to learn more about what is going on in the world, and what it means for my people, and to decide how I can be most useful in the years ahead.

She let no one off the hook, though, criticizing "former liberals," the "reactionary forces" that had "tried to crush me and THE CALIFORNIA EAGLE," and some of her "own people" whom she had helped become successful and who had now "joined forces with the enemy...." This valedictory column, in fact, with considerable detail, subtly moves its author from a definition of "my people" as the Negro people to a definition of "my people" as some Negro people—those who spoke up in defense of Paul Robeson and Dr. Du Bois, for example, plus "the fighters in the ranks of the Progressive Party, the International Workers Order, the Civil Rights Congress, the Marine Cooks and Stewards Union, the United Electrical Workers Union and other people's movements in the nation." These are the inheritors of the heroic revolutionary past, the guarantors of victory against Fascism.

> The future is with them and I am on their side. . . . . I have many plans. And one of the most important will be to assist with every ounce of my strength in the building of that unity of Negro and white Americans without which our country cannot be safe and without which no one of us can be free. (Bass 1960, 177–79)

Bass was soon given another platform for her powerful rhetoric, when she became the nominee for vice president of the United States of America for the Progressive Party in 1952. Nominated for president by that party was a lawyer named Vincent Hallinan, wealthy and encouraged through his wife, Vivian, who had gained both money and fame as a realtor and author of the best-selling *My Wild Irish Rogues,* on Irish American politics and labor in their home city of San Francisco. Hallinan at the time of his nomination had been convicted of contempt of court with a six-month prison sentence, the result of his aggressive defense of a union activist against a charge of communism.

The nomination of Bass for vice president was a surprise, and her short-lived move to New York City was perhaps a way to make the Progressive ticket bi-coastal.

Unsurprisingly, Mrs. Bass's nomination did not get sympathetic coverage in the mainstream press, with *Time* magazine, for example, calling her the

> dumpy, domineering Mrs. Charlotta Bass, Negro, former Los Angeles publisher and, until 1940, a power in California Republican ranks. Childless Mrs. Bass was steered left by a young nephew she adored, became bitterly radical when the nephew was killed in World War II. She visited Russia, dined . . . in Moscow . . . (17 March 1952, quoted in Flamming, 370)

Less understandable and predictable, W. E. B. Du Bois, long-time friend of Bass, one of the people whom she had defended, privately expressed unhappiness with her nomination. Gerald Gill summarizes the reaction in the black press, which, with the exception of the *Chicago Defender*, at least made mention of her candidacy. Ironically, most hostile was the paper Bass had just sold the year before, the *California Eagle*, which "denounced the Progressive party as a 'stooge' and 'stalking horse' for the American Communist Party" (Gill, 113–14).

What were the issues the Progressive Party campaigned on in 1952? Broadly speaking, peace with the Soviet Union, an end to the Korean War, civil rights and women's rights. More emphatically, and with effective rhetorical flourishes, they were the causes which Charlotta Bass held up in her acceptance speech on Sunday, March 30, 1952, at the party's Chicago convention. She began with three short declarative statements, two sentences and a fragment employing parallelism, moving from "I," to her race and her gender, and then to the American political and historical context:

> I stand before you with great pride.
> This is a historic moment in American political life.
> Historic for myself, for my people, for all women.

> It is a great honor to be chosen as a pioneer. And a great responsibility. But I am strengthened by thousands on thousands of pioneers who stand by my side and look over my shoulder—those who have led the fight for freedom—those who led the fight for women's rights—those who have been in the front line fighting for peace and justice and equality everywhere. How they must rejoice in this great understanding which here joins the cause of peace and freedom. (Bass 1952)

Bass then goes on to trace her own history and that of her race—we were here before the *Mayflower*—through its support of the nation in World War II. But now, she laments, "I see the men who lead my government supporting oppression of the colored peoples of the earth who today reach out for the independence this nation achieved in 1776." She lists specifics: South African apartheid, bloody French rule in Indo-China; Dutch repression in Indonesia; and "Churchill's rule in the Middle East and over the colored peoples of Africa and Malaya."

In a powerful series of parallel sentences she sets up the "my people," the Negro people, to "my people," the working people and oppressed of the world metamorphosis of her final *Eagle* column the year before. For forty years, the eagle stirred her nest.

> I have stood watch over a home to protect a Negro family against the outrages of the Ku Klux Klan. And I have fought the brazen attempts to drive Negroes from their homes under restrictive covenants. I have challenged the great corporations which [sic] Negroes in their plants. I have stormed city councils and state legislatures and the halls of Congress demanding real representation for my people.

And now, beyond the eagle's nest, she continued, she would continue to fight for all people "who are oppressed and who are denied their just share of the world's goods their labor produces." She would walk the picket lines for men and women of all races for the right to organize. She would cry out against police brutality as she did in the zoot suit riots, "when I went into dark alleys and reached scared and badly beaten Negro and Mexican American boys." And, she said, she had not hesitated to face "that most un-American Un-American Activities Committee," and she would face them again if need be: "I shall continue to tell the truth as I know it and believe it as a progressive citizen and a good American."

So I should probably retire, Bass continued. But how could I "when I saw that slavery had been abolished but not destroyed," when "to retire meant to leave this world to these people" (she lists many specifics) "who carried oppression to Africa, to Asia, who made profits from oppression in my own land. To retire meant to leave the field to evil."

And she, Charlotta Bass, believed "in a world of good and not of evil." She had been "called . . .to lead the fight against evil, the fight for human life and human dignity." And always with the specifics, to hold up her visionary statements, she asks, one can imagine with a sly grin in her heart if not her face:

> Can you conceive of the party of Taft and Eisenhower and MacArthur and McCarthy and the big corporations, calling a Negro woman to

lead the good fight in 1952? Can you see the party [of] Truman, of Russell of Georgia, of Rankin of Mississippi, of Byrnes of South Carolina, of Acheson, naming a Negro woman to lead the fight against enslavement?

And her finale: a longer paragraph, and then a shorter one:

> I make this pledge to my people, the dead and the living—to all Americans, black and white. I will not retire nor will I retreat, not one inch, so long as God gives me vision to see what is happening and strength to fight for the things I know are right. For I know that my kingdom, my peoples of all the world, is not beyond the skies, the moon and the stars, bur right here at our feet—acres of diamonds—freedom—peace and justice—for all the peoples if we will but stoop down and get them.
>
> I accept this great honor. I give you as my slogan in this campaign— "Let my people go." (Bass 1952)

We could say with considerable accuracy for the 1952 campaign of Progressive Party candidates Vincent Hallinan for president of the United States and Charlotta Bass for vice president, as well as for "third-party" candidates ever since, that Bass's other repeated statement: "Win or Lose—We Win By Raising the Issues" is the operative rallying cry. She crossed the country by rail six times in her campaign, distributing literature, making long, passionate speeches, usually accompanied by campaign manager C. B. Baldwin and his wife, Lillian, for Hallinan began his jail term in April and so was not free to campaign until shortly before the election.

Predictably, the Progressive ticket received "embarrassingly few votes" (Flamming 2005, 371) and Republican Dwight D. Eisenhower with his running mate Richard Nixon were swept into office. But, as Douglas Flamming says, the list of seemingly utopian dreams Bass articulated in that campaign—federal laws against racial segregation; equal employment opportunities for racial minorities and women; assurance of the black vote in the South; the end of colonial rule and the arms race; the end of apartheid in South Africa; cooperation with communist countries—are much less dream than reality today. Gerald Gill points out that several arguments in regard to foreign affairs raised by the Progressives in 1952 were later "espoused by J. William Fulbright, then chairman of the Senate Foreign Relations Committee, in *The Arrogance of Power* and have since been implemented by American foreign policy makers" (Gill 1978, 1997, 118).

The key? Flamming insightfully pulls together the history of Charlotta Bass, of Los Angeles, of Black America, and of America and the world:

It was not Progressive Party radicalism that moved Bass's definition of freedom to the center of national politics, [but] the insistent activism of blacks and voters in the West and North after they joined Roosevelt's Democratic Party. When New Deal liberalism first blossomed, racial equality was not on the liberal agenda. Black activists such as those in L.A. put racial liberalism on the Democratic table and made sure it stayed there. (Flamming 2005, 372–73)

We win, one can hear Charlotta Bass say, by raising the issues—and in our tiny two-hundredth gnat-like size, by nudging those humungous elephants and donkeys in the directions they need to go.

Further Reading

Bass, Charlotta A. *Forty Years: Memories from the Pages of a Newspaper.* Los Angeles, CA. Published by Charlotta A. Bass, 1960.

Bass, Charlotta. "Acceptance Speech for Vice Presidential Candidate of the Progressive Party." 1952. Accessed at www.blackpast.org, An Online Reference Guide to African American History. Quintard Taylor, University of Washington, Seattle. A shortened form of the speech is in Suzanne McIntire, ed. *American Heritage Book of Great American Speeches for Young People.* New York: John Wiley and Sons, 2001: 187–189.

Cairns, Kathleen A. *Front Page Women Journalists.* Lincoln: University of Nebraska Press, 2003.

Charlotta Bass and the California Eagle. Southern California Library for Social Studies and Research. www.sociallib.org/bass/story/index.html

Flamming, Douglas. *Bound for Freedom: Black Los Angeles in Jim Crow America.* Berkeley, CA: University of California Press, 2005.

Freer, Regina. "L. A. Race Woman: Charlotta Bass and the Complexities of Black Political Development in Los Angeles." *American Quarterly* 56: 607–632.

Gill, Gerald R. " 'Win or Lose—We Win.': The 1952 Vice Presidential Campaign of Charlotta A. Bass." In *The Afro-American Woman: Struggles and Images,* ed. Sharon Harley and Rosalyn Terborg-Penn, 109–118. Baltimore, MD: Black Classic Press , 1997.

Johnson, Gaye Theresa. "Constellations of Struggle: Luisa Moreno, Charlotta Bass, and the Legacy for Ethnic Studies." *Aztlan* 33: 155–172.

Leavitt, Jacqueline. "Charlotta A. Bass, The California Eagle, and Black Settlement in Los Angeles." In *Urban Planning and the African American Community: In the Shadows,* ed. June Manning Thomas and Marsha Ritzdorf, 167–186. Thousand Oaks, CA, London, New Delhi: Sage Publications, 1997.

Streitmatter, Rodger. "Charlotta A. Bass: Radical Precursor of the Black Power Movement." In *Raising Her Voice: African-American Women Journalists who Changed History,* 95–105. Lexington, KY: The University Press of Kentucky, 1994.

Tolbert, Emory J. *The UNIA and Black Los Angeles.* Los Angeles: UCLA Center for Afro-American Studies, 1980.

Shirley Chisholm, January 25, 1972, announcing her candidacy for the Democratic Party's presidential nomination. (Courtesy of the Library of Congress, LC-U9-25383–33.)

CHAPTER 4

Shirley Chisholm
A Catalyst for Change

MAXINE D. JONES

The next time a woman runs, or a black, a Jew or anyone from a group that the country is "not ready" to elect to its highest office, I believe he or she will be taken seriously from the start. The door is not open yet, but it is ajar.

(Shirley Chisholm)

Born in 1924, only four years after the Nineteenth Amendment gave women the right to vote in national elections, Shirley Anita St. Hill Chisholm had to hurdle the barriers of racism and sexism all her life. Her parents, Ruby Seale and Charles St. Hill, welcomed their eldest child into a world where one was often judged on the basis on their skin color and not on the content of their character or abilities. It was a United States rampant with racial discrimination and violence. Blacks all over the country struggled to earn decent wages to support their families and many cowered in the face of white opposition that kept them from participating in the political process. Unlike many faced with the same challenges, Chisholm refused to allow sexism or racism to handicap her. In 1968, voters from the Twelfth Congressional District in Brooklyn, New York, elected her to represent them in the U.S. Congress. In fact, she considered it "foolish" that she was both famous and a national figure because she was "the first person in 192 years to be at once a congressman, black, and a woman. . . ." She was not in Washington long before she decided to seek the presidency of the United States, not because she thought she could win, but to shake things up a little.

Shirley St. Hill Chisholm was an unusual human being. Her critics often labeled her stubborn, hard to handle, and a maverick, but Chisholm was intelligent, smart, compassionate, perceptive, outspoken, and sometimes impatient. Once involved in politics, it did not take long for her to figure out how the game was played. Problems arose when she refused to play by the rules. Chisholm spent her first three years in Brooklyn, New York, but economic hard times convinced her struggling parents in 1928, that their three daughters might be better off in Barbados with their maternal grandmother; just until they could save enough money to buy a house and afford a college education for their children. Chisholm and her sisters did not return to their parents in Brooklyn until 1934, but the years in Barbados were not wasted. Chisholm attended school there, "in the strict, traditional, British-style schools." She attributes that system for laying the foundation for her speaking and writing skills and for her valuing education.

Ruby Seale St. Hill was a strict parent, and Charles St. Hill less so. Shirley and her mother butted heads most of the time. Chisholm wrote in her autobiography that her mother was "thoroughly British in her ideas, her manners and her plans for her daughters. We were to become young ladies—poised, modest, accomplished, educated, and graceful, prepared to take our places in the world." Chisholm adored her father, who, she claimed, was handsome, a voracious reader and conversationalist and "would have been a brilliant scholar if he had been able to go to college." A Garveyite, Charles St. Hill was proud of his own West Indian background. He instilled race pride in his daughters and the importance of education. He was determined that they make something of themselves. Charles St. Hill also encouraged his wife, with little success, to be less controlling with Shirley.

Shirley graduated high school in 1942 with scholarship offers from Oberlin and Vassar, but remained home to attend the tuition-free Brooklyn College. She claimed that she took the only route open to a young black woman at that time and decided to become a teacher. The young realist took a major in Sociology and a minor in Spanish and graduated cum laude in 1946. Because she looked much younger than her twenty-two years, it was difficult to get a job after college. She was finally hired as a teacher's aide in a Harlem childcare center and began to take night classes at Columbia University toward a Master's in early childhood education. In 1949, Shirley St. Hill married Conrad Chisholm.

Shirley St. Hill had led a sheltered life. In college, she began to notice how whites treated blacks and resolved to do something about it one day. When she became involved with New York's political clubs she noticed that women as well as blacks were exploited. New York's political clubs found an astute and observant student in Shirley Chisholm. She observed that these clubs, organized by state assembly districts, often traded some type of aid or assistance in return for votes. All powerful, these organizations controlled politics and elected local officeholders, state senators, city councilmen, and assemblymen. The various political clubs often joined together to pick those who would run for judgeships and congressional seats. In the Seventeenth Assembly District, where she was schooled in politics, she watched how councilmen and political brokers treated those who came to club meetings for help. She considered it degrading, insulting and disrespectful. Angered by their treatment, she often challenged local officials by asking why they had not delivered on their promises or why white communities received services that black neighborhoods did not. Her questions were designed to "show how little they did or cared for the people who kept them in office." Chisholm had nothing to lose because she did not depend on local officials for her job.

She joined the Seventeenth Assembly District Democratic Club and experienced success early when she became a cigar box decorator and served on the card party committee for the club's annual fund raising affair, which included a party and a raffle. The club operated largely on the proceeds from this event. It was in this role that she convinced the women, who planned and put on the event without a budget, that they were being exploited. The women, who were members and wives of the male members, followed Chisholm's counsel and demanded and received operating expenses to the dismay of the men. Already some of the power brokers had pegged Shirley St. Hill Chisholm as a troublemaker, and in an effort to control her they elected her to the Seventeenth Assembly District Democratic Club's board of directors and later a third vice president.

Chisholm, however, failed to fall in line with club leadership. The young black woman, still in her twenties, and very active in trying to solve community problems, continued to ask questions and challenge club leaders and local officials about issues they ignored. Finally realizing that Chisholm could not be controlled, they kicked her off the board and out of the club. But Chisholm knew why she had been placed on the board. She wrote:

> The experience contained lessons that were valuable over and over. Political organizations are formed to keep the powerful in power. Their first rule is "Don't rock the boat." If someone makes trouble and you can get him, do it. If you can't get him, bring him in. Give him some of the action, let him have a taste of power. Power is all anyone wants, and if he has a promise of it as a reward for being good, he'll be good. Anyone who does not play by those rules is incomprehensible to most politicians.

Chisholm's involvement with club politics in New York was the beginning of her understanding of politics as practiced in the United States. "It is a beautiful fraud that has been imposed on the people for years, whose practitioners exchange gilded promises for the most valuable things their victims own, their votes."

The Seventeenth Assembly District Democratic Club was just one of several community organizations that engaged the young activist. For a time she continued to attend Democratic club meetings to harass the leadership, but eventually concentrated her efforts in the League of Women Voters, the NAACP and the Bedford-Stuyvesant Political League (BSPL). Chisholm served as vice president of the BSPL and gained a reputation as a local leader. She led delegations to city hall, spoke at rallies and in 1958 ran for president of the BSPL against a close friend and mentor. At the end of the process she had lost both the race and her political mentor, Wesley "Mac" Holder. Chisholm held to the principle that she had as much of a right to seek the position as anyone, "that was what democracy was all about."

Chisholm had the energy to hold a full-time job, serve as a wife and community activist, and earn a graduate degree from Columbia University. After losing the 1958 BSPL leadership race, she devoted her attention fully to her career in childcare. No longer a teacher's aide, she had served as director of several childcare centers before leaving in 1959 to work as a consultant for the city of New York. For almost two years, Chisholm remained out of politics, but in 1960 she and five others formed the Unity Democratic Club with the sole purpose of challenging the Seventeenth Assembly District Democratic Club for control of the district. The Unity Democratic Club joined forces with the Nostrand Democratic Club and ran a black candidate for state assemblyman. Their platform included more jobs for blacks and Puerto Ricans, better health care, housing, and schools. Though unsuccessful, their candidate garnered 42 percent of the vote.

This only encouraged Chisholm and the Unity Club to keep their grass-roots campaign going and to prepare for the 1962 election. In the fall 1962 election, their candidates for the state assembly seat and district co-leader received 60 percent of the vote. Chisholm considered this a historic moment because their victory added much needed diversity to the county committee. The Unity Democratic Club became the official Democratic organization for the Seventeenth District with Chisholm as one of the leaders, who she claimed "were now in a position, for the first time, to exert some leverage on the party and the state legislature in behalf of the people who had been second-class citizens all their lives." For Chisholm, it was never about power for personal gain or to hold sway over others. It was about making government truly representative and giving people a voice.

In 1964, Shirley Chisholm ran for a vacant Seventeenth District state assembly seat. Though she met resistance from every corner, including from men and members of the Unity Democratic Club, Chisholm decided that she had more than paid her dues, was qualified for the seat, and that it was time for a change. She refused to be denied the opportunity because of her sex. Both men and women questioned her decision to seek a position outside of the women's sphere, and reminded her that her place was at home taking care of her husband. Chisholm claimed that she understood why black men lashed out at black women who seemingly were overstepping their bounds, "in a society that denied them real manhood, I was threatening their shaky self-esteem still more." She patiently explained to them that she only wanted the opportunity to protect their interests on the state level.

Chisholm easily won the primary, but faced money problems in the general election. The Unity Democratic Club could provide support, but very little of it financial. She made do with the $4,000 she withdrew from her personal savings. Determined not to allow the lack of money, racism, or sexism to keep her from going to Albany, Chisholm campaigned hard and easily defeated her two challengers. She became only the second woman to represent an assembly district and was one of eight blacks to be sworn in as members of the New York State legislature. Redistricting contributed to the increased black representation. However, because of the ever-changing district boundaries Chisholm had to seek reelection in 1965 and in 1966.

Assemblywoman Shirley Chisholm puzzled the Democratic power structure in Albany, because they could never predict how she would vote on an issue. She was not a conformist, but being a maverick, as she asserted, did not keep her from being an effective assemblywoman. She earned the respect of many of her colleagues who sometimes gave her their vote, though they disagreed with her. Three of the measures she introduced her first year in Albany passed. During her four-year tenure she introduced fifty bills, with eight of them passing. Chisholm lobbied for state aid to day care centers, for increasing the amount spent per pupil in local school districts, and for assistance for disadvantaged youth to attend college. If being involved in ward and county politics back home in Brooklyn was equivalent to an undergraduate degree, then Chisholm's four years in Albany can be likened to graduate work. She took her job seriously, studying and preparing for debates. Chisholm stated, "I did not like a great deal of what I learned." She witnessed firsthand:

> Men whose consciences urged them to one course of action were forced to take another by the political dynamics of the situation. A man might be against a bill, but one phone call from a boss, advising him that his political future rests on his being for the bill, would turn him around. I have even seen a man cry because he was not permitted to do what he knew was right.
>
> It is what the system does. There are so many ways for those in power to control someone who strays. They jealously guard their power and

use it to make sure that they call the shots; they are the ones who benefit from the system.

Though often frustrated by the failure of representative government, Chisholm's tenure in Albany was productive. She learned several valuable lessons that would prepare her for the next stage in her political career. Chisholm learned that "if you decide to operate on the basis of your conscience, rather than your political advantage, you must be ready for the consequences and not complain when you suffer them." The assemblywoman determined that "there is little place in the political scheme of things for an independent, creative personality, for a fighter. Anyone who takes that role must pay a price." A woman of integrity, Shirley Chisholm was willing to suffer the consequences, but she remained optimistic that representative democracy could work.

A potential seat in Congress opened for Chisholm when a new Twelfth New York Congressional District was created in 1967. A citizens' committee and the Unity Democratic Club endorsed Chisholm, but her reputation of being "hard to handle" cost her the support of the county machine. That was okay with Chisholm, who welcomed the return of mentor, Mac Holder, to organize her campaign. Conducting an old-fashioned campaign, Chisholm spent ten months walking and talking to the people in Crown Heights, Williamsburg and Bedford-Stuyvesant. She worked hard, determined to show that "it was possible for someone with decency and a fighting spirit to overcome the system by beating it with its own weapons." Her slogan, "Fighting Shirley Chisholm—Unbought and Unbossed," described the young activist and assemblywoman perfectly. In a three-person race, Chisholm won the primary election and carried four white districts. Her Republican competition in the general elections was James Farmer who had made a name for himself in the Congress of Racial Equality (CORE). Farmer had a reputation and money with which to conduct his campaign. Sexism reared its ugly head in a competition that should have been about issues. The opposition painted Chisholm as a "bossy female." Mac Holder and Chisholm decided to use this to their advantage, by appealing to the women voters in the district who outnumbered male voters more than two to one. "It was not my original strategy to organize womanpower to elect me" Chisholm asserted, "it was forced on me by the time, place, and circumstances. I never meant to start a war between women and men." The ability to speak fluent Spanish also aided Chisholm in her campaign again Farmer. Chisholm carried the Puerto Rican districts in her decisive victory over Farmer and a Conservative party candidate.

Shirley Chisholm, the gentlewoman from New York, entered the Ninety-first Congress as the first black woman elected to that august body. She hired an experienced all-female staff and challenged her appointment to the Agriculture Committee and her placement on its rural development and forestry subcommittees. Chisholm had come to Washington to represent her urban and largely poor district, and while the Agriculture Committee was not among the three committees she coveted, it did oversee the food stamp and surplus food program and was concerned with migrant workers, all areas of relevance to her constituents. Nevertheless, the first-year congresswoman broke all protocol when she asked Speaker of the House, John McCormack, to change her assignment. McCormack reminded her to be a good soldier and she would eventually be rewarded. Chisholm retorted, "it does not make sense to put a black woman on a subcommittee dealing with forestry. If you do not assist me, I will have to do my own thing." Confused, McCormack asked, "Your what?" And in true Chisholm fashion, she responded, "It means I will do what I have to do, regardless of the consequences. Doing your thing means that if you have strong feelings about something, you do it."

Chisholm's actions offended McCormack, Wilbur Mills, chairman of the Ways and Means Committee and the chair of the Agriculture Committee, W. R. Poage. When they did not assist her, she took her concerns to the House against the advice of her colleagues who warned her that to do so would be political suicide. When Chisholm was not acknowledged after repeated attempts in the session, she walked down to the well and waited until Mills and Carl Albert of Oklahoma recognized her. She explained to them that she could not meet the needs of her predominantly black and Puerto Rican constituents by serving on the forestry subcommittee. Next, she offered a resolution removing her from the Agriculture Committee and requesting a new assignment. Mills asked Chisholm to withdraw her resolution because of procedural problems, but promised that she could offer it later. Her amendment passed and she was later welcomed to the Veterans' Affairs Committee by its chairman, Olin "Tiger" Teague of Texas, and placed on its education and training subcommittees.

The media both praised and criticized Chisholm for her actions. Shirley Chisholm knew the rules of the game. She realized that there might be repercussions stating, "politicians have long memories for a slight or challenge and can wait a long time to even things." But Chisholm had never played by the rules. She would be as disappointed with her colleagues in Washington, D.C., as she had been with her fellow assemblymen and women in Albany. But she strongly believed that

sometime somebody has to start trying to change things, start to say something, do something, be politically expendable. My little rebellion was not intended to sink the system; I was simply mad at being put where I would be wasted, and I could not keep quiet about it.

Chisholm intended to work for the people she represented in the best way that she could, including those who were not in her district, because they were being neglected by their own elected officials. The legislation to make the country better and to insure equality had already been passed, but Congress and the administration, according to Chisholm, did not allow them to work. She described her role in Congress as such:

> So I do not see myself as a lawmaker, an innovator in the field of legislation. America has the laws and the material resources it takes to insure justice for all its people. What it lacks is the heart, the humanity, the Christian love that it would take. It is perhaps unrealistic to hope that I can help give this nation any of those things, but that is what I believe I have to try to do.

Chisholm's maiden speech, given in March 1969, called for an end to U.S. involvement in Vietnam and denounced military spending. Cutting social programs to fund the war and to build an ABM system was wrong, Chisholm said, when so many Americans were suffering. This speech attracted the attention of the nation's college students. Voters reelected Shirley Chisholm to Congress in 1970, 1972, 1974, 1976, 1978, and 1980. In addition to calling for an end to the war in Southeast Asia, and a focus on poverty, racism, and other problems that plagued the United States, Chisholm became the voice for the poor, minorities, and women. One of the founders of the National Organization of Women (NOW), Chisholm lobbied for and sponsored the Equal Rights Amendment, telling her male colleagues "As a black person, I am no stranger to race prejudice. But the truth is that in the political world I have been far oftener discriminated against because I am a woman than because I am black." Chisholm claimed that men and even some women refused to believe that prejudice against women existed because it was invisible. The congresswoman also supported a woman's right to have an abortion. Shirley Chisholm went to the nation's capital to be what she had always been—an activist and an advocate for blacks, browns, reds, yellows, whites, the poor, and women. Because of her stance on the issues mentioned above, she quietly gained a national constituency. It did not take long for the gentlewoman from New York to become disillusioned with her congressional colleagues, many of whom she believed had no conscience. She concluded that there was not much she could do in Congress in a legislative way.

It was during Chisholm's second term as a representative from New York that she began to entertain the idea of running for the presidency of the United States of America. College students who supported her anti-war stance on the Vietnam War invited her to their campuses. Between 1969 and the end of her second term in Congress, Chisholm gave speeches on more than one hundred campuses all across the country. She often spoke of her frustration with the legislature and the administration. On one campus in the South, a white male student asked her to run for president, to break the "tradition." This was the first of many such requests and promises of support. Chisholm began seriously to ponder the question during the summer of 1971, but she knew what she would be up against. An honest appraisal convinced her that lack of money, and her race and sex were at the top of the list of reasons not to run.

Shirley Chisholm never backed away from challenges and she would face many just in making a decision to run for the country's highest office. Opposition to her candidacy came from the black community and the Congressional Black Caucus (CBC). A group of black leaders and politicians met in Chicago in late 1971 to formulate a strategic plan for blacks to follow in the 1972 presidential election. There was little support for Chisholm at this meeting. Many of the black men attending this session supported the sentiment of one in attendance who told a reporter, "In this first serious effort of blacks for high political office, it would be better if it were a man." Others believed that she would be a candidate for women and not for blacks. With two exceptions, Chisholm's colleagues in the CBC gave little encouragement.

Chisholm, very much aware of the feelings of black men about her possible candidacy, boldly asserted at an Operation Breadbasket Black Expo in Chicago in October 1971 that she did not expect the endorsement or support of black men. Claiming, "they would never endorse me. They are the prisoners of their traditional attitudes, and some of them are just plain jealous, because they have been wounded in their male egos." She told them, "Get off my back!"

> If I make the race, I want it clear that it will be without seeking anyone's endorsement. The endorsements I have so far have come from those who are not regarded as leaders, men who play a role in the decision of who will run for President. My backing is coming from just plain people, and that is enough for me. That will be my inspiration, if I do make the decision to accept the challenge, and see whether I can be a catalyst for change in this country, an instrument the people can use to shake up the system.

Chisholm believed that women's talents were being wasted in the struggle for liberation because of black male vanity and insecurities. How could they question her commitment to black causes?

Shirley Anita St. Hill Chisholm announced her candidacy for the Democratic nomination for the presidency of the United States on January 25, 1972, at the Concord Baptist Church in Brooklyn, New York. "I am not the candidate of black America, although I am black and proud," she told her audience. "I am not the candidate of the women's movement of this country, although I am a woman, and I am equally proud of that." Chisholm declared, "I am not the candidate of any political bosses or special interests. . . . I am the candidate of the people." The field for the Democratic Party's nomination was a crowded one. Edmund Muskie, George McGovern, George Wallace, and Hubert Humphrey were the big front-runners. But there were others seeking the nomination as well, including Chisholm's friend and New York colleague John Lindsay, who had only recently switched his registration from Republican to Democratic; Henry "Scoop" Jackson; and Wilbur Mills. Several black colleagues sought to earn delegates as favorite sons, including Walter Fauntroy.

So, for the first time in the history of the United States, a black woman sought the presidential nomination of a major political party. She was not the first woman to seek such a nomination; Margaret Chase Smith established that precedent when she announced for the Republican nomination in 1964. Senator George Aiken of Vermont placed her name in nomination at the Republican National Convention held in San Francisco. Smith reminded voters often that she was not a feminist. She ran on her record as a senator, "not a woman senator." At the beginning of the primaries, Chisholm was not the only woman seeking the Democratic Party's nomination. Patsy T. Mink, a congresswoman from Hawaii, was on the ballot in a few states, including Oregon and Wisconsin, but by May had withdrawn from the competition.

Chisholm was not "ego-tripping" as some of her critics claimed. She knew her chances of winning the Democratic Party's nomination were slim and unrealistic. But here was a woman who refused to be trapped by her race and her sex. Shirley Chisholm believed that she had the potential to fashion a coalition that included blacks, women, young voters, and older whites who were disillusioned with the existing political landscape. She considered herself the strongest black candidate available and acknowledged that she was not just a black candidate. Her positions on the Vietnam War, Women's Rights, abortion, and social issues attracted many supporters, including those who had just gained the right to vote with the passage of the Twenty-sixth Amendment.

LaVerne McCain Gill in *African American Women in Congress* claims that the above issues made Chisholm's campaign a feasible one. Chisholm even thought that she had a chance of garnering about 85 percent of the black vote if black leaders backed her. But without financing to run a national campaign and the support from crucial groups the effort was doomed. Those who urged Chisholm to run and those who believed that she could make a difference, even if she could not win, contributed approximately $95,000 to her campaign. Campaign expenses totaled $300,000.

The Congressional Black Caucus did not endorse Shirley Chisholm and neither did the National Black Political Convention, which met in March 1972. Many of Chisholm's friends in NOW and other women's groups applauded and supported her right to seek the office, but only a few even considered the congresswoman a serious candidate. Chisholm did not expect men of any color to support her, but she was surprised by the lack of support from Bella Abzug and disappointed with the half-hearted initial support from Gloria Steinem and Betty Friedan. It was the grassroots support that fueled and sustained Chisholm's campaign.

Loyal supporters with more time than money worked hard for Chisholm in Florida. Chisholm spoke before large and enthusiastic crowds in the Sunshine State, including two thousand students at Florida State University. Black state representative Gwendolyn Sawyer pledged her support and befriended Chisholm. Alcee Hastings, a black attorney with a political future, attacked Chisholm and correctly predicted "she would get the heck beaten out of her in this state." Despite the stumping she did across Florida, Chisholm received only 4 percent of the votes cast in a field crowded with thirteen candidates. Florida was only the first state in which Chisholm actively campaigned. She also campaigned in New York, New Jersey, California, Minnesota, Michigan, Massachusetts, and North Carolina. In the Massachusetts primary Chisholm earned seven delegates; and eight more in Minnesota. When the primaries ended Chisholm had twenty-eight committed delegates. Margaret Chase Smith had won sixteen.

The Democratic National Convention was held July 10–13, in Miami Beach, Florida. Even with all the behind the scenes maneuverings, the outcome of the convention was obvious. Nevertheless, a historic script was allowed to unfold when Percy Sutton placed Congresswoman Chisholm's name into nomination. On the first ballot, McGovern received enough votes to win the party's nomination, but Shirley Chisholm received 151.25 votes. Chisholm became the first black and the first black woman to seek the nomination of a major political party. Though criticized throughout her campaign she stayed the course, claiming, "Once I was in the campaign, I had to stay all the way to the end, all the way to the night at the convention. Nothing less would have shown that I was a serious candidate."

Shirley Chisholm knew from the beginning, as did her supporters, that she would not become the Democratic Party's choice to run against the Republican incumbent, Richard Nixon. Their intent was to force the party to be more responsive to the needs of the poor, minorities, and women. There was also hope that they could have some influence in crafting the party's platform and in selecting a vice presidential running mate or even cabinet members if the Democrats won the November election. But the Chisholm campaign faced too many hurdles and challenges. She could never convince the American people to take her candidacy seriously. Even those voters who agreed with Chisholm believed that their votes would be wasted if they voted for her. According to Chisholm,

> politics in this country is a game that most people feel should be played to win, and it was hard for me to persuade them to use their votes to "shake up the system within the system," as I kept urging.

Black leaders doubted Chisholm's commitment to black causes and refused to endorse her. And unfortunately within her camp, blacks and whites and men and women fought each other for control. This rivalry between her black male and white women campaign workers apparently became very bitter and hostile in California. Chisholm explained that it was a competition over which group was "going to own me and my candidacy." The infighting did not help. From day one, the Chisholm campaign was plagued with disorganization, lack of finances and of a national strategy. She failed to earn critical support from black leaders and her own colleagues in the Congressional Black Caucus. Black women have always been forced to choose between race and sex. For generations, black women chose race. Shirley Chisholm refused to play that game, even though it cost her. She wrote in *The Good Fight*: "It is important to remember that I never made the rights of women or of blacks a primary theme of my campaign but insisted on making my role that of a potential voice for all the out-groups, those included."

A critical appraisal of Shirley Chisholm's efforts to earn the 1972 Democratic Party nomination for president remains to be written. Ronald Walters concludes in *Black Presidential Politics in America* that Chisholm's candidacy never matured or developed legitimacy. She failed to gain the bargaining leverage that she hoped her campaign would produce. In her assessment of Chisholm's presidential campaign, Julie Gallagher notes that Chisholm remained an outsider by choice when she failed to make "overtures of accommodation," with national black leaders. She appeared content to remain outside the circle of blacks who were planning a national strategy to approach the 1972 presidential campaign. This decision was costly.

After the Democratic National Convention, Chisholm worked to elect George McGovern. She returned her attention fully to her duties as Congresswoman and continued to serve, until her retirement in 1982, as a voice for women, minorities, and the poor. In 1993, President Bill Clinton offered Chisholm the ambassadorship to Jamaica, but for health reasons she declined. She watched as others would attempt to follow the blueprint that she left: "The next campaign by a woman or a black must be well prepared and well financed; it must be planned long in advance, and it must aim at the building of a new coalition."

In a sense, Shirley Chisholm achieved what she set out to do—"to shake up the system." When asked by the producer of a documentary about her 1972 campaign how she wished to be remembered, Chisholm stated:

> When I die, I want to be remembered as a woman who lived in the twentieth century and who dared to be a catalyst of change. I don't want to be remembered as the first black woman who went to Congress. And I don't even want to be remembered as the first woman who happened to be black to make a bid for the presidency. I want to be remembered as a woman who fought for change in the twentieth century. That's what I want.

Shirley Chisholm died January 1, 2005, but she left the door ajar for the candidate who would follow her blueprint.

Further Reading

Chisholm, Shirley. *Unbought and Unbossed.* Boston: Houghton Mifflin Company, 1970.
——. *The Good Fight.* New York: Harper & Row Publishers, 1973.
Duffy, Susan, comp. *Shirley Chisholm: A Bibliography of Writings by and about Her.* New York: Scarecrow Press, 1988.
Gallagher, Julie A. "Women of Action, in Action: The New Politics of Black Women in New York City, 1944–1972." Ph.D. Dissertation. University of Massachusetts, Amherst, 2003.
Gill, Laverne McCain. *African American Women in Congress: Forming and Transforming History.* New Brunswick, NJ: Rutgers University Press, 1997.
Gutgold, Nichola D. *Paving the Way for Madam President.* New York: Lexington Books, 2006.
Walters, Ronald. *Black Presidential Politics in America: A Strategic Approach.* New York: SUNY Press, 1988.
Walton, Hanes, Jr., ed. *Black Politics and Black Political Behavior: A Linkage Analysis.* Westport, CT: Praeger, 1994.

A campaign poster for Andrew Pulley, vice presidential candidate for the Socialist Workers Party during the 1972 race. (Courtesy of the Library of Congress, POS 6—U.S., no. 790 (C size).)

CHAPTER 5

The Socialist Workers Party and African Americans

DWONNA NAOMI GOLDSTONE

It's useless to stay in Democratic or Republican Parties.
(The Militant)

On September 1, 1919, Otto Huiswoud, an immigrant from Surinam, became the first African American to join the newly formed American Communist Party after the Socialists split into three groups. Active in the Harlem Twenty-first Assembly District club of the Socialist Party, Huiswoud became close friends with Arthur P. Hendricks, an immigrant from British Guyana and a theology student with strong interest in Marxist theory. Sharing a similar colonial background, the two men joined the Socialist left wing, which was about to be expelled because of its refusal to deal with the "Negro problem." Hendricks died of tuberculosis that spring, and in June 1919 Huiswoud attended the National Left Wing Conference and was among the group that met to found the Communist Party on September 1, 1919.

Joining the Communist Party was a shift in the black political ideology of the time. The early, pre-Civil War Marxists had a "sense of urgency of the slavery issue and its portentous implications for white labor." Post-Civil War labor leaders, like William Sylvis, tried to reach out to black workers, but he was not successful because he could not "breach the prejudices of the members of his own molders' union." By the turn of the twentieth century, the Socialist Party had adopted a "pure" class outlook in which the "liberation of wage labor through socialism would automatically solve the problems of race and racism." Eugene Debs, Socialist Party candidate in 1912 and 1920, promised that the "Negro would rise as the working class rose." Still, many African Americans believed that the Socialist Party did not understand the "distinctive dimensions" of the black experience and that they ignored the "special needs and demands" of the community.

In Harlem, a socialist current emerged as West Indian immigrants and native black Americans laid a foundation that was strengthened by the West Indians who had carried into the city a sensitivity to the social stratification of their Caribbean homelands. Their relatively extensive colonial schooling and sharp class awareness made many of them anti-imperialist and opposed to capitalism. The West Indians teamed with African American Socialists Hubert Harrison, A. Philip Randolph, and Chandler Owen. Harrison, who was active in the party from 1911 until his departure in 1920, was a brilliant speaker who electrified crowds by condemning capitalism as the source of racism. He urged blacks to "embrace socialism even though Socialists had not yet embraced blacks." Inspired by the Bolshevik Revolution in Russia, the Harlem Socialists organized the interracial Twenty-first Assembly District Socialist Party club in the summer of 1918 and also launched the People's Educational Forum, which focused on socialist analysis. The Socialist Party's refusal to address the issues of black Americans, however, caused many of them to join the American Communist Party.

Black communists, however, would soon become disenchanted with their party. Although the Communist Party believed that African Americans had "withstood systematic and special oppression" from capitalism, some black communists believed differently. In his 1939 essay "The SWP and Negro Work," Trinidadian Marxist C. L. R. James wrote that many interested African Americans were turned off by the Kremlin's creation of black leaders whom they then used for political purposes unconnected with black struggles.

> With its latest turn beginning in 1935, [James wrote] the CP has become openly a party of American bourgeois democracy. Not only to expand but merely to exist in this milieu demanded that it imbibe and practice the racial discriminations inherent in that society.

The Socialist Workers Party would soon become a viable alternative for black Americans seeking equality in the United States.

The Socialist Workers Party (SWP) dates back to the Communist League of America (CLA), which was established in 1928 by members of the Communist Party USA. These members had been expelled for their support of Russian Communist leader Leon Trotsky, who had gained momentum for developing his own theoretical branch of Marxism. In 1934, the CLA merged with the American Workers Party and formed the Workers Party of the United States. Three years later, a rift between the "official" Socialists and the Trotskyist faction led to the forming of a new political organization—the Socialist Workers Party. Rooted in Trotskyism, the SWP focused its attention on overthrowing capitalism and establishing a proletarian rule led by workers of all colors. Because their plan for a new political system specifically included the equality of African Americans, James and other African Americans departed the Communist Party in favor of the Socialist Workers Party. The SWP continued to gain popularity in the black community into the 1960s when Black Nationalism and "Black Power" reigned over the black political consciousness of many African Americans.

It is no coincidence that beginning with the presidential election of 1964—and in every presidential election thereafter save 1984—the SWP included an African American on its presidential ticket. Perhaps no document highlights the political significance of 1964 more than Malcolm X's April 3, 1964 speech, "The Ballot or the Bullet." As Malcolm told the crowd in Cleveland, Ohio:

> If we don't do something real soon, I think you'll have to agree that we're going to be forced either to use the ballot or the bullet. It's one or the other in 1964. It isn't that time is running out—time has run out! 1964 threatens to be the most explosive year America has ever witnessed. . . . Why? It's the year when all of the white politicians will be back in the so-called Negro community jiving you and me for some votes. The year when all of the white political crooks will be right back in your and my community with the false promises, building up our hopes for a letdown, with their trickery and their treachery, with their false promises which they don't intend to keep.

For Malcolm X and many black Americans, the Republican and Democratic Parties offered little hope that life would change for African Americans. One reason Malcolm X and black members of the Socialist Workers Party developed such a close relationship was because Malcolm was a black nationalist who publicly spoke out in favor of socialism as the best system for bringing equality to black Americans. "While I was traveling I noticed that most of the countries that had recently emerged into independence have turned away from the so-called capitalistic system in the direction of socialism," Malcolm said in a speech following a trip to the Middle East and to Africa. Malcolm also believed that the only way to do away with racism was to do away with capitalism. "It's impossible for a white person to believe in capitalism and not believe in racism," he said.

You can't have capitalism without racism. And if you find one and you happen to get that person into a conversation and they have a philosophy that makes you sure they don't have this racism in their outlook, usually they're socialists or their political philosophy is socialism.

Many black nationalists turned to the Socialist Workers Party because the SWP proposed that its black members collaborate with other militant African Americans in order to form a black party dedicated to civil rights. The SWP's foray into the black civil rights struggle led the FBI to begin engaging in decades of illegal disruption activities against the party. In a secret October 1961 memorandum, the FBI announced that it was creating the SWP Disruption Program on the grounds that the party had been openly talking about its policies on a local and national level, running candidates for public office, supporting such causes as Castro's Cuba, and fighting for integration in the South. Launched during President Kennedy's administration, the goal of the SWP Disruption Program was, in part, to "block legal political activity that depart[ed] from orthodoxy" and to undermine the civil rights movement. According to Nelson Blackstock, J. Edgar Hoover concocted the Cointelpro plot not so much to disrupt socialist election campaigns but because the socialist candidates were "openly talking to people about their ideas."

One political candidate the FBI targeted was Clifton DeBerry, a longtime leader of the Socialist Workers Party. In 1964, the SWP nominated DeBerry as its presidential candidate, making him the third African American to run for president of the United States. He did reasonably well, winning some 28,500 votes after appearing on eleven state ballots. DeBerry's foray into politics began in the 1940s, when he participated in union-organizing drives in the South and labor struggles in the North. In Chicago, DeBerry took a job at the International Harvester plant, where he became actively involved in the Farm Equipment Workers Union. In 1953 DeBerry joined the Socialist Workers Party, and four years later, he was elected to the party's National Committee and served on the party's Control Commission for twenty-five years. DeBerry's activism was not limited to simply promoting the ideals of the party and the working class. He participated in the national civil rights movement, helping to organize a mass protest meeting in Chicago after the murder of Emmett Till in Money, Mississippi, in August 1955. During the 1956–57 Montgomery bus boycott, DeBerry worked with members of the Montgomery Improvement Association to organize the Station Wagons to Montgomery Committee. DeBerry also joined civil rights marches in Selma, Alabama, and in Memphis, Tennessee, where he supported the sanitation workers in their strike for job safety, better wages and benefits, and union recognition.

As the 1964 presidential candidate for the SWP, DeBerry fought for the safety of black and white civil rights workers, arguing that President Lyndon Johnson needed to send troops to the South, and not to North and South Vietnam. "If as Johnson claims their purpose is to 'protect democracy,' then send them to Mississippi and let them do some protecting of Black Americans there," DeBerry said (Blackstock, 4). DeBerry was particularly concerned about the FBI's "complicity" with white law enforcement officers after the disappearance of three civil rights workers—James Chaney, Andrew Goodman, and Michael Schwerner—in Philadelphia, Mississippi, on June 21, 1964. Cecil Price, a Neshoba County deputy sheriff and a member of the White Knights of the Ku Klux Klan, had arrested the three civil rights workers and then released them that evening to fellow Klansmen who abducted, tortured, and killed them. DeBerry told his supporters that while the three kidnapped youths were in jail in Philadelphia, Mississippi, their coworkers became fearful for their safety and telephoned the FBI in Jackson and that the FBI agent refused to help.

DeBerry's public criticisms of the FBI led to his becoming a "favorite target" of the SWP Disruption Program. In fact, of the nearly 1,000 pages of Cointelpro files that have been released, more named DeBerry than any other person. The FBI noted in one secret memorandum, for example, that a review was being conducted of DeBerry's file in order to determine whether or not there was anything disparaging in his background which might cause embarrassment to the SWP if publicly released. They found—and did—such on a December 6, 1963 tour stop in Chicago. There, the FBI arranged to have DeBerry arrested in order to create a scandal that they might use to harm his reputation. Just before DeBerry was to address a SWP meeting, the Chicago police stormed into the building where he was speaking and they took him to the station where they booked him on charges of nonsupport of his ex-wife. The FBI followed up his arrest with "enormous attention" to try to get the news media to report this incident and DeBerry's earlier arrests for labor trouble.

The FBI continued its harassment of DeBerry. In April 1964, the New York office of the FBI recommended and the federal office approved the Crime Records Division to release to certain news mediums derogatory information concerning DeBerry. This derogatory information referred to previous arrests for nonsupport of his wife and children and to the fact that he was living with the daughter of the National Secretary of the SWP. After the SWP nominated DeBerry as its candidate for the 1965 New York City mayoral election, the FBI—worried that DeBerry would use radio and television to "spread the SWP propaganda"—again approved the release of more derogatory information regarding him. The FBI planned to disseminate the information to the press or in an anonymous mailing. DeBerry lost that election, but he continued to speak in favor of social and economic justice around the world. He supported the African liberation struggles, demanded withdrawal of U.S. troops from Vietnam, and defended the Cuban Revolution.

On occasion, DeBerry joined with Malcolm X to convey the latter's "revolutionary nationalist perspectives" more widely than might have been possible. DeBerry first made contact with Malcolm when he was still the main spokesman for the Nation of Islam, and in late 1963 he went on a speaking tour with him. After Malcolm's break with the Nation of Islam in early 1964, DeBerry continued to meet with Malcolm almost every Saturday. During those meetings, the two would discuss politics and often compared notes and checked up on what the others had heard about the "developing nationalist response among Blacks." At the suggestion of Malcolm X and his collaborator, James Shabazz, DeBerry spoke at a couple of classes at the Muslim Mosque, Inc., which Malcolm headed. Because they were often touring at the same time, DeBerry's and Malcolm's paths would often "crisscross," and DeBerry would attend Malcolm's speeches when he could.

The relationship between SWP African American candidates and Malcolm X extended beyond DeBerry. In 1968, Paul Boutelle, another black radical influenced by the ideas of Malcolm X, entered the national spotlight. That year the SWP nominated Fred Halstead—a forty-year-old cloth cutter—as its presidential candidate, and Boutelle—a thirty-five-year-old African American "transportation executive from New York City" (cab driver)—as its vice presidential candidate. The ticket embodied the two main concerns of the party: the continuing war in Vietnam (one of their main campaign slogans was "Bring the G.I.'s Home Now") and the fight for black liberation ("Black Control of the Black Community"). Born in Manhattan, Boutelle was a strong proponent of the Black Liberation movement. In 1963, he founded the all-black Freedom Now Party, which was built on the ideal that African Americans needed to create their own political organizations if they were to have any hope of ending racial prejudice. The "radical Negro Party" was a "minor force" in New York but had some supporters in Michigan, and it fielded thirty-nine candidates for federal and local offices in the two states, including Boutelle's candidacy for state senator in the Twenty-first District. Though the Freedom Now Party survived just two years, it engendered fear in the white community in part because of a leaflet it handed out. Entitled "American Democracy—A Damned Lie," the leaflet said:

> White racists like Wallace, phony liberals like Rockefeller, members of the John Birch Society and many others are free to speak throughout the country, ... But a black man born and raised in Harlem and the choice of a black-led and controlled political party cannot speak to his people. (Montgomery, 1)

Boutelle joined the Socialist Workers Party in 1965—though he was under great pressure to not join a "white" organization—and was the SWP's candidate for borough president of Manhattan that year. In 1966, he was the SWP candidate for New York State attorney general, and in 1969 Boutelle was the SWP's candidate for New York City mayor. In an attempt to undermine his campaign and fracture the SWP, the FBI operated a secret campaign against Boutelle, castigating him and his friends as "monkeys" in an attempt to "polarize blacks and whites within the SWP." In another attempt to anger Boutelle over the racism within the party, the FBI was granted permission to prepare an anonymous letter on commercial stationery to send to Boutelle's home. This letter said, in part

> "Comrade" Paul—Some of us within the Party are fed up with the subversive effect you are having on the Party, but since a few see your presence as an asset (because of your color only) not much can be said openly. . . . Why don't you and the rest of your fellow party monkeys hook up with the Panthers where you'd feel at home? Maybe then we could get on with the job Trotsky had in mind for us. (Blackstock, 10–11)

The FBI hoped that such a letter would create a split within the SWP and that such action would result in Boutelle's resignation from the SWP along with other members who supported him, thereby halting the SWP hopes for expanding its membership. Such did not happen, however.

In the 1968 presidential election, the primary focus for Boutelle was "black power." "Black power," Boutelle said, "means that the black communities should be controlled by the black people who live there." A supporter of the Black Panther Party and other groups "seeking self-determination," Boutelle said that neither he nor the SWP advocated violence but "rather change by any means necessary." President Johnson and the government, Boutelle argued, advocated violence, not the people. Boutelle and Halstead toured throughout the United States, appearing on numerous radio and television programs. At a campaign stop sponsored by the Jack London Society—Students for a Democratic Society at California State College in Fullerton, Boutelle told a group of 300 students and faculty that the U.S. government was the "enemy of freedom seeking people all over the world" and that the capitalist system was the cause of the world's problems. When asked about the war in Vietnam, Boutelle said that he saw America as "imperialistic and criminal" for going into Vietnam and that China and Russia had the "right and moral obligation" to give the North Vietnamese all the support they could muster. He also believed that the United States needed to "keep [its] hands off Cuba" and support the struggles of the people in Latin

America, Asia, Africa, and in the Arab world, arguing that Cuba was one of the most democratic countries in the world today.

Boutelle continued speaking out against the Vietnam War in his campaign stops, and controversy often followed him, especially on college campuses. Perhaps the most controversial stop was on October 16, 1968, at the University of Oklahoma. Boutelle—whom the student newspaper described as a Marxist and a black nationalist—arrived in Norman for a two-day stay during which he planned to participate in a Vietnam teach-in and speak on "How to Achieve Socialism in America." Though Boutelle had stopped at several college campuses in the South and Southwest, his speeches were hardly noticed and not well attended. At the University of Oklahoma, however, Boutelle drew his largest crowd after Oklahoma state legislators threatened economic sanctions at OU because they believed that a Marxist like Boutelle who also "spoke so deprecatingly and harshly of American society and its political and social practices" should not be speaking on a college campus. The state legislators argued that a tax-supported institution should not allow "such people" to speak.

Although Boutelle admitted that the Socialist Workers Party had no chance of winning and that he only sought to expose its views, his speech filled Meacham Auditorium. According to Paul Galloway's article "The Boutelle Incident," Boutelle's talk was "nearer to a harangue at times, was immoderate and occasionally inflammatory" at others. Galloway also noted that Boutelle's "attacks" on President Lyndon Johnson were nothing worse than one might hear from the Republican or Democratic candidates in the previous presidential election. Boutelle called the American flag "a rag," which Galloway said was "a distasteful thing to say," but he noted that Boutelle was "an angry young man" and that he "reflected an anger and a hate which pervades the dispossessed, who live with despair and oppression, in our urban ghettos." Galloway believed that Boutelle had something important to say and that students should listen to him so that they could understand his perspective. Students at the University of Oklahoma, Galloway believed, simply wanted an opportunity to "hear it like it is," and they resented others telling them whom they could and could not hear. Boutelle's appearance led to the Board of Regents passing a rule that restricted who could—and could not—speak on college campuses.

Boutelle continued his campaign stops at colleges and universities throughout the United States. Asked about the Republican and Democratic candidates for president, Boutelle labeled Hubert Humphrey as a "fox" and George Wallace and Richard Nixon as "wolves" when it came to their political philosophy, arguing that all of the major party candidates were from the same "rotten system." Boutelle called Minnesota senator Eugene McCarthy an "undercover racist" with no plans for breaking free from the Democratic

Party or for seeking freedom for African Americans or to make "worthwhile changes" to American politics. With regards to the Biafra situation in Nigeria, Boutelle was critical of both Democrats and Republicans, whom he saw simply as capitalists who wished to control the wealth in Asia and in Africa and the rest of "Black America." Boutelle also took his presidential campaign overseas, promoting the SWP and its political agenda in Canada, England, Scotland, and France. He argued that the "enemy" was "worldwide," and he named NATO and SEATO as "enemies of the people of the world."

Boutelle's support for the Castro Revolution caused problems in the United States. On October 16, 1968, "Anti-Castro Cubans" bombed the headquarters of the Southern California Socialist Workers Campaign Committee, doing extensive damage to the stairway and a store and knocking out a door and a window. In a joint statement issued with his running mate Fred Halstead, Boutelle and Halstead spoke out against the bombing of the campaign headquarters and blamed the "violence-breeding policies of the government and the Democratic and Republican parties" for creating a "climate where right-wing groups and individuals are encouraged to carry on their own 'anti-communist' campaigns." The two men believed that the "terrorist goons" were simply imitating the "terrible violence" that Washington had unleashed against Vietnam and in the failed Bay of Pigs invasion of Cuba. Boutelle hoped that the terrorist bombings would unify SWP supporters across the country by "redoubling their efforts to build the antiwar and black liberation movements," as well as a movement to end the capitalist system that caused this violence. Although the 1968 SWP presidential ticket only appeared on twenty-one states (ten more than it had in the 1964 presidential election), it received 41,500 votes. In contrast, the Communist Party—which had African American bookkeeper Charlene Mitchell as its presidential candidate—only received 1,100 votes.

Boutelle continued being active in politics after the 1968 presidential election, and he spoke often against the Vietnam War. One such speech came in New York City on October 16, 1969, at a "day of moratorium," a simultaneous protest on hundreds of college campuses throughout the United States to pay honor to the nearly 40,000 American soldiers who had died in Vietnam. New York City mayor John Lindsay spoke on the steps of Low Library at Columbia University to a crowd of nearly 10,000 students, many of whom were wearing black armbands. Mayor Lindsay told the crowd that they could not "rest content with the charge from Washington that this peaceful protest is unpatriotic," arguing that their dissent was the highest form of patriotism. Following his speech, John Rockwell, a member of Students for a Democratic Society, shouted: "The same Lindsay who is coming on so peaceful is the same Lindsay who sent police into the high schools." Students "booed and hooted down" Rockwell, but the tide turned when Boutelle spoke. Boutelle "berated" the students for "booing the radical" and then said: "Let Lindsay repudiate his support for Nixon-Agnew last year! Let him repudiate the Gulf of Tonkin resolution" (Weinraub, 1). To this, the crowd "applauded wildly."

In 1969 Boutelle again ran for mayor of New York City, and his campaign headquarters was bombed with fifteen workers inside. The New York Board of Elections removed the SWP ticket from the ballot after the mayor's supporters challenged the validity of Socialist Workers Party signatures. In an open letter to New York mayor Lindsay, Boutelle said that the removal was "a slap in the face of every fair-minded individual in the city." In 1970, Boutelle ran as the SWP candidate for Congress in the Eighteenth Congressional District in Harlem. Seeking the seat held by Representative Adam Clayton Powell, Boutelle's platform was based on "black control of the black community" and "Puerto Rican control of the Puerto Rican community." Boutelle was also the keynoter at the New York Conference to Build a Black Political Party, ran for mayor of Oakland, California, supported Angela Davis after her arrest and imprisonment, and was number five on the House Panel's List of 65 "Undesirable Radical Speakers."

Another SWP candidate entered leftist politics through his attraction to the words of Malcolm X. Andrew Pulley, while stationed at Ft. Jackson, South Carolina, was introduced to some tapes of Malcolm X, and after several days of listening to these tapes, Pulley and the other black soldiers were hooked. In an interview, Pulley said that the tapes helped them to see that not only were African Americans being oppressed but so were the Indians. They also realized that the working class was "being oppressed and exploited by the ruling class" and that they, as black GIs, were being oppressed and exploited more than any other group of people because they were asked to risk their lives for something in which they did not believe. Pulley and his fellow soldiers turned their focus to instilling "pride and integrity" among the other black soldiers and to committing themselves to the antiwar struggle. Shortly thereafter, the eight soldiers founded G.I.'s United Against the War in Vietnam, and when their superiors placed them on kitchen patrol in order to keep them from organizing and speaking out against the war, the "Fort Jackson Eight" hired lawyers. They were eventually arrested and held in the stockade for incitement to riot, but they never wavered in their cause. The Fort Jackson Eight said that the first thing they signed when they entered the service was a pledge to protect the U.S. Constitution, and they believed that there was no better way to protect the Constitution than by utilizing it. The charges were eventually dropped, and all of the soldiers were discharged from the army.

After leaving the army, Pulley began to tour nationally and speak out against the War in Vietnam and racial prejudice in America. He told a crowd in Colorado Springs, Colorado, that he was convinced "the Establishment" would not end the war in Vietnam until the citizens told them to end the war. He joined the Socialist Workers Party shortly after being discharged from the army, and in 1972 Pulley ran as the Socialist Workers Party candidate for vice president of the United States. With SWP presidential candidate Linda Jenness, the two received almost 37,000 votes. Pulley was also the SWP candidate for president in 1980, and he continued to speak out against U.S. imperialism and racism at home. During a two-day campaign stop in Miami, Pulley told the crowd that both the Democratic and Republican parties ignored the needs of the black community. He also said that both Ronald Reagan and James Carter "support a law and order" that resulted in the murder of African Americans throughout the United States. Pulley and his running mate—Matilde Zimmerman—received some 40,000 votes in that election.

The Socialist Workers Party continued its fight to protect working people from "soaring prices, layoffs, wars, racial oppression, and sexism." "The Socialist Workers Party is campaigning for a new society—a socialist society—where wars, racism, sexual oppression, and other forms of human degradation and exploitation no longer exist," a 1976 statement from the party exclaimed. And, the SWP continued selecting candidates for the presidential election to give voters options outside of the Republican and Democratic parties. The 1976 Socialist Workers Party "Bill of Rights" stated that neither the Republicans nor the Democrats offered voters a solution and that both Houses of Congress were only interested in shifting the responsibility and escaping the blame. In the midst an economic, political, and social crisis in the United States, the SWP nominated Peter Camejo, a thirty-six-year-old computer programmer, as its 1976 presidential candidate, and Willie Mae Reid, a thirty-five-year-old African American social activist from Chicago, as his running mate. Both agreed to support the party's program and platform, which called for (1) busing for school desegregation; (2) a suspension of interest payments on all federal borrowing; (3) an end to military spending; and (4) the support of abortion reform. Other programs of the party included

> a massive public works job program; a 30-hour work week with no cut in pay; opening all files of the Federal Bureau of Investigation Agency and the Central Intelligence Agency; ratification of the equal rights amendment; and free medical care and education through college. (Walton, 272)

Although both Camejo and Reid were active and vocal candidates, Reid was more of a local organizer. A product of the segregated South, Reid grew up in

Memphis, Tennessee, and in 1958 she joined with other civil rights workers to end the segregated busing policy in Memphis. She worked as a hospital kitchen worker, a hotel worker, and a garment worker in Memphis before moving to Chicago, where she worked as a garment worker, an office worker, and a computer programmer. While in Chicago, Reid attended Loop Junior College and joined the Afro-American society, where she, too, was influenced by the ideas of Malcolm X after hearing his speeches. Reid continued to be active in the struggle to better conditions in Chicago for the African American community. She was also a supporter of women's liberation and helped to organize the Chicago Women's Abortion Action Coalition, a group that supported a woman's right to an abortion. In 1971, Reid joined the SWP party and was a candidate for the U.S. Congress. In 1975, Reid had challenged the "entire [Richard] Daley machine" when she announced her candidacy for mayor of Chicago as a candidate of the Socialist Workers Party. Though Camejo and Reid lost the 1976 election to Democrat Jimmy Carter, the two received the Socialist Party's greatest number of votes in a presidential election—90,310.

Willie Mae Reid was also the vice presidential candidate in 1992, though she shared that title in some states. James "Mac" Warren was a former steelworker and journalist who ran as the SWP's presidential candidate in the 1988 and 1992 elections. His running mate in 1988 was Kathleen Mickells, and in 1992 he had two—Estelle DeBates and Willie Mae Reid, depending on the state. In 1988, Warren—then a Jersey City resident—received 11,435 votes. Though the national campaign was "grueling," he said that it was "a very interesting experience." He told reporters that most of the people he spoke to were those who had lost all interest in the political process and that they saw the other candidates as "Tweedledee and Tweedledum." After the 1988 election, Warren moved to Chicago, where he said he would consider running again, which he did in 1992. In the 1992 election, Warren said that he was the only real alternative to the Republican and Democratic parties' presidential candidates.

At a campaign stop in Salt Lake, Utah, Warren said that he hoped that voters who were frustrated with the economy would not turn to independent candidate Ross Perot. Warren told reporters that Perot's campaign was merely a diversion from the most important question facing the working class and that the United States was faced with "the crisis of capitalism"—the failure of the Republican and Democratic parties to provide adequately for the working class. Warren believed that all of the candidates—Perot, President George Bush, and Democratic nominee Bill Clinton—were asking working people to make sacrifices. He told listeners that this would lead to working people paying a higher price for economic recovery and that the Socialist Worker Party's platform was intended to meet their needs. The

1992 SWP platform included a massive public works program beginning with the rebuilding of communities in Florida that had been destroyed by Hurricane Andrew; a reduction of the work week from 40 hours to 30 hours with workers still being paid the same amount of money; and insuring that the costs of jobs, health care, and other needs were paid for by "those the party blame[d] for the economic crisis," not by the working class. In this election, Warren and his running mate(s) appeared on the ballot in fourteen states, and they received some 22,000 votes.

The 1996 and 2000 SWP presidential platforms also featured socialist candidates whose politics were separate from the Democratic and Republican parties that they believed represented the ruling class and put profits "before human needs." James Harris, SWP presidential candidate for both elections, believed that workers should confront problems as a class rather than as individuals. Born in Cleveland, Ohio, to working-class parents, Harris first became politically active in the 1960s when his family joined other African American families in setting up "Freedom Schools" to study African American history. After graduation, Harris attended Cleveland State University, where he was a founding member of the Black Student Union. He also organized demonstrations against racism at the university as well as against the War in Vietnam. Harris joined the Young Socialist Alliance and in 1969 ran for the school board in Cleveland on the Socialist Workers ticket, and soon after Harris joined the SWP.

Harris's life-long work in the SWP is an extensive one. He supported Cuba's socialist revolution, and in 1969 he participated in the second "Venceremos Brigade to Cuba" along with hundreds of other students from the United States. In an expression of solidarity with the millions of working people in Cuba, Brigade members cut sugar cane for a couple of weeks to maximize sugar production. In 1977 Harris moved to New York to join the staff of the National Student Coalition Against Racism, which was instrumental in mobilizing for school desegregation. Harris worked at a Ford auto plant in New Jersey, where he was a member of the United Auto Workers. He later worked in a garment factory in Los Angeles, where he helped the party branch out to the growing numbers of workers coming into the United States. Harris defended the Nicaraguan Revolution in the mid-1980s, and he joined a delegation to visit Grenada in the early 1980s to "tell the truth about the first revolution to take power in a Black and English-speaking country in the Caribbean." He served as the national organization secretary for the SWP and was a staff writer for the *Militant*, the socialist newsweekly. Harris' writings covered the struggles to abolish apartheid in South Africa as well as the 1989–91 strike by machinists against "union busting" Eastern Airlines.

In both presidential elections, Harris often spoke about encouraging African Americans to support the SWP, telling them that both the

Republicans and the Democrats represented the "ruling class that perpetuates racism." In an interview with the *Atlanta Daily World,* Harris told the reporter that he would work to advance the "political power of working people against the ruling class." In 2000, Harris joined workers in Florida who were defending affirmative action from attacks by the state government, and he spoke out against the "racist death penalty." In the 1996 and 2000 presidential campaigns, Harris and his running mate—Willie Mae Reid in 1996 and Margaret "Maggie" Trowe in 2000—brought a "revolutionary socialist perspective" to the fight for racial equality, imperialism, and to working-class politics. Harris believed that the SWP was the most realistic campaign, and he explained that the cause of the problems workers faced was capitalism. Workers and farmers, Harris said, needed socialist solutions, and to achieve that, the two groups needed to "make a revolution and take political power." The SWP appeared on the ballot in thirteen states and the District of Columbia and won fewer than 9,000 votes in both elections.

"It's not who you're against, but what you are for!" was the slogan of the 2004 presidential campaign. Arrin Hawkins, the vice presidential candidate for the SWP ticket, believed that Republicans and Democrats were "twin parties of imperialist war, economic depression, and racist oppression." Though only twenty-eight years old and therefore constitutionally ineligible to serve if she won (her presidential running mate—Róger Calero—was also constitutionally ineligible to serve because he had been born in Nicaragua), Hawkins said that the Socialist Workers Party campaign was to support a workers' right to organize unions and to defend workers against the bosses' attacks on "jobs, wages, benefits, working conditions, and dignity." During a campaign stop, Hawkins said that the cause of the United States' worsening economic and social crisis was not President George Bush or the Republican Party but the capitalist system and a small number of "billionaire families" who maintained their power at the expense of the vast majority. At another campaign stop at Bloomsburg University in Pennsylvania, Hawkins chided people for voting for Kerry simply because he was a "lesser evil," and she instead implored people to support the SWP ticket. She said that Democrats who believed that it was necessary to "defeat Bush" at all costs by voting for Kerry were wrong, and that the only way to "defeat the Bush agenda" was to organize working people to fight for their interests independently of the "twin capitalist parties."

Like other African American socialists, Hawkins came to the SWP because of the party's willingness to embrace the multiple identities of their African American members. Hawkins joined the SWP while a student at the University of Minnesota, where she served as a leader in the youth wing of the party. She participated in the conference of the Organization of Latin American and Caribbean Students in Havana in 2000 and was part of an international delegation to Cuba for the Cuba–US Youth Exchange in 2001 and 2003. In 2001 Hawkins represented the Young Socialists at the World Festival of Youth and Students in Algiers, Algeria, and afterwards she visited the camps of the Polisario independence fighters in Tindouf, Algeria. An advocate for women's rights, Hawkins spent time in Senegal studying the role of women in African society, and in 2004, she helped organize the March for Women's Lives in Washington, D.C., where hundreds of thousands of people marched to defend a woman's right to an abortion.

In the 2008 presidential election—an election in which Republican presidential candidate John McCain accused Democratic presidential candidate Barack Obama of being a socialist—the Socialist Workers Party did, in fact, run their own candidates. Arguing that Barack Obama was the furthest thing from a socialist, Róger Calero, the SWP's presidential candidate, said that under the SWP's plan, the vast majority of workers would have a quality lifestyle as opposed to under capitalism where a small elite shared in the profits at the expense of the majority of people. Calero's running mate was Alyson Kennedy, a fifty-seven-year-old garment worker originally from Indiana. A socialist and trade union fighter for more than thirty years, Kennedy worked in the coal mines in Alabama, Colorado, Utah, and West Virginia. She joined the United Mine Workers of America (UMWA) in 1981, and from 2003 to 2006 Kennedy was "the leading militant" in a battle to organize a union at the Co-Op coal mine outside Huntington, Utah. In Huntington, Kennedy fought to allow immigrants from Mexico to be represented by the UMWA to work for safer working conditions, an end to abuse by the bosses, and better wages. Although the miners did not win in their battle against the coal bosses' "profit drives," their struggle became an important example for how working people might fight fatal working conditions.

Originally from Indianapolis, Kennedy was a long-time fighter against racism and discrimination. She was part of the fight to desegregate public schools in Louisville, Kentucky, in the mid-1970s, and in the 1980s she joined in the battle to fight apartheid in South Africa. Kennedy joined the socialist movement in 1973 and was a member of the garment workers' union UNITE (Union of Needletrades, Industrial and Textile Employees), United Steelworkers, and other trade unions. She was also active in the fight against imperialism. In the 1970s, she fought against the war in Vietnam and has joined in demonstrations calling for an end to the U.S. wars in Iraq and Afghanistan. As a union organizer, Kennedy was actively involved in the Coal Employment Project, an organization founded in 1977 that worked to get women hired in the coal mines and opposed sexual harassment on the job. Kennedy has remained active in fighting for women's rights, working to protect a woman's right to an abortion as well as defending clinics from "rightist attempts to shut them down."

All of the African Americans who were candidates for president or vice president on the SWP ticket believed that black Americans—as well as other "oppressed people"—had a "right to control the schools, hospitals, parks, and other institutions in their communities" as well as a right to "determine how federal and state funds" would be used in those communities. Many of them had been influenced by Malcolm X and the black nationalist fervor of the 1960s, yet they were successful in balancing the needs of the black community with the needs of the working class. As C. L. R. James wrote, the SWP was the "most likely means of bringing the masses of Negroes into political action, which, though programmatically devoted to their own interests, must inevitably merge with the broader struggles of the American working-class movement" (James, 3). It was this "audacity of hope" that inspired African Americans to join the Socialist Workers Party and to work for an equal America for all Americans.

Further Reading

"A Bill of Rights for Working People," http://marxists.anu.edu.au/history/etol/writers/camejo/billofrights.htm (accessed March 4, 2009).

"Alyson Kennedy, Socialist Workers Party Candidate for U.S. Vice President." *The Militant* 72 (January 14, 2008): 1–2.

Blackstock, Nelson. "Early Years of the FBI's Secret War on Political Freedom." *Tribe.* December 24, 2007. http://tribes.tribe.net/speak-easy/thread/21cfa0d5-6bef-46bf-b351-a2f58412d7b2 (accessed January 29, 2009).

"Calero and Hawkins, Socialist Candidates." *The Militant* 68 (July 6, 2004): 1–2.

Chomsky, Noam. "Early Years of the FBI's Secret War on Political Freedom." *Tribe.* December 24, 2007. http://tribes.tribe.net/speak-easy/thread/21cfa0d5-6bef-46bf-b351-a2f58412d7b2 (accessed January 29, 2009).

"COINTELPRO—Socialist Workers Party (1961–1970)." *Paul Wolf.* http://www.icdc.com/~paulwolf/cointelpro/swp.htm3 (accessed February 14, 2009), 3–11.

Drabble, John, and Christopher Vaughan. "Fighting Black Power—New Left Coalitions: Covert FBI Media Campaigns and American Cultural Discourse, 1967–1971." *European Journal of American Culture* 27 (June 2008): 65–91.

"For Some Seeking Presidency, Winning Isn't the Only Thing." *New York Times* (February 16, 1992): 1.

Galloway, Paul. "The Boutelle Incident." *Sooner Magazine* (n.d.): 25–27.

Halstead, Fred. "Antiwar GI's Speak: Interviews with Fort Jackson GIs United Against the War." *International Socialist Review* 30, (July–August 1969), http://www.marxists.org/history/etol/writers/halstead/1969/07/gis.htm (accessed March 13, 2009).

James, C. L. R. "The SWP and Negro Work." July 11, 1939. http:// Marxists. architexturez.net/archive/james-clr/works/1939/07/negro-work.htm (accessed February 24, 2009).

Johnson, Cedric. *Revolutionaries to Race Leaders: Black Power and the Making of African American Politics.* Minneapolis: University of Minnesota Press, 2007.

Kihss, Peter. "Trotskyite Party Assails Police." *New York Times* (March 30, 1976): 1.

Montgomery, Paul L. "Speaker at Rally in Harlem Seized." *New York Times* (August 9, 1964): 1.

"Socialist Workers HQ in L. A. Bombed by Anti-Castro Cubans." *Black Panther 10* (October 26, 1968): 16.

"Socialist Workers Party Names Antiwar Slate for '69 Election." *New York Times* (August 31, 1967): 1.

Titcomb, Caldwell. "Black Blood in the White House." *The Harvard Crimson,* January 18, 1972, http://www.thecrimson.com/article.aspx?ref=134190 (accessed February 19, 2009).

Walton, Jr., Hanes. "Black Female Presidential Candidates: Bass, Mitchell, Chisholm, Wright, Reid, Davis, and Fulani." In *Black Politics and Black Political Behavior,* ed. Hanes Walton, Jr. Westport, CT: Praeger, 1992.

Weeks, Tony. "Boutelle Covers Political Spectrum, Attacks U.S. on Foreign Policy Position." *The Titan 11* (October 1, 1968): 1.

Weinraub, Bernard. "Campuses Remember Slain G. I.'s." *New York Times* (October 16, 1969): 1.

X, Malcolm. "It's the Ballot or the Bullet." In *Malcolm X Speaks: Selected Speeches and Statements,* ed. George Breitman. New York: Merit Publishers, 1965.

——. "The Harlem Hate-Gang Scare." In *Malcolm X Speaks: Selected Speeches and Statements,* ed. George Breitman. New York: Merit Publishers, 1965.

Zion, Sidney E. "Ballot Spot Lost by Leftist Party." *New York Times* (September 18, 1969): 1.

A poster promoting comedian and political activist Dick Gregory following his 1968 independent campaign for president of the United States. The poster reads: "Needed: public citizen #1, president of the United States in exile, inaugurated 3–4–69". (Courtesy of the Library of Congress, LC-USZ62–109615.)

CHAPTER 6

Civil Rights Activists and the Reach for Political Power

JEAN VAN DELINDER

This chapter uses the candidacy of a series of black presidential candidates that emerged from the civil rights and black power movements in the late 1960s and then reappeared in 2004 and 2008 to better understand the transformation of race issues into political party politics. The individuals discussed here, principally Martin Luther King, Jr., but also Eldridge Cleaver, Dick Gregory, Julian Bond, Ronald Daniels, Al Sharpton, and Elaine Brown, each made largely symbolic bids for the presidency. Though these candidates acted more on principle than calculated political decision (that is—to win the election), they serve to illustrate how race activists started to channel energies away from the civil rights and black power movements and attempt to leverage their celebrity power into successful political careers.

The era of the civil rights and black power movements fostered a growing desire by race activists to coalesce their activism into a common political agenda. Yet this common political agenda was always uneasy. Civil rights activists were tested by their natural mistrust of any establishment entity's potential to "sell them out" for short-term political gains. The party establishment was in its own right distrustful of these new partners—fueled by the militancy of race activists and fear that the activists were reckless and counterproductive to the party's electoral success.

As African Americans transformed themselves from political outsiders to party insiders, there became a realization of a divergence between the character type necessary to be a successful party leader and that required in being a presidential candidate. The individuals discussed in this chapter provide a forum by which to discuss how different race activists possessed one or the other of the qualities of the race activist and party insider.

Intriguingly, both characteristics are found in President Barack Obama. As the first successful African American presidential candidate, Obama symbolizes the persona and style of an activist outside the political system, while gaining power by means of the tactics and strategies of a party insider. In going forward, this essay then lays a foundation for understanding how future leaders may well be developed.

Historical Antecedents

The ascendancy of race activists with presidential aspirations occurred against the backdrop of the post-World War II era of American dominance as a global power. To better understand how activists—and which activists—transitioned to political power, we must understand three main themes: the specter or fear of communism, the changes undergoing the Democratic Party during the post-war years and the sometimes difficult interaction between local and national organizations and leaders.

The Specter of Communism

One outcome of the political realignment after World War II was the growing threat of the Soviet Union as the instigator of a world communist menace. The policies of the Truman administration reflected a growing reaction to and paranoia about communist infiltration: defended at home with loyalty oaths and abroad with American troops as the bulwark against the "Reds." In the decades following World War II, the United States would use this "climate of fear" to justify hunts for those who were felt to be un-American (meaning not agreeing with the existing political and social order). During these same years, the United States also struggled with the contradiction of defending democracy at home and abroad in spite of its unfair racial discrimination. The rhetoric of the Truman administration portrayed democracy as morally superior to communism, largely ignoring its failure to incorporate non-white peoples into its political institutions and to participate equally for its economic rewards.

While the United States fought communism at home and abroad, decolonization in Africa and Asia rapidly became a fertile terrain for communist expansion among oppressed non-white peoples. An ideological battle raged on the world stage between the emancipatory rhetoric of Marxism versus Democracy. If democracies such as the United States systematically excluded people of color, why would emerging new nations in the third world want to align with their former colonial masters and allies?

Renowned American civil rights leaders, such as singer and actor Paul Robeson and writer W. E. B. Du Bois, were outspoken, articulate advocates of the superiority of communism in alleviating the downtrodden economic condition of African Americans.

This shift in focus toward regional concerns was also fueled in part by fears of communist infiltration of the national Democratic Party. As the South industrialized in the late 1930s and 1940s, it not only feared the rise of a labor movement but also communist-affiliated labor union organizers, particularly in its larger cities such as Birmingham, Alabama. The tenuous affiliation of communist sympathizers with New Deal Democrats also fueled concerns about the shift in national policies toward targeting racial inequality, which, in the South, had the potential to disrupt the economic, political and social factors sustaining white supremacy, their whole way of life.

Though Senator Joseph McCarthy of Wisconsin went too far in trying to extend the communist label to more liberal Democrats, his actions resulted in an eventual decoupling of New Deal liberalism from communism in the 1950s. This fissure in the left would continue to grow in the late 1950s and 1960s as older anti-communist New Deal liberals attempted to create an uneasy alliance with younger and openly pro-communist race activists during the civil rights movement.

While advocating anti-communist legislation, American political leaders advocated a more laissez-faire approach toward racial parity using the executive branch to cautiously enter into altering the racial status quo. For example, in 1946 Truman appointed a Committee on Civil Rights to make recommendations to the Department of Justice on ways to stop voting discrimination and racial discrimination in employment. Truman also used his power through issuing executive orders to begin desegregating the military, which would take well over a decade to accomplish. These initial efforts to address racial discrimination were largely directed toward advocating black assimilation into the dominant white society. It characterized democracy as morally superior to other political forms of government. But these efforts largely failed to address the economic consequences of centuries of racial discrimination, the enduring poverty and limited economic mobility of African Americans. Additionally, these policies were devoid of any understanding of black self-sufficiency and empowerment.

When considered within the context of virulent anti-communism, the civil rights movement fueled suspicions about it being a communist front threatening Southern moral and religious values.

In addition to the mounting criticism of the Vietnam War, the coalition between the more radical young race activists and older white Democratic liberals was also being strained by the specter of communism. The substantial changes being pushed by the civil rights movement concerned Southern political leaders that the Democratic Party was being infiltrated by communism via the young, black SNCC members. Southern political leaders also tried to discredit Northern civil rights workers by calling attention to the communist or "Red diaper babies" who filled the ranks of Freedom Summer white volunteers in 1964. At the grassroots level, the more militant SNCC leaders found themselves in an oppositional position from the national leadership interests. The split between the older white Democratic liberals who dominated the party leadership at the national level and younger black militants leading local and regional change is illustrated by SNCC's refusal to listen to the national leadership in accepting the help of the communist-backed National Lawyers Guild.

Changes in the Democratic Party

Between 1946 and 1968 the ideals and values of racial equality were eventually taken up as policies by the national Democratic Party. Gradually white Americans came to terms with the fact that racial inequality was not just a Southern problem but a national dilemma.

The dismantling of racial segregation was also strongly opposed by Southern Democratic Party leaders, particularly Alabama governor George Wallace (who had national political and presidential aspirations). Resistance to racial equality was not limited to the South however, as evidenced by Wallace's strong showing among Northern voters during the 1964 presidential race, capturing almost half of the vote in three Democratic primaries.

This disconnect between the national agenda of racial integration and regional concerns with economic problems exacerbated by the lack of access to grassroots political processes would fuel the growing insurgency of African Americans for several decades to come.

In the years immediately following World War II, Southern black Americans' best hope was aligning with the Democratic Party, if and when they were allowed to vote. The growing rift between Southern white Democrats and the national party leadership would also fuel Southern resistance to national desegregation efforts, causing an eventual re-alignment of Southern white political elites away from continuing support of national policies, as it had with New Deal liberalism.

The postwar era also saw the realignment of the racial and constitutionally conservative Southern Democrats from the national Democratic Party. During the Depression, Southern Democrats, who primarily represented the interests of its regional business elites, supported Roosevelt's New Deal programs since the South needed economic assistance from the federal government. But in the greater prosperity after World War II, Southern Democrats were less inclined to support the national party, particularly as race issues supplanted economic concerns after the 1954 *Brown* decision.

In the less segregated North, racial segregation was viewed more of a moral embarrassment, a practice contradicting American democratic values. In the South, maintaining racial segregation was synonymous with defending an idealized version of Southern values and its way of life. The resulting sectional politics meant that while the national Democratic Party moved toward defending racial integration it alienated its Southern allies, a significant power base for the national party. Though the resulting political realignment of the South would take several decades to solidify, it would have significant consequences for Democratic Party presidential candidates. Though the demographic shift from northern cities to the south was just a trickle at this time, it would have long term consequences as the south became more populated and therefore increasingly more important for delivering electoral votes in presidential elections. The lack of Southern support for racial programs meant the national Democratic leadership was increasingly more at odds with members of its own party in trying to enforce federal civil rights legislation.

Though the Democratic Party was the dominant political party in the South, there was a growing mistrust over whether or not it was a credible representation of African Americans. Prior to voter registration drives, particularly Freedom Summer in 1964, the fact that blacks could not record their dissatisfaction through the ballot also meant blacks mistrusted any white-controlled political system. Though this emphasis on electoral politics would not come to fruition until after the 1965 Voting Act, its antecedents can be seen in the formation of a new multiracial party in 1964, the Mississippi Freedom Democratic Party (MFDP). The formation of this political party to represent civil rights issues, including a growing sense of black nationalism, also signaled a growing impatience with the Democratic Party, foretelling a strategy shift toward creating an alternate, third party.

On the other hand, white Southern Democrats were dissatisfied with the national party's enforcement of civil rights legislation in their region. At the 1964 Democratic convention in Atlantic City, Southern Democrats threatened to back Republican candidate Barry Goldwater if Johnson recognized the Freedom Democrat delegates. President Lyndon B. Johnson sought a compromise with both camps by seating the all-white delegates but promising to make civil rights issues part of the party platform. Termed the "Atlantic City Compromise," Johnson's short-lived attempt to reconcile the different factions in his party resulted in a mistrust of the political system by the younger, more militant African Americans. These splits were later to become all too present during the 1968 elections.

Struggle between National and Local: Martin Luther King

Due to racial segregation in the South and almost total exclusion from white society in the North, African Americans were forced to utilize their own leaders and community institutions to channel insurgency. These "race activists" were predominately drawn from the ranks of lawyers, educators, and ministers. The dominant message was one of racial assimilation and integration. Leadership during this era is typified by people like Supreme Court Justice Thurgood Marshall and Rev. Martin Luther King, Jr. This was not unsurprising as the mass base of the civil rights movement is attributed to the organizational structure of Southern local communities which revolved around segregated churches, schools, and civic institutions. This organizational structure is reflected in organizations like SCLC (Southern Christian Leadership Council), founded in 1957, which used local churches for mobilizing mass protests. The emergence of SCLC as a vehicle to foster grassroots protests and demonstrations directly challenged the more staid legal tactics of the older, more established NAACP (National Association for the Advancement of Colored People) founded in 1909. During this period black leadership was divided over whether to pursue the lawyer-led approach that produced *Brown* or whether the display of public dissatisfaction using "mass boycotts and demonstrations" would be more effective.

Growing federal support for racial integration facilitated a strategy shift towards using mass demonstrations in the South by the late 1950s. Prior to the civil rights movement mass mobilizations and protests were largely ceremonial ones carried out in the North, such as the NAACP-led marches against lynching on the streets of Harlem in the 1930s and the March on Washington Movement first proposed in 1941 and actualized in 1963.

Using the logic of civil disobedience and nonviolent action, the civil rights movement directly challenged the legality of racial segregation in all aspects of public life. In addressing "the most flagrant failure of American society" its leadership took the moral high ground seeking reconciliation and not revolution. Nonviolence was a deliberate tactic to gain national exposure through the expected counter-violence drama by local law officials.

Within a few years, SCLC would itself be challenged and supplanted by other more radical organizations such as Student Nonviolent Coordinating Committee (SNCC) and the Black Panther Party. SCLC was more mainstream, raising awareness about the moral injustice of segregation and pushing for integration at the local level. SNCC and later the Black Panther Party were more politically oriented, organizing voter registration drives and putting forward black candidates for local, state, and eventually national political office.

The internal tensions within the black community over which direction to move in was reflected in the intersection of three different campaigns in the civil rights movement: freedom rides, sit-ins, and voter registration drives. Planned by yet another civil rights organization pre-dating the 1950s, Congress of Racial Equality (CORE), the 1961 "Freedom Rides" organized to test laws outlawing discrimination in public transportation. The attempt of two integrated groups of college students to ride a bus from Washington, D.C. to New Orleans resulted in a violent reaction by white vigilantes who severely beat many of the riders. The freedom rides provided Northern whites with a visual image about racial oppression. For Southern blacks, the freedom rides generated civil rights activity that helped galvanize the black community for protest.

Though this did not result in making the South enforce its antidiscrimination laws, it did succeed in catching the attention of the Kennedy administration. After 1961, the federal government placed increasing pressure on civil rights organizations to channel their efforts into voter registration activities rather than public demonstrations.

This almost grudging acknowledgement by the federal government indicates that these mass demonstrations were having some of their desired effect on political policies. Realizing that the black vote would help bring about Southern blacks' equal democratic participation, voter registration drives were organized across the South by SNCC. Though blacks nominally had the right to vote, few were registered due to white intimidation. For example, in Mississippi only 6 percent of the state's black population was registered in the early 1960s.

Ways in which civil rights organizations could sometimes work against each other is illustrated by what happened in Albany, Georgia in 1961 and 1962. Located in southern Georgia, Albany was a thoroughly segregated city and had a population of 56,000, 40 percent of which was black. Both SNCC and SCLC planned campaigns in Albany at about the same time, but SNCC organizers arrived first, having selected Albany in the summer of 1961 for a voter registration drive. Things quickly got out of hand as public demonstrations were organized after five students from Albany College, a local black college, were arrested for sitting at the bus station lunch counter. A few weeks later, nine black "freedom riders" got off the train from Atlanta and were arrested for sitting in the white waiting room.

The local police chief, Laurie Pritchett, did not want mass demonstrations to take over Albany, so he quickly made arrangements with surrounding counties to jail the protesters. The desired mass arrests of black activists did not have the desired effect of overburdening the local facilities, as detainees were sent to other towns, thus defusing the police station as a target. Pritchett also neutralized the melodrama of racial injustice by ordering his police to not allow themselves to be antagonized by the protesters, especially when members of the media were present.

Against the objections of the SNCC, Martin Luther King, Jr. was invited to

Albany to speak at a rally. King's organization, the SCLC, had also been interested in launching a boycott in Albany similar to what had been done in nearby
Montgomery, Alabama. King led a protest march and was quickly arrested. He
refused bond and remained jailed with hundreds of other demonstrators.
Arrangements were quickly made to get King released from jail and out of
Albany before he tried to speak for everyone and thereby "compromise away
many of their accomplishments" (Ricks, 6). SNCC's worst fears were realized,
for upon his release from jail, King made a verbal agreement to cease demonstrations, effectively stalling desegregation efforts in Albany for several more
years. King would be derisively labeled "DeLawd" by SNCC insiders for his
sanctimonious stance and ability to derail more radical protests.

Events in Albany illustrated the tensions between grass-roots black organizers in the South and national leaders like Martin Luther King, Jr. This case
also illustrates two types of black leadership, one leading mass mobilizations
protesting specific local issues and the other pushing forward broader
national concerns. After the 1955 Montgomery Bus Boycott made him a
national leader, Martin Luther King, Jr. soon began directing his attention
away from leading grassroots nonviolence activities toward changing the
racial configuration of elected officials. In May 1957, on the third anniversary of the 1954 *Brown* decision, King outlined an extraordinary leadership
plan for black politics (Walters and Smith, 119):

> Give us the ballot and we will no longer plead to the federal government
> for passage of an anti-lynching law; we will by the power of our vote
> write the law on the statute books of the southern states . . . Give us the
> ballot and we will fill our legislative halls with men of good will, and
> send to the sacred halls of Congress men who will not sign a Southern
> Manifesto, because of their devotion to the manifesto of justice.

King's words foreshadowed a shift from the strategy of civil rights demonstrations to electoral politics. As a race activist as well as an important figure
in the national arena, he is also a transitional type of black political leader
away from focusing on specific race issues. Instead, he recognized that there
were broader, systemic social problem, such as poverty and unemployment,
that not only plagued African Americans but other oppressed groups as well.

As racial integration became more of a possibility after the *Brown* decision, King realized there was no logical place for it to stop. Once African
Americans obtained the right to freely participate in society the next step was
to "redefine the character of American society" (Walters and Smith, 117). As
a political minority at the national level, African Americans needed to focus
their attention on building coalitions with other groups in order to address
some of the other social problems mentioned above. On the other hand, at

the grassroots level, African Americans were using integration or the right to participate in their local communities to build cohesion within their own communities in order to solidify their power.

This bifurcation in policies between the local and national level created an enduring "oppositional character" of black leadership (Walters and Smith, 116). As a national civil rights leader more and more concerned with broader economic problems, King often found himself at odds with grassroots leaders. His leadership tactics in the early 1960s exemplified a strategy shift away from the "issue" leadership of race advancement and civil rights toward strategies that brought greater political representation.

As a national leader, Martin Luther King's interests shifted from specific civil rights issues toward increased African American political participation and power. The divergence between national and local leaders became more obvious once SNCC's radicalized leadership aligned with the Palestinians during the 1967 Six Day War. In an attempt to link struggles against racism at home with the plight of Palestinians, SNCC alienated many American Jews who had initially funded many of their civil rights initiatives. Staying focused on the civil rights movement and interested in pursuing increased political power for African Americans, King did not want to antagonize white liberal supporters. Instead, he turned his attention toward more pressing economic issues such as poverty and unemployment.

However, the funding for the War on Poverty was eclipsed by the soaring cost of the Vietnam War. As American involvement in Vietnam intensified, King could no longer remain silent and aligned himself with the anti-war New Left, claiming a commonality between civil rights at home and opposition to the war in Vietnam. "This madness must cease," King proclaimed. In a speech delivered in Los Angeles in February 1967, King linked "racism, extreme materialism, and militarism" as the three evils tearing American society apart (Radosh, 33). His stance was a moral one and it caused a rift among the national civil rights leadership. As a major civil rights leader, King was running the risk of jeopardizing the movement by speaking out against American involvement in the Vietnam War and de facto sympathizing with communists abroad and at home.

King's opposition to the Vietnam War further alienated him from the Democratic Party and he soon found himself at the center of the New Politics Convention discussion of a third-party presidential ticket in 1967. Though he eventually refused to consider running as a third-party presidential candidate, he did continue to press for Vietnam peace talks. After his assassination in April 1968, the Freedom and Peace Party asked King's widow, Coretta Scott King to serve as its vice-presidential candidate, but she also declined to seek political office. Instead, she turned her attention to continuing King's work on nonviolence and combating racism.

"From asking to telling": Black Self-determination and Presidential Candidates

By the end of the 1960s there was a splintering of the civil rights movement into radical factions, fueled in part by a growing disaffection with the Democratic Party support for the Vietnam War and the rising authority of black self-determination. The grasp of more moderate organizations advocating nonviolence and integration disintegrated. New, younger, and more radical organizations and leaders emerged, advocating racial separatism as a means of empowerment. There was also growing endorsement of violent behavior and the use of militant tactics to bring about social change.

Once a mainstream organization, the Student Nonviolent Coordinating Committee (SNCC) took on the more radical rhetoric of black self-determination, rejecting the premise of bi-racial coalitions. The black power movement also began to emerge, providing a more militant voice arguing for separatism and community control as opposed to the integration and nonviolence characterized by the now almost non-operational civil rights movement.

The emergence of this more radical black political and social activism is linked to a rising national racial consciousness of African Americans that became highly politicized by 1968. The younger generation had lost patience with the ability of peacefulness and passivity to bring about a change in race relations. The founding of the Black Panther Party in 1966 also signals the twilight of the legitimacy of mainstream nonviolent protests and the beginning of more revolutionary and aggressive rhetoric and violent tactics.

The following section discusses race activists whose political aspirations were shaped through religious, civil rights, and community organizations. Three black presidential and vice presidential candidates who initially worked for SNCC—Eldridge Cleaver, Julian Bond, and Elaine Brown— were shaped by the emerging rhetoric of black power and the rising disillusionment with America's neo-imperialist involvement in the Vietnam War. Of these three candidates, Cleaver and Brown were deemed more radical due to their involvement in the Black Panthers, while Bond remained in the mainstream, advocating integration as the road toward black self-sufficiency. As discussed later in this chapter, the political careers of Al Sharpton and Ronald Daniels were routed through more unconventional means.

Eldridge Cleaver and Dick Gregory

In particular, 1968 was a watershed year for black politics with the brief appearance of four black presidential and vice presidential candidates: Eldridge Cleaver, Julian Bond, Coretta Scott King, and Richard C. "Dick" Gregory. Though, as third-party candidates, Cleaver and Gregory were unlikely to be elected in 1968, it is important to consider their actions within the historical context of the 1960s. As race activists, these four candidates also represent four distinctly economic, political, and social directions.

Cleaver and Gregory were both originally affiliated with the Peace and Freedom Party (PFP). The PFP, a loose configuration of Marxists and libertarians, grew out of discontent with the Democratic Party's support for the war in Vietnam and failure to effectively support the civil rights movement. Holding its first and only national convention in Ann Arbor, Michigan, in August 1968, the PFP party was soon split into competing factions. Cleaver was nominated for president over Dick Gregory. Cleaver, a convicted felon and Black Panther leader, was only thirty-four years old and technically not eligible to run. Gregory also ran for president, forming a competing Peace and Freedom party and receiving more votes than Cleaver in the November election (47,097 to 36,623).

Both branches of the PFP represented the interests of black militants and white liberals. Cleaver's race activism and black socialism were shaped by his prison experiences. While an inmate in San Quentin, he began reading books on black civil rights and was particularly influenced by black nationalism and the writings of Malcolm X. After being released from prison, Cleaver joined the Black Panther Party in 1967 (founded in Oakland, California in October, 1966) and was appointed Minister of Information. Through the Black Panthers' newspaper, Cleaver called for an armed insurrection and the establishment of a black socialist government. His political aspirations were cut short after he went exile after his April 1968 shootout with Oakland police.

As a political leader, Cleaver represented the underclass and the disenfranchised. His affiliation with the Black Panthers allowed him to assume the mantle of militant black self-determination advocating separatism instead of integration. His rise to power was also fueled by a growing dissatisfaction with the moderate tactics used in the civil rights movement. Using "the style of the street," Cleaver and the Black Panthers took on a "folk hero" status as the "young, tough, crime-seared 'brothers on the block' replaced the 'band of brothers in a circle of love'" (Gitlin, 350). By the late 1960s, the Black Panthers' rhetoric of communist revolution grew more strident as its alliances with the liberal white left crumbled in light of the unfilled promises of the economic and political equality that were supposed to accompany racial integration. After Cleaver went into exile, the window of opportunity closed for any serious antiestablishment national political candidacy to come out of the Black Panthers for several decades until Elaine Brown's nomination in 2007.

Cleaver's competition for the presidential nomination on the Peace and Freedom Party ticket in 1968 was Richard "Dick" Gregory. Gregory used his considerable performance skills and social acumen to promote civil rights and eventually run for political office. Born and raised in St. Louis, Missouri, Dick Gregory was shaped by his early exposure to poverty and violence. An acute social critic, he used humor to point out the hypocrisy of racial segregation to both black and white audiences. As a faction of the counterculture movement of the 1960s, Gregory promoted civil disobedience using his sense of theater as a comic. Gregory's oratory skills were initially directed against racial discrimination, but he soon openly opposed American involvement in Vietnam. He also called for economic reform and sought to bring attention to the rising problem of drug use among African Americans. His provocative rhetoric is illustrated by the title of his best selling autobiography, *Nigger*, published in 1964.

As a founding member of the "Yippie" Movement (Youth International Party) in December 1967, Gregory joined Abbie Hoffman and Jerry Rubin in creating absurdist political manifestos and obscenity-laced diatribes against mainstream society (Gitlin, 235). Despite his input to the theatrics of political absurdism, Gregory took his activism seriously. He began his political career by running against Richard J. Daley for mayor of Chicago in 1967. Like other race activists who came of age during the era of the civil rights and black power movements, Gregory attempted to use his celebrity status to launch a political career. As a comic and social critic, Gregory had made a career of pointing out the faults of the current political system, largely controlled by white elites. As a party outsider, Gregory had little chance of electoral success, but the pattern of channeling race activism into political aspirations would be more successful with others who followed him, like Julian Bond.

Julian Bond

Julian Bond's involvement in politics grew out of his civil rights activism from which he was able to launch a political career. His political ambitions in the mid-1960s also illustrate a strategic shift among grassroots leaders away from the issue politics of Myrdal's "race men." The eclipse of "race men" leadership, motivated by an ideology of racial uplift but not necessarily full equality, was now being supplanted by race activists like Julian Bond. Realizing that African Americans needed to gain a political presence if they were to sustain their civil rights initiatives, Bond ran for political office at an early age. As a voter registration worker, Bond realized access to the ballot was necessary to full equality for African Americans. He also learned the basics of community organizing within the black community and this experience enabled him to run a successful campaign for state office.

Bond's early political victories later became a classic example of how to run a grassroots campaign. Bond was first elected in 1965 to a one-year term in the Georgia House of Representatives. Because of his outspoken opposition to the war in Vietnam, members of the House voted not to seat him. Bond was elected two more times before the Supreme Court ruled unanimously that the Georgia House had violated Bond's rights in refusing him his seat. He was elected to the Georgia Senate in 1974 and served until 1987, when an unsuccessful congressional race in 1986 prevented him from seeking reelection to the Senate. In 1968, Bond was nominated for the vice presidency at the Democratic convention, but stepped down because he did not meet the age qualification. In 1995, Bond was elected to his fourth term on the National Board of the National Association for the Advancement of Colored People, the nation's oldest and largest civil rights organization. Bond has served as chairman of the NAACP since 1998.

Ronald Daniels

Ronald Daniels, a 1992 third-party presidential candidate for the Peace and Freedom Party (PFP), is a black community organizer in the tradition of E. D. Nixon (a labor organizer for the Brotherhood of Sleeping Car Porters who managed the Montgomery Bus Boycott in 1955–56). Daniels exemplifies a type of black political leader often overlooked in studies of leadership due to "fluctuations in his or her roles . . . involved in 'floating coalitions' of activity (Walters and Smith, 114). As a type of leader often at odds with national black leaders, community organizers often step in and fill the void left by national organizations, taking on responsibility for discrete, local concerns. During the 1960s, community organizers were given some legitimacy through federally funded Community Action Programs. Their oppositional stance to mayors and members of city councils often resulted in mobilizations and protests, reaching a high point from the mid-1960s to mid-1970s. Eventually, their funding was eliminated and by the early 1990s most community organizers had been shunted to the side by institutional leadership drawn from national organizations such as the NAACP, SCLC and Jesse Jackson's Rainbow Coalition.

Daniels is a transitional race activist figure in black presidential candidates. His experience and considerable skill as a community organizer gave him insight into grassroots problems and issues. But, unlike Julian Bond, he has not been able to use this expertise to launch a successful political career. Instead, he has been the most successful in using his community organizing skills to direct national civil rights organizations, such as serving as executive director of the Center for Constitutional Rights (1993–2005). His community organizing and leadership skills were used in Jesse Jackson's unsuccessful 1984 and 1988 presidential campaigns. Now serving as executive director of the new Black World Institute Twenty-first Century (BWI) a reconstitution of the original BWI founded in 1970, Daniels continues to use his expertise as a community organizer to help local groups by linking them up to necessary information and resources.

Al Sharpton

A 2004 African American presidential candidate, Reverend Al Sharpton represents another type of black political leader that has emerged in the past twenty years. Sharpton's flair for the dramatic makes him a controversial figure among current race activists. In some ways, he resembles the "race men" of an earlier era, when black leaders used their oratory skills to draw attention to the injustices of segregation. Like other black religious leaders, Sharpton's rhetoric can be effective in drawing attention to racial injustice, but it can also alienate moderates. Though it is sometimes difficult to see the person behind Sharpton's theatrics, he first developed his unique leadership style as a performer, billed as the "wonder boy preacher" touring at age ten with famed gospel singer Mahalia Jackson. By age fourteen he was serving as youth director for Jesse Jackson's Operation Breadbasket, using his theatrical skills to strategically "stage" protests against the A&P stores, a national grocery store chain.

Born in the mid-1950s during the ascendancy of the civil rights movement, Sharpton's fame as a national civil rights leader is tied to his skillful use of the media, rather than substantive work as a minister or grassroots community organizer. In the 1980s, his involvement in two high-profile cases in the New York City area served to keep media scrutiny as much on himself as on the racially based murder of a black teenager named Michael Griffith in 1986 and the Tawana Brawley case in 1987. Though the Brawley case was later dismissed by a grand jury due to lack of evidence, Sharpton's reputation was damaged after being fined for making slanderous remarks against the district attorney. While his personal life seemed to spin out of control, he remained dedicated to his activism, raising awareness about police brutality in New York City.

After one unsuccessful run for the New York State Assembly in 1978, Sharpton decided to run for national public office in 1992 and 1994, seeking a U.S. Senate seat. When Sharpton began to set his sights on the presidency, the controversial twists and turns of his race activist career gave him a name recognition problem of high name recognition but low favorable opinion in polls. Sharpton's 2004 ineffective campaign for the presidency failed to garner enough support to become a contender for the Democratic Party nomination.

Sharpton remains an important black leader in his commitment to racial justice. Though he has failed to be elected to any political office, he uses his institutional base, National Action Network (NAN) to link activists with resources. He regularly appears in the media as a champion for those who have no voice, such as speaking out for the nameless victims of Hurricane Katrina.

Elaine Brown

Women's contributions to race activism are obscured as they often took on leadership-like roles without being formally acknowledged as a "leader." In the rare cases when women were in the forefront, their activism is often obscured by other factors in their personal lives. For example, Ella Baker's involvement in the 1964 Democratic Party convention would be later discredited by her ties to the American Communist Party and involvement in the Southern Conference Education Fund (SCEF). And while Martin Luther King went on to national prominence as an influential political leader, Rosa Parks is largely remembered as the symbolic representation of the Montgomery Bus Boycott rather than for her extensive participatory role in the broader civil rights struggle.

In the early years of the civil rights movement, women were excluded from formal leadership positions due in part to the dominance of the black church in civil rights organizing. For example, the 1955 Montgomery Bus Boycott was also supported by the Women's Political Council (WPC), one of several women's organizations that worked "parallel" with the male-dominated Montgomery Improvement Association (MIA) helping to coordinate and sustain the boycott. Later, during Freedom Summer in 1964, African American women found a way around gender constraints and hierarchies by extending their family and community roles by coordinating the housing and feeding of civil rights workers.

One woman who defied convention as a race activist is Elaine Brown, former Black Panther Party insider. A tireless race activist for over thirty years, Brown sought the 2008 Green Party presidential nomination before resigning from the party in December 2007. Brown grew up in North Philadelphia and moved to Los Angeles to pursue a career in music. In 1967, Brown joined the Black Panther Party and began to channel her musical talents toward the cause of racial justice. In 1971, Brown became a member of the party's Central Committee as Minister of Information, replacing the expelled Eldridge Cleaver.

Brown's work in the Black Panther Party eventually led her to make a bid for public office in 1973, unsuccessfully running for Oakland city council. After Black Panther Party leader Huey Newton fled to Cuba in 1974, he appointed Brown as his proxy. Brown was chairman of the Black Panther Party from 1974 until 1977. Brown fought many gender stereotypes in trying to lead the Black Panthers in supporting community schools and representation in electoral politics.

As a race activist Brown fought a battle on two fronts, one against racism and the other against sexism within and outside her race. Though only a handful of race activists were women, their contributions are often obscured by the types of activities they engaged in. Brown's race activism was primarily channeled into community organizing. Like Ron Daniels, working at the grassroots level, Brown's work was less concerned with national politics and more focused on trying to improve African Americans' access to quality education, jobs, and decent housing. In her 1992 autobiography, Brown notes how as a woman in a militant and fringe civil rights organization, she had to negotiate her leadership within the contradictory roles of being an African American and a feminist (Brown):

> A woman in the movement was considered, at best, irrelevant. A woman asserting herself was a pariah. If a black woman assumed a role of leadership, she was said to be eroding black manhood, to be hindering the progress of the black race. She was an enemy of the black people.
> . . . I knew I had to muster something mighty to manage the Black Panther Party.

Brown's affiliation with the Black Panther Party placed her at odds with national black leaders. The Black Panthers' community work at the grassroots level is often overshadowed by their strident rhetoric and militant tactics. As a woman, Brown was further marginalized within her own organization, making it even more difficult to overcome the obstacles of racism.

Conclusion

This chapter examined the candidacy of a series of black presidential candidates to better understand the transformation of race issues into political party politics. In channeling their political aspirations, the individuals discussed here—Martin Luther King, Jr., Eldridge Cleaver, Dick Gregory, Julian Bond, Ronald Daniels, Al Sharpton, and Elaine Brown—were staunch social justice advocates and affiliated either through the Democratic Party or a related third party. The trend since emancipation has been for strong black voter attachment to one party, such as the Republican Party after the Civil War and the Democratic Party well into the twentieth century. Recent decades have seen some voter attachment to other parties, primarily third parties such as the PFP and the Green Party, and the recent candidacy of Alan Keyes indicates that his conservative and Christian fundamentalist issues might have the ability to outweigh race issues. The candidates considered in this chapter emerged out of the post-World War II era of black activism and the creation of coalitions addressing racial inequality.

The political aspirations of the race activists considered in this chapter were undermined by the decline of civil rights as a national agenda. After the Democratic Party fell out of power after 1968, several race activists tried to fill the gap in party leadership by trying to run for national political office. The recent election of Obama reflects his ability to use his outsider status, his nonpartisan vision in inspiring "hope" and "change" for all Americans, regardless of race and economic status. Obama's community organizing experience combined with his political acumen to finally be elected president of the United States reflects his ability to combine the divergent talents of many of the race activists discussed in this chapter.

Further Reading

Branch, Taylor. *At Canaan's Edge: America in the King Years, 1965–68.* New York: Simon & Schuster, 2006.

Brown, Elaine. *A Taste of Power: A Black Woman's Story.* New York: Doubleday, 1992.

Gitlin, Todd. *The Sixties: Years of Hope, Days of Rage.* Toronto: Bantam Books, 1987.

Hodgson, Godfrey. *America in Our Time.* New York: Vintage Books, 1976.

Kuumba, M. Bahati. "'You've Struck a Rock': Comparing Gender, Social Movements, and Transformation in the United States and South Africa." *Gender & Society* 16 (2002): 504–523.

Payne, Charles. *I've Got the Light of Freedom: The Organizing Tradition and the Mississippi Freedom Struggle.* Berkeley: University of California Press, 1995.

Radosh, Ronald. *Divided They Fell: The Demise of the Democratic Party, 1964–1996.* New York: Free Press, 1996.

Ricks, John A. "'DeLawd' Descends and is Crucified: Martin Luther King, Jr. in Albany Georgia." *Journal of Southwest Georgia History* 2 (1984): 3–14.

Robnett, Bernice. "African-American Women in the Civil Rights Movement, 1954–1965: Gender, Leadership, and Micro-Mobilization." *American Journal of Sociology* 101 (1996): 1661–1693.

Singh, Nikhil Pal. *Black Is a Country: Race and the Unfinished Struggle for Democracy.* Cambridge, MA: Harvard University Press, 2004.

Walters, Ronald W. *Freedom Is Not Enough: Black Voters, Black Candidates, and American Presidential Politics.* Lanham, MD: Rowman & Littlefield, 2005.

Walters, Ronald W., and Robert C. Smith. *African American Leadership.* Albany: State University of New York Press, 1999.

Walton, Hanes. *African American Power and Politics: The Political Context Variable.* New York: Columbia University Press, 1997.

Walton, Hanes, and Robert C. Smith. *American Politics and the African American Quest for Universal Freedom.* 3rd ed. New York: Pearson Longman, 2006.

Zinn, Howard. *A People's History of the United States.* New York: Harper Collins Publishers, 2003.

Jesse Jackson in July 1983, a few months before he began his first campaign for the Democratic Party's presidential nomination. (Courtesy of the Library of Congress, LC-U9-41583-29.)

CHAPTER 7

Jesse Jackson

Run, Jesse, Run!

JAMES M. SMALLWOOD

Barack Obama made history in 2008 when he won the American presidency, becoming the first African American to do so. Yet, he had many precursors who earlier tilled the political garden for him. Prior to his rapid rise politically, a number of blacks had contested for the presidency or vice presidency. Most were candidates of fringe parties (the Socialist Workers Party, for example) and had no realistic chance to win America's highest political office. But, in 1972 Democratic congresswoman Shirley Chisholm became the first African American female to stand for the presidency as a member of a major political party before her campaign stuttered early in the primary season due to lack of both supporters and funds. Even though hers was a brief campaign, Chisholm in many respects set the stage for Jesse Jackson's campaigns. However, Jackson's 1984 and 1988 attempts to win the White House were different. In his efforts, he had a reasonable chance to gain control of the Democratic Party, one of the two national parties that controlled the office since Franklin Pierce's victory in 1852. After entering the Democratic primaries in 1984, Jackson tried to move his political colleagues to the left, especially on issues vital to the country's poor in general and to the African American community in particular. When he won the Michigan caucus vote in 1988, Jackson clearly established himself as a force in the Democratic Party. The win announced his arrival.

Just who was this man who helped prepare the United States for the day when a black man could, indeed, win the highest office in the land? In part, he revealed to millions of television viewers (those lucky enough to have chosen the right television network to watch the election wind down) who he was in 2008 during the post-election celebrations in Chicago, home to both Obama and Jackson. A camera-man swept his viewer over a large crowd of happy people and, at one point, "zoomed" in on Jesse Jackson. He was not the star of the scene. Unlike his son, Congressman Jesse Jackson, Jr., he had no official role to play during the celebration. He was not scheduled to speak. He was just one of the enthusiastic spectators. He would have been easy to miss had not the camera-man recognized who he was. What was he doing when the camera caught him in a close-up? He was crying. Undoubtedly, it occurred to many people that the scene had to be bittersweet for him, a black man who had earlier tried to grab the brass ring only to see someone else win. Many of Jackson's longtime supporters were prouder of him at that moment than ever before. It was the time for his tears—tears of joy even if bittersweet. He was a shock trooper who helped prepare the way. He had been a major leader of the civil rights movement when Obama was but a child, only to watch someone else win the biggest political prize in the United States, a prize that he had contested for twice. Yet, he must have been happy for Obama and joyous that a Democrat had once again captured the White House.

Like some other people, I was astounded by Obama's rapid rise post-2004 and his 2008 victory. I knew that one day a black person would become president, just as one day voters will elevate a woman to that office—but I did not believe that I would live to see such developments in my lifetime. Born in 1944, I was more than amazed because I lived through the latter years of American's Age of Segregation, in Jim Crow's America, and took part in early civil rights efforts in my hometown. I lived in a small town in Northeast Texas (Terrell) where east–west railroad tracks divided the races, whites on the north side, blacks on the south. All on the white side appeared exactly as you might expect; the streets were paved, and the homes had modern conveniences such as indoor plumbing and access to electricity and natural gas. On the black side of town was degradation. One saw dirt streets (that were turned into quagmires when rains came) and shacks where blacks were forced to live, hovels that had no plumbing, no electricity, and no natural gas for cooking and heating. The white slum lords who owned those shacks refused to make improvements, preferring instead to maximize their short-term profits. Unless members of the black community worked on the white side of town (having jobs as domestics, for example), they could not cross the tracks without inviting police scrutiny and possible arrest, the exception being Saturday morning from 8:00 a.m. to 12:00 noon when they could venture to Moore Street, the downtown street parallel and one block north of the tracks. Blacks had four hours to shop and to give white merchants their precious money before they had to scurry back south of the tracks to avoid confrontations with whites, including the all-white police force.

Jesse Jackson was a black leader who tried to change Terrell, Texas, and all the segregated towns and cities like it. He was one who tried to secure justice for blacks in the United States. Destined to become a premier African American crusader for civil rights, he was born Jesse Louis Burns on October 8, 1941—just before the United States entered World War II—in segregated Greenville, North Carolina. His mother Helen Burns was unwed. His father Noah Lewis Robinson, a relatively prominent man in the local African American community who was married, was one of Helen Burns's neighbors. After the birth, he refused to become involved in his son's life. Early on, Jesse considered Charles Henry Jackson his father because that man married Helen in 1943 and helped her raise her son whom he later adopted; whereupon, Jesse proudly took the Jackson name.

Educated in segregated public schools in Greenville, he became a student leader and an all-around athlete. Upon graduating in 1959, Jackson received an offer to play professional baseball but turned down the opportunity to focus on football, a sport in which he excelled as a quarterback. The integrated University of Illinois offered him a football scholarship, and he quickly accepted. However, once on the college's practice field, he played behind another black quarterback. Apparently, he believed that he would never be a college football star while sitting on a bench at game time. Further, he fell behind in his studies. As a result, university administrators placed him on academic probation. After one disappointing year in Illinois, Jackson transferred to North Carolina A&T, a predominantly black school in Greensboro, North Carolina, where he emerged as a star quarterback and excelled as a student. After receiving his Bachelor's degree, he briefly attended Chicago Theological Seminary before deciding to devote more of his time to the ongoing civil rights movement (he was ordained a Baptist minister in 1968 without degree).

Jackson began his civil rights career while still a student in Greensboro. He joined the Congress on Racial Quality (CORE) and became an activist in its local Greensboro chapter. Quickly becoming a leader, he organized street marches and sit-ins in 1963 and was arrested several times for challenging the segregated practices of local restaurants and theaters. His work was rewarded when the North Carolina Intercollegiate Council on Human Rights chose him as their president. Perhaps more important, he became the field director of CORE in its southeastern campaign. In 1964, he was a delegate to the Young Democrats National Convention where he continued lobbying for black rights. The next year, he joined Martin Luther King's protest in Selma, Alabama, where authorities beat demonstrators, some under-age children, and set attack dogs on them in full view of television cameras. Such barbarities made gruesome viewing on nighttime news on major network channels. This incident proved to be the turning point in the civil rights movement because many whites—who had been apathetic—rallied to the movement since the actions of the authorities were so extreme.

When a racist sharpshooter killed Viola Liuzzo, a white volunteer from Detroit, Michigan, who used her car to transport people from Selma to Montgomery during King's "March on Montgomery," President Lyndon B. Johnson appeared on national television. He was clearly enraged at the nefarious act and demanded that Congress pass the Voting Rights Act which guaranteed all adults, regardless of color, the right to vote.

When King's Southern Christian Leadership Conference (SCLC) launched its Chicago Freedom Movement in 1966 in an effort to expand the civil rights struggle out of the South, Jackson organized marches in all-white neighborhoods, protesting against segregated housing. He coordinated Operation Breadbasket, an economic movement that urged white-owned grocery stores to stock more products familiar to African American customers; to hire more black workers; and to buy from African American companies who produced foodstuffs and other goods; or risk "selective buying," a none-too-subtle code-word for boycott. Such pressure brought results as many white owners negotiated with Jackson rather than lose a significant part of their consumer base. After Jackson had worked the Chicago market for a year, King promoted him to national director of Breadbasket.

Jackson continued to work with the SCLC until the aftermath of King's assassination on April 4, 1968, which caused more than one type of controversy. Jackson claimed to be with King when he was shot; whereas, other leaders said that he was in the parking lot of the Memphis motel where the charismatic leader was staying when he was shot down. Whatever the exact facts, Jackson must have rushed to the scene, for he came away with King's blood on his turtleneck sweater, which he wore the next day in his appearance on *Today*, a popular television program. Some critics believed that Jackson was grandstanding and doing so on the wrong occasion. Afterwards, he clashed with Ralph Abernathy who emerged as the new leader of the SCLC. Finally, the young firebrand left the organization in December of 1971 when Abernathy suspended him for "administrative improprieties" and "violations" of the SCLC's policies. Jackson had an aggressive and impatient personality that apparently alienated other SCLC leaders. He supposedly made a number of decisions and took pursuant actions without consulting other SCLC leaders. Later in December, Jackson and his supporters organized Operation PUSH (People United to Save Humanity), and in subsequent months, he proved to be, as always, an effective organizer and a brilliant lobbyist for black rights. The New Yorker Al Sharpton, a close associate of Jackson, also left the SCLC and joined PUSH in addition to forming his own National Youth Movement.

Before his "suspension," Jackson led hunger marches in Illinois that culminated with a march on the state capital to raise awareness that, even in America, the "underclass" witnessed starvation. As a result, the state increased funds for school meal programs, but Chicago mayor Richard Daley was not cooperative. Consequently Jackson ran for the mayor's job in 1971, a political contest that he lost. Nevertheless, some analysts opined that he laid the "groundwork" for Harold Washington's successful race in 1983 wherein he became Chicago's first black mayor.

During the 1970s, Jackson continued to promote his issues while leading various campaigns. He had a weekly radio program and established awards which he bestowed on notable African Americans who had excelled in one venue or another and who thereby could be role models for all blacks, especially younger people. Jackson established PUSH-Excel, a program designed to keep ghetto children in school and to help them find employment once they had their high school diplomas. The program had a checkered history of pluses and minuses until it was abandoned. Meanwhile, Jackson turned to the international community.

By the late 1970s, Jackson had become a self-appointed spokesperson for the oppressed worldwide. He went to South Africa in 1979 and criticized its policy of rigid segregation (called *apartheid*). The same year, he went to the Middle East to talk peace to both the Israelis and the Palestinians. In a dramatic episode, he flew to Damascus, Syria in 1983 to treat with Syria's government for the release of Lieutenant Robert Goodman, a black naval aviator who had been shot down in the skies over Lebanon while trying to target Syrian military positions there. After discussions with Jackson, Syrian president Hafez al-Assad released the American pilot. When Goodman returned to the United States, President Ronald Reagan invited both the aviator and Jackson to the White House on January 4, 1984, a gesture that ended up honoring the pilot and insulting his savior.

Reagan operated with a heavy hand. According to civil rights advocate Richard Hatcher, the president was not inclined to honor a Democrat—and a black one at that. Holding a press conference in the Rose Garden, Reagan intended that he would lead the session and speak and that Goodman would say a few words, but, according to Hatcher, Jackson was to be seen and not heard. Apparently upset that Jackson had operated outside the proper diplomatic channels, Reagan allowed him to be present but refused to give him credit for the good deed that he had done. Refusing to be shunned, the black firebrand managed to grab the microphone and to speak—regardless of what Reagan wanted. According to Hatcher, Jackson already had a habit of "speaking truth to power."

Soon active internationally again, Jackson went to Cuba after being invited by Cuban president Fidel Castro—who in 1959 had swept down from the hills around Havana and overthrown a government supported by the United States. Once there, Jackson met with the dictator. They spent time together talking about the state of affairs between their two countries and about the poverty that entrapped many African Americans in the states. Later, Jackson focused on his major mission of securing the release of American prisoners held in Cuba. His talks with the one-time guerrilla warrior had positive results. Castro released twenty-two Americans then being held in a lock-up. Next, Jackson toured Central America to talk to various leaders in hopes of bringing peace to warring parties in several countries in the region.

Even after his unsuccessful runs for the presidency, Jackson remained active on international fronts. In 1990, he became the first man to rescue Americans from Iraq and Kuwait after the Gulf War. He met with Iraq's dictator Saddam Hussein and made an appeal that brought positive results. Later, after he became close to President Bill Clinton and his wife Hillary, he treated with Kenya's President Daniel Arap Moi in 1997 about ensuring fair democratic elections in his country. Two years later found him in an interfaith delegation that went to Belgrade during the Kosovo War to negotiate with the genocidal international criminal, Yugoslav president Slobodan Milosevic. The Americans asked for the release of three of their countrymen captured in Macedonia, an effort that was ultimately successful. Still, controversy developed before the trip. Sandy Berger, national security advisor to Clinton, told Jackson that, as a private citizen, he could not represent the United States diplomatically. American law forbade that. Berger also told him that his safety could not be assured, that Jackson, himself, could be captured or killed.

Despite such warnings, Jackson continued the mission and brought three Americans home. The United States Senate noted the achievement and awarded Jackson a Senate Commendation. May of 1999 found the black leader in Africa's war-torn Sierra Leone where he arranged a cease fire in a civil war that had pitted President Tejan Kabbah's forces against rebel challenger Foday Sankoh and his supporters. While there, Jackson secured the release of more than 2,000 prisoners of war. Because the cease fire was later violated, Jackson returned. Year 2000 found him in Sierra Leone again, continuing to spread words of peace to the region while trying to arrange another armistice.

Jackson opposed President George W. Bush's war in Iraq, and spoke out against the coming conflict. After giving sundry anti-war speeches in the United States, on February 15, 2003 Jackson spoke in London, England to approximately one million people during a protest of President George

Bush's plans to invade Iraq. Remaining active worldwide, to Ireland Jackson went in 2004, with hopes of defusing the conflict there between Protestants and Catholics, a civil war replete with terrorist attacks, a war that had been ongoing for centuries. August of 2005 found him in Venezuela, treating with President Hugo Chavez.

*   *   *

Despite his successful work domestically and overseas, in the early 1980s, Jackson decided to seek a new forum so that Americans could hear his voice for change. In November of 1983, he announced for the presidency, launching his bid to become the Democratic Party nominee. Initially few took his efforts seriously, but his campaign was surprisingly effective. He offered an alternative to the conservative administration of Ronald Reagan, and to the less than exciting Democratic challengers. Jackson's 1984 election campaign coalesced around his Rainbow Coalition, envisioned as an alliance of those excluded from power: African Americans, Hispanics, the poor, the elderly, family farmers, and women. The movement was modeled on the black struggle. The campaign goals of peace, freedom, and justice had broad appeal, and attracted the support of many white progressives.

Jackson's more specific platform embraced a comprehensive set of liberal policies. Borrowing from the New Deal, Jackson promised to establish a public works program to address the nation's infrastructure and provide jobs for all, and he offered a solution to the small farmers' economic problems based on the New Deal agricultural programs. He addressed the health, education, and welfare needs of Americans by promising to repeal the Reagan tax-cuts for upper-income Americans, and using these funds to expand social welfare programs; providing universal healthcare through a single-payer system, and increasing federal funding for public education and making community college education free to all Americans. He proposed to reverse priorities in the War on Drugs by shifting the emphasis from arresting drug users to attacking the supply side of the illegal drug system including the financing and money laundering operations. In defense and foreign policy Jackson promised to cut defense spending by 15 percent, institute an immediate nuclear freeze and initiate disarmament negotiations with the Soviet Union, isolate the apartheid South African regime, and support the creation of a Palestinian state in the Middle East. In the area of civil rights Jackson endorsed the Equal Rights Amendment for women, promised increased enforcement of the Voting Rights Act, and advocated a system of reparations to compensate African Americans for slavery and racism.

Jackson's 1984 campaign showed that his message had legs. He was one of ten Democratic politicians to enter party primaries, and he came in third, overall. Walter Mondale, the eventual nominee, had a total of 6,952,912 votes, while second-place finisher Gary Hart received 6,504,842. Ahead of such candidates as John Glenn, George McGovern, and Alan Cranston, Jackson finished third with 3,283,431, although he cut his campaign short after seeing he could not win. In a remarkable but under-funded campaign, he won primaries or caucuses in Washington, D.C., South Carolina, Virginia, Louisiana, and one of two separate races in Mississippi, all regions of heavy black population.

Jackson's campaign faced a number of weaknesses. He was handicapped by a lack of resources and a weak and inexperienced campaign staff. These deficiencies were particularly troublesome because Jackson was running an unconventional campaign that was part protest politics and part more traditional electoral politics. This duality required both the mobilizations of masses of hard core supporters for the rallies and the polls, and the more traditional tasks of fund-raising, obtaining endorsements, and developing a database of supporters.

Jackson's background in protest politics generated a certain excitement for his campaign, but it also led to problems. Most notably Jackson's campaign was marred by comments he made to a reporter from the *Washington Post*, wherein he referred to New York City as "Hymietown." According to civil rights activist Richard Hatcher, Jackson's use of that anti-Semitic racial slur threw a "wet blanket" over his entire campaign. Strong supporters, including money donors, began winnowing away. And, although Jackson apologized publicly several times, the apology did not satisfy everyone, including many Jews who were emotionally inflamed by Jackson's use of the derogatory term. The negative comment proved to have long legs and an even longer life. It later dogged Jackson in his 1988 run for the presidency when New York mayor Ed Koch resurrected the term, saying that any Jew who supported the black leader had to be crazy. Jackson was also harmed by his perceived association with radical Black Muslim Louis Farrakhan, one more issue that damaged his campaign.

* * *

One fruit of his surprising campaign was an invitation to speak at the Democratic National Convention. Taking the podium on July 18, 1984, shortly before the delegates would nominate Walter Mondale, Jackson's oratory was spellbinding. Jackson responded with an electrifying address. He opened with a definition of the party's mission: "to feed the hungry; to clothe the naked; to house the homeless; to teach the illiterate; to provide jobs for the jobless; and to choose the human race over the nuclear race." The heart of the speech then focused on his vision of the Rainbow Coalition:

Our flag is red, white and blue, but our nation is a rainbow—red, yellow, brown, black and white—and we're all precious in God's sight.

America is not like a blanket—one piece of unbroken cloth, the same color, the same texture, the same size. America is more like a quilt: many patches, many pieces, many colors, many sizes, all woven and held together by a common thread. The white, the Hispanic, the black, the Arab, the Jew, the woman, the native American, the small farmer, the businessperson, the environmentalist, the peace activist, the young, the old, the lesbian, the gay, and the disabled make up the American quilt.

Even in our fractured state, all of us count and fit somewhere. We have proven that we can survive without each other. But we have not proven that we can win and make progress without each other. We must come together.

In spite of his success in the campaign and his speech at the convention, none of Jackson's campaign planks, save one, were incorporated into the Democratic platform. The party did endorse Jackson's call to isolate South Africa's racist regime.

Four years later Jackson again entered the race for the Democratic nomination for president. His surprising strength in 1984 made him a more credible candidate, although few pundits gave him much of a chance to win. Again, though, he did much better than expected and surprised many of his detractors.

Jackson's 1988 campaign was better financed and better organized than his 1984 effort. Still he lacked the infrastructure of more experienced and organized campaigns. For example, he lacked a sophisticated database of supporters, volunteers, and potential donors that his strongest opponents possessed. Still, Jackson showed even more staying power than in 1984. This time he finished second to Michael Dukakis in the Democratic primaries and caucuses, with 6.9 million votes. He won primary victories in Washington, D.C., Alabama, Louisiana, Mississippi, South Carolina, Georgia, Delaware, Vermont, Virginia, Puerto Rico (all states with a large minority population), and—in a surprise—Michigan with 55 percent of the caucus delegates. He also won caucus victories in four other states, and split victories (winning either the caucus or delegate convention or the primary) in two others.

Jackson's Michigan victory was the shocker of the primary season. It briefly made him the front-runner in terms of pledged delegates. Attempting to build on this momentum Jackson focused his attention on the Wisconsin primary two weeks later. Taking advantage of a bitter labor dispute in an auto plant in the state, Jackson received the support of a United Auto

Workers local, and had hopes of winning. However, he lost Wisconsin badly, with far fewer white votes than the polls had indicated. He also lost Colorado in a close race the day before the Wisconsin vote. These two defeats turned the tide, and Dukakis, who controlled the Democratic machinery and had the support of the Democratic Party's "establishment," eventually overwhelmed him.

Jackson's platform in 1988 was virtually the same as in 1984, and again he was invited to address the convention. Jackson spoke to the Democratic convention on July 19, 1988, but his oratory lacked the fire of his 1984 convention address; he nevertheless again took Reaganomics to task and the Republican Party's philosophy of helping the rich and the corporations. He reported that Reaganomics was "based on the belief that the rich had too little money and the poor had too much." Consequently, the Republicans reversed "Robin Hood"; they "took from the poor and gave to the rich, paid for by the middle class. We cannot stand four more years of Reaganomics in any version, in any disguise." Jackson said that the harm Reagan and his Republicans had done was documented: "Seven years later, the richest 1 percent of our society pays 20 percent less in taxes. The poorest 10 percent pay 20 percent more." Clearly heart-sick about what the outgoing president had done, Jackson added that

> Reagan gave the rich and the powerful a multibillion-dollar party. Now the party's over. He expects the people to pay for the damage. I take this principled position, convention, let us not raise taxes on the poor and the middle class, but those who had the party, the rich and the powerful, must pay for the party.

As he had for most of his public career, Jackson again spoke truth to power. He lamented that the government spent so much on the military when the money could go to far better purposes.

> We are spending $150 billion a year defending Europe and Japan 43 years after the war [World War II, 1941–45]. We have more troops in Europe tonight than we had seven years ago. Yet, the threat of war is ever more remote.

Continuing, the Democratic candidate pointed out that Germany and Japan were creditor nations while the United States was a debtor nation, a development that he had earlier predicted. He advised that we should make Germany and Japan "share the burden of their own defense."

Jackson held that if Americans would trim the military budget, some of that money could be spent for better housing, public education, and health care. "Use some of that money to wipe out . . . slums and put America back to work," he said. "If we can bail out Europe and Japan; if we can bail out Continental Bank and Chrysler and Mr. [Lee] Iaccoca makes $8,000 an hour; we can bail out the family farmer [and others who needed attention]." It made no sense, Jackson thundered, to "close down 650,000 family farms in this country while importing food from abroad, subsidized by the U.S. government. Let's make sense." It made no sense, he added, for the U.S. Navy "to be escorting all our tankers up and down the Persian Gulf, paying $2.50 for every $1 worth of oil we bring out, while oil wells are capped in Texas, Oklahoma, and Louisiana."

Speaking primarily to the underclass, Jackson closed his address with a personal note. "I have a story," he said. "I was not always on television. Writers were not always outside my door . . . You see, I was born of a teenage mother who was born of a teenage mother . . . I know abandonment and people being mean to you and saying you are nothing." Continuing, he said that "I wasn't born in a hospital. Mama didn't have insurance. I was born in the bed at the house." "I was," he admitted,

> born in a three-room house, bathroom in the backyard [called the outhouse], slop jar by the bed, no hot and cold running water [in the house]. . . My mother [was] a working woman. So many of the days she went to work early with runs in her stockings . . . so that [she could buy matching socks] for my brother and I and not be laughed at school . . . Call you outcasts, low down, you can't make it, you're nothing . . . you are from nobody, subclass, underclass. When you see Jesse Jackson, when you see my name [go] in nomination [tonight, for president,] your name goes in nomination.

A vital question left over from the 1988 campaign remains pivotal: why was Jesse Jackson not picked as the vice presidential running mate for Michael Dukakis? Remember, he had the second largest number of delegates going into the Democratic convention. Four years earlier Jackson's presence enabled Walter Mondale to select a woman, Geraldine Ferraro, as the Democratic vice presidential nominee. There are three answers/reasons. First, Dukakis and his followers saw him somewhat as the heir to John F. Kennedy, and since Kennedy chose a senator from Texas, so should Dukakis, as a result Texas senator Lloyd Bentsen became the vice presidential candidate. Secondly, the Democrats assumed that the black vote would go to Dukakis anyway, so why put Jackson on the ticket? And, lastly, Jackson was perceived as divisive, primarily a race man. Essentially these reasons dismissed Jackson too lightly and considered Bentsen too highly. When the Dukakis campaign went into a funk at mid-tide, neither Dukakis nor Bentsen seemed capable of energizing the campaign. It would not have lacked energy or drive with the Reverend Jesse Jackson as the vice presidential nominee. A significant statement and selection was not made; Dukakis and Bentsen, somewhat like Dewey in 1948, snatched defeat from the jaws of victory.

Following the 1988 elections, Jackson moved his home and daily headquarters to Washington, D.C. He had a chance to run for mayor after Marion Berry was bounced from office because of a drug scandal, but Jackson confounded analysts by refusing to make the race. Instead, in July of 1990, he announced that he was standing for the post of D.C.'s "shadow senator" (also called the "statehood senator"), an office that Washington's local government established to prod Congress for statehood and to do so repeatedly in every session of Congress. Elected in January of 1991, he served his six-year term but believed he was stymied by congressional opposition to D.C.'s efforts.

After his decision not to seek reelection as the "shadow senator," Jackson transferred efforts to New York, where he began his "Wall Street Project," which he believed would benefit upper- and middle-class blacks. He and others in his organization lobbied national companies to provide more employment opportunities for African Americans and to give more business to minority-owned companies. He lobbied black investors to exert their power to influence the companies in which they had bought stock. Jackson believed that many such minority investors did not realize the economic leverage they had as stockholders. He told *Black Enterprise* that when shareholders go into a company meeting, "you now have the right to the floor." Continuing, he said that "now you can walk into a board meeting" and ask major questions about the company and its hiring program, for example. Are they hiring minorities, or do they discriminate based on race? Are they fair? "We empower politically with our vote. Now we must empower economically with our dollar." As Jackson told *Ebony*: "We have gone from sharecropper to shareholder." To corporate America, we say, "we don't want to be just consumers and workers, but investors and partners."

Jackson remained active in presidential politics following the 1988 election, although never again as candidate. While he was not a strong supporter of Clinton as a candidate he eventually became a political ally and helped build Clinton's support within the African American community. During the Clinton years Jackson became a close advisor of the president, and Clinton awarded Jackson the Medal of Freedom, the nation's highest honor bestowed on civilians. Early in the new century Jackson devoted energy to his son's political career. Jesse Jackson, Jr. won election to Congress from Illinois in 2002. In 2004 Jackson chose not to endorse either of the African American candidates (Al Sharpton and Carol Moseley-Braun) who were seeking the Democratic Party nomination. While he never endorsed any candidate, he did seem to favor Dennis Kucinich, a congressman from Ohio. Jackson invited Kucinich to address a Rainbow-PUSH political forum during the primary campaign and generally spoke favorably of the candidate.

In the 2008 presidential election Jackson endorsed Obama early in the campaign, but he played no formal role in the campaign. In contrast, Jesse Jackson, Jr. served as the national co-chair of the Obama campaign. There were reports of behind the scenes clashes between Jackson Sr. and Obama during the campaign. This rumored tension became public. While speaking "privately" before an open mike, Jackson observed that Obama was "talking down to black people" for his comments criticizing black men on Father's Day. Jackson then added, "I want to cut his nuts off." These comments created a brief firestorm. Jesse Jackson, Jr. sharply criticized his father's comments. Jackson, Sr. personally apologized to Obama, but many cited the differences as reflecting the emergence of a new generation of African American leadership—and the passing of the old leadership class.

* * *

One is struck by the similarities and the issues involved in Jackson's campaigns in the 1980s and Obama's quest in the new millennium. Jackson was a "dark horse" candidate as was Obama in the early going. And many of the issues were/are the same, as if the country had solved no problems from the 1980s to circa 2009. Both followed conservative low-tax Republican presidents. Both shared some of the same political objectives—to adjust the tax rate to shift the burden to the wealthiest Americans, address the health care system, rebuild the nation's infrastructure with public works, and pursue a foreign policy based on inter-nation cooperation and negotiation rather than confrontation. It is therefore not surprising that election night brought tears to the eyes of the elder Jackson. His goals were vindicated—but he was on the sidelines watching.

And Americans should remember that Jesse Jackson was at least a quarter-century before his time. He was a prophet who saw our future, yesterday.

Further Reading

Barker, Lucius J., and Ronald W. Walters, eds. *Jesse Jackson's 1984 Presidential Campaign: Challenge and Change in American Politics.* Urbana: University of Illinois Press, 1989.

Bruns, Roger. *Jesse Jackson: A Biography.* Westport, CT: Greenwood Press, 2005.

Callahan, Linda Florence. "A Fantasy-Theme Analysis of the Political Rhetoric of the Reverend Jesse Louis Jackson, The First Serious Black Candidate for the Office of President of the United States." Ph.D. dissertation, Ohio State University, 1987.

Clemente, Frank and Frank, Watkins, eds. *Keep Hope Alive: Jesse Jackson's 1988 Presidential Campaign.* Boston: South End Press, 1989.

Frady, Marshall. *Jesse: The Life and Pilgrimage of Jesse Jackson.* New York: Simon & Schuster, 2006.

Gibbons, Arnold. *Race, Politics, and the White Media: The Jesse Jackson Campaigns.* Lanham, MD: University Press of American, 1993.

Hatch, Roger D., and Frank E. Watkins, eds. *Straight From the Heart: Jesse Jackson.* Philadelphia: Fortress Press, 1987.

Henry, Charles. *Jesse Jackson: The Search for Common Ground.* Oakland, CA: Black Scholar Press, 1991.

Landress, Tom, and Richard M. Quinn. *Jesse Jackson & the Politics of Race.* Ottawa, IL: Jameson Books, 1985.

Loewenstein, Gaither, and Lyttleton T. Sanders. "Bloc Voting, Rainbow Coalitions, and the Jackson Presidential Candidacy." *Journal of Black Studies* 18 (September 1987): 86–96.

Morris, Lorenzo, ed. *The Social and Political Implications of the 1984 Jesse Jackson Presidential Campaign.* New York: Praeger, 1990.

Reed, Adolph L., Jr. *The Jesse Jackson Phenomenon: The Crisis of Purpose in Afro-American Politics.* New Haven: Yale University Press, 1986.

Reynolds, Barbara A. *America's David: Jesse Jackson, the Movement, the Myth.* Washington, DC: JFJ Associates, 1985.

Stone, Eddie. *Jesse Jackson.* Los Angeles: Holloway House, 1988.

Walters, Ronald W. *Black Presidential Politics in America: A Strategic Approach.* Albany: State University of New York Press, 1988.

Walton, Hanes, Jr., ed. *Black Politics and Black Political Behavior: A Linkage Analysis.* Westport, CT: Praeger, 1994.

———. *African American Power and Politics: The Political Context Variable.* New York: Columbia University Press, 1997.

Lenora Branch Fulani during a Harlem street festival celebrating the twentieth anniversary of her 1988 race for the presidency as the nominee of the New Alliance Party. (Courtesy of the Committee of a Unified Independent Party (CUIP) Archives.)

CHAPTER 8

Lenora Branch Fulani

Challenging the Rules of the Game

OMAR H. ALI

Unable to restructure the whole of American politics to make it more inclusive and participatory, largely because we were politically attached to the Democratic Party . . .we instead fought for little pieces of access to a system that was controlled from the top . . . Identity politics came to dominate. Black Americans became a part of special interest politics. Ironically and tragically, race relations worsened as a result . . . My own involvement in third party politics was based on wanting to create a way out of being essentially held hostage to a two-party system that was not only hostile to us but hostile to the democratic participation of all the American people.

(Dr. Lenora B. Fulani, 1997)

In 1988 developmental psychologist Lenora Branch Fulani became the first woman and the first African American to get on the ballot in all fifty states as a candidate for president of the United States. She ran with the New Alliance Party, among other progressive third parties, including the Peace and Freedom Party in California and the predominantly black United Citizens Party in South Carolina. Approximately one quarter of a million people voted for her as a third-party or independent candidate. Other African Americans had launched presidential campaigns (from George Edwin Taylor in 1904 to civil rights leader Reverend Jesse Jackson in 1984); other women had run for president (from women's suffragist Victoria Woodhull in 1872 to New York Congresswoman Shirley Chisholm in 1972); none appeared on the ballot in every state of the nation running for president.

Fulani's 1988 campaign was a milestone in terms of gender and race. But when asked whether it was more difficult running for president being black or being a woman, Fulani responded by saying that it was more difficult *running as an independent*. Getting on the ballot across the country required extensive grassroots fundraising and logistical coordination, and only after gathering nearly 1.2 million signatures and winning eleven lawsuits against election authorities did her campaign achieve the task. Bipartisan (Democratic and Republican) imposed legal and political barriers to independent and third-party candidacies include restrictive ballot access, exclusion from candidate debates, and campaign finance laws that favor the two major parties. In essence there is one set of legal requirements for the two major parties, and another set for independents and third-party candidates.

A pioneer in the creation of "black and independent alliances" (largely disaffected black Democrats working with white independents), Fulani would in creating such alliances for political reform forge the development of a postmodern independent black leadership in the United States. This new leadership—most powerfully expressed in Senator Barack Obama during his 2008 presidential campaign (by his reaching out to independents and Republicans, in addition to rank-and-file Democrats)—is less identity-based and ideologically driven than traditional black politics, much of which had become tied to the Democratic Party since the mid-1960s. Instead, the postmodern black leadership-in-the-making that Fulani was developing two decades before Obama launched his presidential campaign was focused on reforming the electoral process itself.

The creation of black and independent alliances for political reform that began in 1988 took more discernible form during Fulani's second presidential campaign in 1992. Both of her campaigns were designed to spur the growth of independent politics nationally towards breaking up the bipartisan electoral monopoly of the Democratic and Republican parties. In 1992 Fulani launched her campaign by reaching out to white independents in New Hampshire; she would then urge voters to also support Texas billionaire Ross Perot, who entered the race as an independent. He personally invested tens of millions of dollars to promote his candidacy (nearly 70 million dollars in all). Fulani welcomed the opportunity presented by Perot's entrance into the race to build an independent movement, even though she was politically progressive (on the left) and Perot was conservative (center-right). The "postmodern" in this was Fulani's willingness to break ideological boundaries by creating an on-the-ground pro-reform coalition between her multiracial progressive networks of support (much of which was black) and the largely white and conservative networks of support that Perot had helped to inspire.

In the wake of the 1992 election, which saw nearly twenty million voters cast their ballots for Perot (including over half a million African Americans),

Fulani sought to build organizations that could carry on the desire for political independence and political reform that Perot had tapped into and helped to unleash. Over the next sixteen years she built networks of independent activists around the country and promoted independent and insurgent political reform-oriented candidates (for president she supported Perot in 1996, John Hagelin in 2000, Ralph Nader in 2004, and Obama in 2008). Throughout the 1990s and into the 2000s Fulani also spearheaded multiple campaigns to promote structural political reforms, including term limits, ballot access, initiative and referendum, nonpartisan municipal elections, and open primaries—all designed to empower voters. Among the different political parties and organizations that she co-founded were the Patriot Party, the Reform Party, the Independence Party of New York, and the Committee for a Unified Independent Party—each of which attempted to build across a wide geographic, ideological, and demographic spectrum of Americans.

Biographical Background

Born Lenora Branch on April 25, 1950 in Chester, Pennsylvania, Fulani grew up in the working-class black community of her birth located to the southwest of Philadelphia. Her mother, Pearl Branch, was a domestic worker before becoming a nurse; her father, Charles Lee, was a baggage carrier on the Pennsylvania Railroad. As a child, Fulani briefly participated in the public school desegregation process following the *Brown v. Board of Education* decision in 1954. Northern forms of institutional racial discrimination, whether in public schools or other public services, mirrored aspects of southern Jim Crow—and often with tragic results: The ambulance service that was called when Fulani's father had a heart attack when she was twelve years old refused to come into her black neighborhood; neighbors scrambled to carry her father to the hospital on a makeshift stretcher, but he died on the way. Fulani's response to such fatal consequences of poverty and racism was to become active in her community. A youth leader in the black Baptist Church, she decided in her teens that she wanted to become a psychologist to help those in her community deal with their emotional pain.

In 1968 Fulani won a scholarship to Hofstra University on Long Island, New York, where she majored in psychology. Fulani had begun to be influenced in college by the writings of Frantz Fanon, the revolutionary black psychiatrist from Martinique who worked in Algeria during that nation's anti-colonial struggle against France. It was the late 1960s and the Black Power movement was underway on campuses and in communities across the United States. She graduated, married, and had two children, Ainka and Amani. However, she divorced when her children were young and became a single parent. Reflecting her pride in being of African descent, she changed her last name to Fulani—the name of a West African people. She continued with her studies, completing a Master's degree at Columbia University Teachers' College and then pursuing a doctorate. In 1984 she received her Ph.D. in developmental psychology at the Graduate Center of the City University of New York. Her dissertation, "Children's Understanding of Number Symbols in Formal and Informal Contexts," was an exploration of the ways in which poor black children learn mathematics inside and outside of school. It reflected her growing interest in the discoveries of the early-twentieth century Soviet methodologist Lev Vygotsky, whose work in education and psychology she had been introduced to as a researcher at Rockefeller University during the mid-1970s.

At Rockefeller Fulani specialized in the interplay between social environment and learning, with a particular focus on African Americans. She began to question the value of efforts to reform traditional psychology—including black, feminist, and gay psychologies—when these very reform efforts perpetuated key, if not foundational features of it, such as labeling and fixed identities. In 1978 Lois Holzman, a colleague at Rockefeller, introduced Fulani to Fred Newman, a Stanford-trained philosopher of science who left his academic career in the late 1960s to build community-based services and programs in some of New York's poorest neighborhoods. Newman became Fulani's mentor and collaborator over the next three decades in the work of creating educational, therapeutic, as well as political alternatives for the black community. Such efforts were a direct challenge to the Democratic Party and its traditional liberal programs and spheres of political influence. Many of these liberal programs were viewed as ineffective in the black community, despite tens of millions of dollars spent on them.

In the areas of psychology and education Fulani worked with Newman, Holzman, and others to create a performance-based clinical approach to curing emotional pain, which they called social therapy. Grounded in the early writings of Karl Marx, Vygotsky, and the philosopher Ludwig Wittgenstein, this approach informs the All Stars Talent Show Network—a supplementary education program for inner-city youth which Fulani helped to found in New York in 1981. Since then the program has spread to Newark, Philadelphia, Boston, Chicago, Atlanta, Los Angeles, and the San Francisco Bay Area. Fulani also helped to found the All Stars' sister program, the Development School for Youth, a leadership training school for young people based in New York, Newark, and Los Angeles. Together, the programs involve approximately ten thousand young people each year.

Despite the praise Fulani has received for her work in the field of supplementary education by some of the nation's most prominent black scholars and educational innovators—including Columbia University's Edmund

Gordon, Harvard University's Henry Louis Gates, Jr., Princeton University's Kwame Anthony Appiah, and New York University's Derrick Bell—she remains a controversial figure. However, Fulani's controversiality derives only partially from her work in building educational and therapeutic approaches and programs that challenge traditional (explanatory and diagnostic) psychology and cognitively driven pedagogy, in favor of activistic, performance based practices. It has been her challenges to the bipartisan establishment—and, in particular, the Democratic Party—for its political monopoly while insufficiently addressing poverty in the nation that have produced the most searing vitriol against her.

The 1988 Campaign: Fulani and Jackson

By the mid-1980s an idea inaugurated at the 1972 National Black Political Convention in Gary, Indiana, to create an all-black political party in the National Black Independent Political Party, had run its course. The question on the table in the 1980s for many progressive African Americans was what kinds of new political alliances could be built given that even if an all-black party was to gather the support of every single black voter, it could not compete effectively on a national basis without white and other Americans' support. Fulani joined the New Alliance Party in 1980. The party had been formed the year prior in the South Bronx, New York as a progressive multiracial party whose goal was to challenge the authority of the Democratic Party in New York City's black and Latino communities. Fulani ran for lieutenant governor on the New Alliance Party line in 1982 and then campaigned on behalf of its 1984 presidential candidate Dennis Serrette, a black trade union leader. She herself became the party's presidential candidate in 1988 and then again in 1992 (the New Alliance Party folded into the larger independent political movement underway after 1992; many of its members would join local affiliates of the national Patriot Party).

Between 1988 and 2008 Fulani was the nation's leading black voice for independent politics. She urged African Americans to diversify their political options as a way of both gaining greater leverage with elected officials and creating new alliances that could take the country in more developmental, democratic directions. At the core of her call was the need for political reform—or "fair elections" as she described. In 1988, running on the New Alliance Party ticket, Fulani campaigned under the slogan "Two Roads Are Better than One." Defying convention, she ran with six vice presidential candidates, representing different constituencies, including black, white, Latino, and Native American running mates. Fulani's "Two Roads" strategy entailed encouraging voters to support Rev. Jesse Jackson in the

Democratic primaries and then to support her in the general election in the event that Jackson did not receive the Democratic nomination.

Jackson did not win his party's nomination, and proceeded to lend his support to Massachusetts Governor Michael Dukakis. Dukakis, in turn, rejected Jackson (who received over seven million votes in the primaries) as a vice presidential running mate, choosing Senator Lloyd Bentsen of Texas instead. Fulani strongly urged Jackson to run as an independent to no avail despite there being support for him to do so. In a poll taken by the University of Michigan's Institute for Social Research, two out of three voters who supported Jackson in the primaries said that they would have voted for him as an independent candidate had he decided to run as such. He did not. Republican George H. W. Bush handily won the election that year. Meanwhile, Fulani continued to demonstrate the support that existed for independent politics.

That fall, not only did Fulani get on the ballot in all fifty states (and the District of Columbia), but she also became the first African American woman to receive federal primary matching funds. On election day she received two percent of the national black vote and two percent of the national gay vote—peeling away elements of key constituencies of the Democratic Party. The New Alliance Party emerged as the nation's fourth largest party that year; the right-of-center Libertarian Party, founded in 1971, remained the third largest. Underscoring the purpose of her run for office was her officially registered campaign name: "Lenora B. Fulani's Committee for Fair Elections." Again challenging convention, the standard registered name for a presidential campaign is the candidate's name followed by "for President." Fulani's campaign made clear the purpose of what they were doing, which was focused on political reform.

The electoral playing field is tilted against third-party and independent candidates. Getting on the ballot in all fifty states had required Fulani's campaign to collect more than thirty times the number of nominating petition signatures than either of the major party presidential candidates. Moreover, Fulani was excluded from each of the presidential debates, and the media paid little attention to her campaign. Fulani and her associates in the New Alliance Party would lobby Congress and state assemblies, as well as file multiple law suits to challenge ballot access restrictions, among other electoral inequities. As *Ballot Access News* editor Richard Winger noted in 1992, "The New Alliance Party has done more for ballot access reform than anyone else."

Ballot access was only one obstacle to fairness in the electoral process; another was the exclusion of independent and third-party candidates from the nationally televised presidential debates. The organization that sponsors the debates, the Commission on Presidential Debates (CPD), was established in 1987 by the two major parties. They effectively wrested control of the debates from the nominally nonpartisan League of Women Voters. Fulani's attorneys had argued in federal court that the CPD was not entitled to tax-exemption because it is not nonpartisan, as the law requires (it is bipartisan). In 1988, the CPD said that Fulani was ineligible to be included in its general election debates because she was not a "legitimate" candidate. In June of 1991, a three-judge panel finally ruled that Fulani "lacked standing" to challenge the tax-exempt status of the CPD for excluding her from the debates three years prior—despite the fact that she was on the ballot in all fifty states and had received federal primary matching funds. However, one of the federal judges, Chief Judge Abner Mikva, dissented from his two fellow judges. As he put it, "The government of any democracy, let alone one shaped by the values of our Constitution's First Amendment, must avoid tilting the electoral playing field, lest the democracy itself becomes tarnished." It was a rare judicial acknowledgement of the electoral injustices either written into the law or practiced by the Democratic and Republican Parties.

Fulani was again an independent candidate in 1990 when she ran for governor of New York on the New Alliance Party line and was endorsed by the civil rights activist (and fourteen years later, Democratic presidential candidate) Rev. Al Sharpton and the Nation of Islam's leader Minister Louis Farrakhan. In 1989 Fulani and Sharpton, who at her urging later entered electoral politics but rejected running as an independent, led a series of marches through the Bensonhurst section of Brooklyn, New York to protest the murder of a black teenager, Yusuf Hawkins. Hawkins had been killed by a group of white youth in a racially motivated incident; the white community of Bensonhurst refused to acknowledge any wrongdoing or sympathy for the young African American who happened to get off at the wrong subway stop. Fulani's constant presence in the black community encouraged black and Latino families to call on her for support in subsequent cases of racially motivated violence, especially those involving police brutality. In August of 1991 she played an instrumental role in preventing the escalation of violence in the Crown Heights section of Brooklyn when she placed herself between the police and young black men rioting in response to the hit-and-run death of Gavin Cato, a young black boy. Meanwhile, Fulani's All Stars Talent Show Network was working with thousands of black and Latino youth to create developmental opportunities in many of the same communities in which violence raged alongside chronic levels of poverty.

Instead of being supported by white liberals and black Democrats for her work in communities of color, Fulani came under fire for challenging their party's claim as the party of the poor and working class—that is, the party of African Americans, the most loyal constituency of the Democratic Party. It was in the build-up to Fulani's 1988 presidential campaign that the Democratic Party took targeted measures to ostracize Fulani and undermine her efforts to challenge Democratic authority in black and Latino communities. One such effort began in 1987 with John Foster "Chip" Berlet, who worked for the Democratic Party-affiliated Political Research Associates. Berlet wrote a pamphlet entitled "Clouds Blur the Rainbow" which was widely distributed to liberal and left-leaning organizations and newspapers around the country. The pamphlet became the primary source of all subsequent attacks on Fulani, which stated that her social therapy practice was an instrument of the Newman "cult" used to "brainwash" unwitting patients into membership in the New Alliance Party. Despite repeated attacks and accusations, Fulani continued to build avenues for independent politics and within four years the nation would witness an independent voter revolt on a scale unprecedented in American history.

The 1992 Campaign: Fulani and Perot

Fulani launched her 1992 campaign by going to white New Hampshire, the first state in the nation scheduled to hold presidential primaries. Convention held that overwhelmingly white states like New Hampshire would not support black candidacies. However Fulani believed that she could reach white independent-minded voters by engaging in new kinds of conversations that were not over-determined by partisanship, race, or other forms of identity-based politics; instead she would focus on the need for political reform. Sixteen years later, Obama pursued a similar strategy by going to white Iowa (where the first caucuses in the nation take place) and sought independent support around an agenda for political reform.

As a tactic, Fulani entered the Democratic primary in New Hampshire to help expose the extent to which the Democratic Party—in collusion with the Republican Party—would exercise undemocratic control over the electoral process. The situation was reminiscent of efforts by black civil rights activists a generation earlier pushing accepted social and political boundaries by sitting in "whites-only" counters in Greensboro, North Carolina, or attempting to register to vote in Jackson, Mississippi. In a sense, Fulani was exposing a new kind of Jim Crow in America—one not based on race, but on political affiliation (i.e. independents and insurgents)—and rallying Americans to move the country in a more democratic and developmental direction.

After she had been denied entrance into the first primary debate in New Hampshire, ten thousand registered New Hampshire voters signed petitions calling for Fulani's inclusion in the debates (she was the only African American and the only woman in the Democratic primary), along with two other fellow insurgent candidates, both of whom were white men. Fulani was joined by Larry Agran (an independent-minded Democrat who had been elected mayor of Irvine in California's conservative Orange County) and

Eugene McCarthy (the anti-war insurgent Democratic candidate in 1968 who had forced the pro-war Democratic President Lyndon Johnson from seeking reelection after winning 43 percent of the vote in the New Hampshire primary)—both of whom were out of favor with the Democratic Party establishment. Drawing further attention to the matter, Fulani led a 500-person demonstration outside of the auditorium of Saint Anselm College in Goffstown, where she, Agran, and McCarthy were being banned from participating in the debate.

With the prompting of the national chairman of the Democratic Party, Ron Brown, both the League of Women Voters and CNN (the sponsoring organizations of the primary debates) continued to exclude Fulani. In response Fulani and her campaign organized voters from two dozen cities to stage protests at League offices. Protesters demanded that the only woman in the primary be permitted to participate in the debates. Fulani had also received $624,000 in matching funds from the federal government by this time, placing her second among the Democratic Party candidates. Fulani's attorneys filed suit in U.S. District Court seeking an injunction while still other protests were launched. Congressmen who had previously supported election reform measures with the urging of Fulani associates of the Washington, D.C.-based Rainbow Lobby firm—notably, Minnesota congressman Timothy Penny, who sponsored the Democracy and Presidential Debates Act (H.R. 791)—were asked to apply pressure on the League to reverse its decision. Penny sent a letter which was co-signed by fellow Democratic congressmen John Conyers of Michigan, James Oberstar and Gerry Silkorski of Minnesota, and Richard Neal of Massachusetts. The multiple protests did not lead to the inclusion of Fulani or her fellow insurgents in the debates, but a small albeit significant number of voters in New Hampshire did register their opposition to the "major" Democratic candidates—Bill Clinton, Jerry Brown, Tom Harkin, Bob Kerrey, and Paul Tsongas—by voting for those who had been excluded from the primary debates. Fulani next took her fight to New York, where the Democratic primary was to take place on April 7 and where in July the Democratic Party would hold its nominating convention; and then came Ross Perot's famous late-night announcement.

On February 20 Perot announced on CNN's *Larry King Live* that he would run for president as an independent if supporters got him on the ballot across the country. But even a billionaire like Perot would have to adhere to the ballot access rules and regulations that discriminated against independent and third-party candidates. Perot called on Fulani's legal team for counsel and took the necessary measures to initiate his independent presidential bid, itself centered on a critique of the two major parties. Although Fulani had long entered the race by that point, Perot's announcement, and the massive resources he could bring to bear in projecting the need for political reform (through paid radio, cable, and television advertising and publicity), offered a significant political opportunity to advance independent politics. In a controversial proposition in black and progressive circles, Fulani called on voters to either support her *or* Perot. Fulani, the progressive, would lend her support to Perot, the conservative, as a way of building what was ostensibly becoming a nationwide independent political movement—and one which spanned much of the ideological spectrum, bringing progressives, liberals, and conservatives under the same banner of "independent." It appeared that such a range of independents could only agree on one thing: the need to reform the electoral system so that more voices could be heard— an issue of democracy.

Leading black Democrats were particularly threatened by Fulani during the 1992 election season for exposing their party's shortcomings. Ron Daniels, who had served as the executive director of Jackson's Rainbow Coalition, became the candidate of the black left to counter both Perot (who was being called everything from a "fascist" to a "lunatic") and Fulani (who had been called a number of derogatory names). At Daniels' behest, the Peace and Freedom Party's Central Committee used its veto power to override the results of the party's statewide primary, which Fulani had decisively won, and handed it to Daniels, who later supported the Democratic Clinton-Gore ticket. Dealing with such antidemocratic maneuvers had become familiar to Fulani—and they took a variety of forms. Two years earlier, Joseph Mack attempted to undermine Fulani's gubernatorial bid in New York by proposing to form an all-black "United African Party." The party, which had been devised to pull votes away from Fulani, however, never got off the ground, having failed to get the minimal number of signatures required to get on the ballot. Fulani therefore not only faced bipartisan-imposed legal obstacles and little media coverage, but attacks from black nationalists and black progressives alike—each ultimately tied to the Democratic Party.

In analyzing the 1992 election, American University political scientist Clarence Lusane noted that "One of the reasons Black leaders have hesitated to associate with any motion to act outside of the parties, specifically the Democratic Party, has been the fear of being marginalized and ostracized by White Democratic officials." Fear of losing patronage or favors—a long-standing tradition among black and white politicians, and not limited to those of the major parties—would override the need to challenge the bipartisan monopoly of the electoral process that was readily acknowledged in growing black circles. As the University of Chicago political scientist Michael Dawson wrote in Hanes Walton, *African American Power and Politics*, "Since 1988 a steadily increasing number of African Americans have classified themselves as political independents . . . This figure reached a high of nearly 40 percent in early 1991." Still, the idea of an independent winning office was inconceivable; it was argued that the Democratic Party was the "lesser of two evils." Nevertheless, in the fall of 1992, many African Americans decided to make a break with tradition.

In November of 1992 over half a million African Americans, many of whom had been prompted by Fulani, became part of the nearly twenty million voters who produced what was the largest electoral outpouring for an independent or third-party candidate in the nation's history by voting for Perot. Fulani herself even received nearly 100,000 votes that year. A CBS News poll in May of 1992 showed that at least 12 percent of African Americans said they supported Perot's candidacy, compared with 22 percent support among all voters (at his campaign's high point, Perot was at 42 percent in the polls). Seven percent of African Americans ended up casting their ballots for Perot. In voting for Perot, black voters (who were overwhelmingly Democratic-affiliated) appeared not only to reject the two major parties, but, more specifically, the politics of the Democratic Party. Democratic Arkansas Governor Bill Clinton won the presidency with 43 percent of the vote (the lowest percentage received by a president in eight decades); Bush received 37 percent; and Perot received 19 percent.

Impact on Future Campaigns

In the wake of the 1992 election Fulani was at the center of efforts to organize black, white, and Latino independents from around the country who sought to create new political alliances that could challenge the bipartisan establishment. Fulani immediately began to reach out to Perot supporters. She traveled across the country, including to some of the most conservative white areas (such as Orange County, California), where she received standing ovations in support of building black and independent alliances for political reform. Out of these efforts in 1994 a new national party—the Patriot Party—was formed, bringing together independents from across the country, and across the ideological spectrum.

One hundred and ten delegates from twenty states, along with dozens of observers, gathered in Crystal City, Virginia for the founding convention of the national Patriot Party. Dr. Jessie Fields, a black physician from Harlem and a close ally of Fulani who had been active in third-party politics since the late 1980s, was elected vice chair of the new party; another Fulani ally, Jim Mangia, a progressive white gay activist from California, became the party's national secretary. The two Fulani allies served alongside a largely white male conservative executive committee, including the party's national chairman, Nicholas Sabatine, an attorney from Pennsylvania who had supported Perot. The Patriot Party, representing a cross-section of America, would effectively serve as a transitional organization. It acted as a bridge between the millions of Perot supporters and preexisting elements of the independent movement that included Fulani's networks, much of which came together in the national Reform Party in 1995.

Like the Patriot Party, Fulani had also helped to found the national Reform Party, from which Perot sought to stage his second run for the presidency. A key element of the new party was the Fulani-organized Black Reformers Network. Among the network's leading members were Dr. Fields of New York, Rev. Lawrence Anderson of Ohio, Drake Beadle of Illinois, Juanita Norwood of Pennsylvania, Diane Williams of Maryland, and Wayne Griffin of South Carolina. The group hosted a multiracial meeting of over 300 Reform Party members at the party's convention in Kansas City, Missouri in November of 1997 to assert the role of African Americans within the independent movement. As Fulani later noted about the meeting, white reformers came "partly out of curiosity, and partly to make a statement that they wanted to build a bridge." For African Americans, the bridge was a way out of Democratic Party dependency. Fulani addressed the Black Reformers Network meeting by detailing the history of black dependence on the Democratic Party and the need for both black and white independence from the two major parties; she would also challenge—in postmodern fashion—the notion that identity politics had helped advance the interests of African Americans:

> Unable to restructure the whole of American politics to make it more inclusive and participatory, largely because we were politically attached to the Democratic Party, which had absolutely no interest in a political restructuring that would threaten their institutional power, we instead fought for little pieces of access to a system that was controlled from the top, by the top. Identity politics came to dominate. Black Americans became a part of special interest politics. Ironically and tragically, race relations worsened as a result. Black Americans felt increasingly frustrated and alone. Black politicians, mainly Democrats, who made their own careers off of the perpetuation of racism, proliferated. They weren't interested in structural change either. Racial inequality keeps them in business. Much of white America felt frustrated too. America was not doing well; everybody took to blaming everybody else. But the real problem was not "we the people," it was big government, unresponsive, corrupt, and irresponsible. Identity-based politics which has shaped much of black participation, only made matters worse. My own involvement in third party politics, which began in the early 1980s with the New Alliance Party, was based on wanting to create a way out of this

bind for Black America—a way out of being essentially held hostage to a two-party system that was not only hostile to us but hostile to the democratic participation of all the American people.

Other events were transpiring that signaled a shift among African Americans away from the Democratic Party in the mid-1990s.

In the wake of the 1995 Million Man March spearheaded by Minister Farrakhan (who called for a "third way" and black voter registration), the Democratic Party began to show itself susceptible. During the 1997 gubernatorial race in Virginia, for example, black voter turnout was markedly down. The Democrat, Donald Beyer, polled 80 percent of the vote among African Americans and lost to Republican Jim Gilmore. This was a notable departure from the usual 95 percent black support that traditionally went to Democrats. Former Democratic governor Doug Wilder (Virginia's first black governor) refused to endorse Beyer, instead remaining neutral.

Perhaps the clearest expression of black voters' disaffection from the Democratic Party came during the New York City mayoral election cycles of 2001 and 2005. In 2001 billionaire Michael Bloomberg—running on both the Republican and Independence Party lines in a fusion mayoral bid—received 30 percent of the black vote. Four years later he received 47 percent of the black vote and 60 percent of the independent vote. Both of his runs for office saw unprecedented levels of black and independent support for a non-Democratic candidate in New York City. He had initially received the nomination of the Independence Party of New York, which Fulani had helped to found, after promising that, if elected, he would create a charter revision commission to explore revising the city's election laws in favor of non-partisan municipal elections. Bloomberg won the election and kept his promise but his efforts to enact non-partisan municipal elections were defeated with strong opposition from Democratic leadership.

Meanwhile, the Independence Party of New York, on whose state committee Fulani served, became the third largest party in the state. Through Fulani's efforts and those of her black, white, and Latino associates, the party was also highly diverse. Upwards of 47 percent of the party's New York City membership was either black or Latino—another sign of the disaffection among traditional Democratic Party constituencies. The party's mission, to "restore democratic choice and electoral accountability," would be pursued by endorsing candidates who called for election reforms, including nonpartisan municipal elections. Nonpartisan elections would actually *diminish* the relative strength of the party next to other third parties with ballot status in New York. However, as Fulani and her colleagues would make plain, the party was formed to serve the interests of the city's voters—including the over one million independent (unaffiliated) registered voters in New York.

Using independent politics to try to secure political reforms took unprecedented form in the 2008 election with Obama's insurgent presidential candidacy. Commenting on the movement surrounding Obama, Fulani noted, "New political voices are emerging, searching for a new paradigm, new partnerships and a new way of doing politics." Black independents, particularly those allied with Fulani, were on the cutting edge. South Carolina independent black leader Wayne Griffin created "Independents for Obama" nearly nine months before there was an "Obama phenomenon" to speak of. By the eve of the South Carolina Democratic primary Griffin was running the following radio advertisement:

> Independents can vote on Saturday, and we've got a lot of reasons to do so. The Democratic Party establishment, now run by Bill and Hillary Clinton, sees the country in terms of old labels, old coalitions, and old tactics. They think change comes from the top. But the change I'm a part of is coming from the bottom. It's coming from ordinary people, young people, and politically independent people. Barack Obama has spoken out for that kind of change, and that's why so many independents like me are supporting him. If we want to change the direction of our country, we have to change the way we do politics. It's that simple.

Here Griffin exemplifies the new kind of independent leadership by calling for a different way of doing politics—neither strictly partisan nor ideologically driven.

In 2008 the postmodern black leadership-in-the-making was focused on garnering independent support for Obama's campaign in open primary and caucus states to advance political reform. Through a combination of African American and white independent support Obama secured the Democratic Party nomination. He won over one dozen caucus and open primary states, including caucuses in Iowa, Minnesota, Texas, and Washington, D.C. and open primaries in Alabama, Georgia, Mississippi, North Dakota, South Carolina, Vermont, Virginia, and Wisconsin. Independents (black and white) laid the groundwork for Obama's victory; they had broken significantly in favor of him in the primaries and then in the general election (with an eight-point margin). Meanwhile, African Americans had overwhelmingly supported Obama in the general election (at rates of 95 percent and above).

Today, upwards of 43 percent of Americans self-identify as politically independent (neither Democrat nor Republican), including nearly 30 percent of African Americans—despite the majority of black voters remaining tied to the Democratic Party. Obama had successfully beaten the Democratic Party establishment's candidate, Senator Hillary Clinton. He did so much to the surprise of black elected officials, virtually all Democrats (many of whom, such as Georgia congressman John Lewis, reversed their endorsement of Clinton under pressure from their constituencies who made clear that they were for Obama). In contrast to traditional black politicians (focused on gaining liberal white support tied to the Democratic Party, to the exclusion of conservative white independents), Fulani had long been forging black and independent alliances on the ground to push for political reform. Obama would adopt a similar approach in reaching out to Americans across the partisan, ideological, and racial divide. In his "A More Perfect Union" speech on March 18, 2008 he would articulate the need to "[forge] the alliances [needed] to bring about real change."

In 2008 a new black and independent alliance had asserted itself. Obama did not acknowledge Fulani for her pioneering work in either breaking the fifty-state ballot barrier as an African American or the creation of prior black and independent alliances, let alone her role in the ones that helped to produce his victories in the primaries. (He would say "it is because people like Jesse ran that I have this opportunity to run for president today.") Nevertheless, *New York Magazine* would go on to characterize Obama as the nation's first "Independent president"—that is, in addition to him being the nation's first African American president.

Fulani's postmodernization of black politics through the development of black and independent alliances has opened up new possibilities—new ways for African Americans (as well as white independents) to engage in electoral politics. It was a process that developed over the course of twenty years and it not only contributed to Obama winning the White House but would point to future directions in American politics. The independent movement which first gained national prominence in 1992 continues to be propelled by black independents in the Fulani networks, in addition to Fulani herself, former Perot activists, a variety of third-party members (including those in the Green, Natural Law, Independence, and Libertarian parties), and tens of thousands of Americans who do not want to identify with *any* party but may be affiliated with some independent voter association.

On January 25, 2009, five days after Obama's presidential inauguration, 500 independents, a quarter of whom were African American, gathered in New York City for a conference entitled "The Post-Election Independent Movement: Principles Intact, Paradigms in Transition, Obama in the White House." The conference, which was organized by the Committee for a Unified Independent Party (co-founded by Fulani in 1994 to advocate for election reform and provide organizational training for independents) was aired on C-SPAN as part of national coverage on the role of independents in the election. Fulani addressed the conference, which included participants from thirty-three states. Other independent black leaders and grassroots activists also took to the stage, mostly as part of panel discussions on their work in building networks of independent voters in their respective states. African Americans featured at the conference included Griffin, representing the South Carolina Independence Party, Tyra Cohen of North Carolina's Independents for Change, and David Cherry of United Independents of Illinois. Still other African Americans spoke from the audience. Each of these activists would represent a unique expression (and path) towards postmodern independent black leadership in the United States.

In 2006, Sharpton—who remains a Democrat—spoke about Fulani's role in developing independent politics in the nation and challenging black political orthodoxy:

> I've known Dr. Fulani for a long time. And she and I have agreed to disagree on any number of issues. But you know, there is a growing sense of independent voters in this country, any poll shows that. And one of the things that I think that a lot of the media here misses, is Dr. Fulani rightfully is one of the pioneers of that, particularly in the African American community . . . Twenty years ago, when [she and her associates] started talking about independence, most people in African American political circles thought they were crazy. Now there is a growing trend. I think that we've got to give her credit for at least being persistent. (Salit, 6)

Persistence is only part of Fulani's contribution in developing independent politics in the United States (Richard Carter of the *Amsterdam News* would call her "the real deal among independents").

Her work in the electoral arena may be best understood, in the Vygotskyian formulation, as both a "tool and result" of her overall work as a postmodernist. That is, her approach to building independent politics both reflects and grows out of her work as a developmental psychologist (as a "postmodern revolutionary"), in that she seeks to create developmental environments where people can go (and grow) beyond themselves by bringing seemingly disparate individuals or constituencies together through shared activities. In politics, the shared activity she has focused on has been on reforming the electoral process (as opposed to simply promoting individual platform issues—healthcare, defense, housing, education, and the like). Fulani has broken convention after convention as an African American leader. She has done so by pushing the boundaries of what is socially and politically acceptable; she has done so in search of a more developmental democracy by charting (indeed, creating) new political territory.

Fulani continues to build her supplementary education programs and advocate on behalf of independent voters. For her innovative educational work she was featured in the documentary *America Behind the Color Line*, a PBS/BBC production by Harvard's Henry Louis Gates, Jr. Her programs have also received acclaim from some of the most powerful and diverse people in politics (including Congressman Charles Rangel, former president George H. W. Bush, former New York governor George Pataki, and New York City mayor Michael Bloomberg). Most of the praise she receives, however, comes from the parents and family members of those who participate in her youth programs, seeing and experiencing the results most directly; business and community leaders concerned with the state of young people from inner cities have equally offered their praise and support over the years. Over the last two decades, Fulani has appeared as a guest on hundreds of radio, television, and cable news programs. Her social and political commentaries have also appeared in a range of daily newspapers as "This Way for Black Empowerment," or other op-ed columns. She is the author of the political autobiography, *The Making of A Fringe Candidate*, the editor of *The Psychopathology of Everyday Racism and Sexism*, and a contributing author to *Postmodern Psychologies, Societal Practice, and Political Life*. But when it comes to African Americans and the U.S. presidency, Fulani's most lasting contribution—beyond getting on the ballot in all fifty states—may very well be to have pioneered the creation of a postmodern independent black leadership. This new leadership not only includes dozens, indeed hundreds of black men and women whose names scarcely appear in print, but it also includes the nation's very first black and "Independent" president.

Further Reading

Ali, Omar H. *In the Balance of Power: Independent Black Politics and Third Party Movements in the United States.* Athens: Ohio University Press, 2008.

——. "Obama's Generational Challenge." In *The Speech: Race and Barack Obama's "A More Perfect Union."* T. Denean Shapley-Whiting, ed. New York: Bloomsbury, 2009: 31–33.

——. "Third-Party Movements: Perot." In *History in Dispute: American Social and Political Movements, 1945–2000.* Edited by Benjamin Frankel, Robert J. Allison. Detroit: St. James Press, 2000: 194–202.

Bell, Derek. *Silent Covenants: Brown v. Board of Education and the Unfulfilled Hopes of Racial Reform.* New York: Oxford University Press, 2005.

Carter, Richard. "Lenora Fulani, The Real Deal among Independents." New York. *Amsterdam New* (April 12–18, 2001).

Falk, Erika. *Women for President: Media Bias in Eight Campaigns.* Champaign: University of Illinois Press, 2008.

Fulani, Lenora B. *The Making of a Fringe Candidate, 1992.* New York: Castillo International, 1992.

——, ed. *The Psychopathology of Everyday Racism and Sexism.* New York: Harrington Park Press, 1988.

——. "Race, Identity, and Epistemology." In *Postmodern Psychologies, Societal Practice, and Political Life*, ed. Lois Holzman and John Morss, 158–163. New York: Routledge, 2000.

Fulani v. Brady, 935 F.2d 1324, 1337 (D.C. Cir. 1991).

Gates, Henry Louis, Jr., ed. *America Behind the Color Line: Dialogues with African Americans*. New York: Warner Books, 2004.

Gillespie, J. David. *Politics at the Periphery: Third Parties in Two-Party America*. Columbia: University of South Carolina Press, 1993.

Goldberg, Phyllis. "The Independent Tradition Gives Birth to America's Premier Black Independent." In *When Democracy Is on the Job, America Works*. New York: Lenora B. Fulani for President, 1992.

Holmes, William N. *The National Black Independent Political Party: Political Insurgency or Ideological Convergence?* New York: Garland Publishing, 1999.

Lusane, Clarence. *African Americans at the Crossroads: The Restructuring of Black Leadership and the 1992 Elections*. Boston: South End Press, 1994.

Salit, Jacqueline. "The Color of the Independent Movement." *The Neo-Independent: The Politics of Becoming*. 3.1 (Spring 2006): 6.

———."Unpopular Partnerships (Bloomberg's Dilemma)." *The Neo-Independent: The Politics of Becoming*. 1.1 (Spring 2004): 13–21.

Salit, Jacqueline, and Gabrielle Kurlander. *Independent Black Leadership in America: Minister Louis Farrakhan, Dr. Lenora B. Fulani, and Reverend Al Sharpton*. New York: Castillo International, 1990.

Siffry, Micah L. *Spoiling for a Fight: Third-Party Politics in America*. New York: Routledge, 2002.

Walton, Hanes, Jr. *Black Politics and Black Political Behavior: A Linkage Analysis*. Westport, CT: Praeger, 1994.

Monica Moorehead ran for president in 1996 and 2000 on the Workers World Party ticket. She is currently the editor of the *Workers World* newspaper. (Courtesy of the Workers World Party.)

CHAPTER 9

Race Activists and Fringe Parties with a Message

CHARLES ORSON COOK

Despite the fact that Shirley Chisholm, Jesse Jackson, Carol Mosely-Braun, and Al Sharpton popularized the strategy of working within the Democratic Party (and Alan Keyes in the Republican Party) to seek self-consciously African American electoral success during the last third of the twentieth century, blacks of various backgrounds and goals continued to launch independent campaigns outside the confines of the two-party system. In fact, in terms of sheer numbers, third-party presidential candidacies remained by far the most popular expression of black presidential aspirations even as mainstream candidates began to assert their influence in the two major parties. But independent candidates, especially black ones, found it frustrating to launch bona fide campaigns in which they had to compete for financing, ballot space, and media coverage with both Republicans and Democrats, neither of which they totally trusted to represent the issues. African American independent candidate Larry Holmes echoed this distrust when, in 2000, he lashed out at the Democratic Party as the "box our movement is locked away in." A final factor at work limiting the effectiveness of black campaigns was that their chosen parties were vulnerable to factious disputes which often limited their cohesion and their longevity. To be sure, few, if any, of these candidates held out any hope of actual election, but most of them had other, sometimes even bizarre, goals.

Isabell Masters, for example, has probably sought the presidency more than any other African American. She was born in 1918, educated in public schools, and claims to have earned a doctorate at the University of Oklahoma. Her principal occupation for most of her life was as a secondary school teacher in Oklahoma and Kansas. In 1981, Masters insists that she had a religious epiphany of some kind in which she was instructed to run for president of the United States. She described herself as an evangelist to the world and became a perennial presidential aspirant. In six successive elections, beginning in 1984, Masters announced her intention to seek the presidency, but only in three of those did she receive any votes. A life-long Democrat who left the party over the issue of abortion rights, she was on the Republican primary ballot in Oklahoma in 1988, 1992, and 1996. In 1996, perhaps her best year as a Republican, she was also on the primary ballot in Kansas.

Masters never came close to primary success, but in 1992 and 1996 she was on the general election ballot as the candidate of the Looking Back Party, whose platform she never fully, nor clearly, articulated. The only hint she gave about her position on the issues was her campaign slogan, "integrated biscuits," which she argued showed her opposition to hunger everywhere. In addition, her six children have sometimes been part of her campaigns. Her son Walter was her Looking Back Party vice presidential running mate in 1992 when he and his mother won 327 votes in Arkansas and two in California. Shirley Jean Masters, her daughter, was on the ticket with her mother in 1996 when the Looking Back Party won 749 votes in Arkansas and two more in California. Masters announced candidacies in 2000 and 2004, but never actively campaigned in either year and did not appear on any state's ballot. Today, Masters is ninety-five and living in Riviera Beach, Florida near her son Thomas. Another daughter, Cora Masters Berry, is the wife of Marion Berry, the former controversial mayor of Washington, D.C. for whom Isabell Masters campaigned in 1994. Her only recent political appearance has been as a protestor against the attempt by the Bush-Cheney Republican campaign to stop the 2000 ballot recount in Florida. Masters supported Barack Obama in the election of 2008.

When the African American comedian and drag queen entertainer, Terence Smith, appeared in a red, white, and blue mini-skirt ensemble on the floor of the 1992 Democratic National Convention in New York's Madison Square Garden, it was the most dramatic moment in his campaign for the presidency of the United States. Accompanied by a camera crew from the local gay cable television station, Smith spirited his outrageous outfit and his small press entourage onto the convention floor with the help of several passes and a good deal of *chutzpah*. He then proceeded to give a full-blown press conference in which he announced his Queer Nation party's platform against the backdrop of astonished Democratic delegates and confused security personnel. One friendly observer described the performance as "part

Guerilla Theatre, part Queer zap-action . . . . For visibility, the event broke new ground. . . ." Pat Buchanan, a candidate for the Republican nomination that same year—and a notorious anti-gay political crusader—condemned Smith's shenanigans on the convention floor as "the greatest single exhibition of cross-dressing in American political history." But Smith—in drag as his famous character, Joan Jett Blakk—had succeeded in capturing the attention his candidacy needed and his personality demanded. Over the next twenty-four hours in New York, he gave a thirty-minute interview on the "Brenda and Glenda" gay television talk show and another on the Gay Cable News. He also appeared on several local network news programs and somehow worked in an appearance at a local gay nightclub, which had helped pay for his travel expenses.

Smith made his first political debut in his native Chicago a year earlier when he ran in opposition to incumbent mayor Richard Daley. His dramatic campaign appearance in a leopard coat and wig in the St. Patrick's Day Parade down Michigan Avenue he described as a bit scary, but, as he explained, "I had forty queers with me," and "most people didn't know what was going on until we'd gone by . . . and I really don't think straight people know what drag queens look like." Joan Jett Blakk's Chicago mayoral campaign was captured for all time on a documentary film entitled "Drag in for Votes." Clearly, part of Smith's motivation was his flair for the dramatic—in seven-inch spike heels—and his incessant urge to perform and shock, but there were also elements in his campaign that were probably more serious.

Smith claimed to represent Queer Nation, a short-lived but militant group that may have been the first organization to address directly gay, lesbian, bisexual, and transgender (GLBT) issues and probably was to a large degree responsible for the frequency and acceptance of GLBT concerns in the 1990s and beyond. Queer Nation was highly decentralized with no formal leadership or organization, and its long-term strategies were often vague and inconsistent, but its reliance on highly visible, media-attractive, and usually outrageous actions such as same-sex kiss-ins in department stores and "Queers Night Out" in local bars brought it a good deal of public attention. These tactics were largely an outgrowth of the frustrations over growing violence toward homosexuals and the lack of governmental protection for the gay community, which drew inspiration from the agenda of the AIDS Coalition to Unleash Power (ACT UP).

Smith's Chicago chapter of Queer Nation urged him to take up political campaigning as another opportunity to publicize their cause, and he was quick to respond. He had already invented the character Joan Jett Blakk to use at fundraisers for Queer Nation and Radical Fairies; and he borrowed the cult song "Drag Queen Blues" as his campaign anthem, and it was an easy transition to have Joan run for political office. Interviews and press conferences were her stock-in-trade (Smith even created a nightclub routine around this format), which gave Joan plenty of opportunities to squeeze off outrageous one-line responses to press questions. Examples of her style abound; here are a few quips from a 1992 election interview published under the title, "Kisses for my President":

On gays in the military: "We don't even need the military, much less gays in it. We'll have Dykes on Bikes protecting the country."

On the military budget: "Switch the education and military budgets now."

On the Supreme Court: "I'm going to revamp the Supreme Court. I'm going to make it a lot more fun and call it the Supremes' Court."

On a running mate: "I want a leather oriented lesbian, a leather dyke."

Four years later Terence Smith had moved to San Francisco, but as Ed Karvoski makes clear in his book on gay humor, Joan Jett Blakk's campaign rhetoric had not changed substantially:

On her political style: "[I am] Oprah on ecstasy—too much make-up and too much jewelry."

On her presidential style: "I would be a President on a skateboard."

On the possibility of losing a second campaign: "I'm just going to declare myself president because I'm tired of waiting."

Smith was never actually on the ballot in any state, and never got more than a handful of write-in votes, but he often argued that he had thousands of supporters. In fact, he once claimed all the non-voters in several states whose support he was certain he had won. Blakk's last foray into politics was in 1998 when she ran unsuccessfully for mayor of San Francisco against incumbent Willie Brown. But Joan Jett Blakk's influence lived on to inspire the short-lived 2008 presidential candidacy of the white drag queen "Hedda Letuce."

Most third-party black candidates have been much more serious in both rhetoric and style than Terrence Smith or Isabell Masters. Among the most active parties in supporting candidates at several different levels was the California-based Peace and Freedom Party which made its first appearance in 1968 when the Black Panthers and California's white anti-Vietnam War activists merged forces to field a number of candidates for state-wide and national offices. The best known of those was Eldridge

Cleaver who ran for the presidency in 1968 (an event which is covered in Chapter 6 of this volume). But other, lesser-known, black presidential aspirants were inspired by Cleaver's campaign even though they rarely approached his popularity. In 1971, the Peace and Freedom Party joined a coalition of other radical groups at a national convention in Dallas, Texas where such leftist luminaries as Gore Vidal and the white physician-turned-radical-activist Benjamin Spock helped create the new People's Party in order to build a broader base of political support for radical causes.

Dr. Spock's anti-war credentials made him an ideal choice to lead the People's Party ticket in 1972, and his campaign created widespread interest in radical circles. But his vice presidential running mate, Julius Hobson, a black—and radical—community activist from Washington, D.C., brought a racial component to the ticket as well. Hobson carried a virtually flawless activist resume from his work in the civil rights struggle in the nation's capital. Born in 1919 the son of school teacher mother and a father who ran a small drug store in Alabama, Hobson attended Tuskegee Institute for three years before joining the Army Air Corps in World War II in which he won three bronze stars. After the war, he finished a degree in engineering at Tuskegee and a Master's degree in economics from Howard University and settled in Washington, D.C. for the rest of his life. Hobson quickly tired of the cautionary tactics of conventional community groups—including the National Association for the Advancement of Colored People (NAACP)—and formed his own chapter of the more radical Congress of Racial Equality (CORE). The young Hobson carried on campaigns against the racist policies of the local school board, led the fight against the city bus company to make them hire black drivers, and opposed apartment owners who refused to rent to African Americans. He once threatened to dump rats in affluent (and mostly white) Georgetown to publicize the woeful public health conditions in Washington proper.

Described by one colleague as "an angry man," Hobson was an uncompromising defender of black rights for the better part of two decades who was profoundly suspicious of all leaders, black and white, and of established political parties. He was also an avowed atheist who sometimes alienated black churches and ministers and a Marxist ideologue who had little use for conventional formulas for black advancement. He could also be at the heart of controversy in other ways. He was widely criticized by many black power advocates for marrying a white woman, and, at one point in his career, rumors circulated widely that he had been an FBI informant. He came to public attention outside Washington in 1970 when he ran for the District's non-voting representative in Congress as an advocate of statehood for the District of Columbia.

Hobson and running mate Benjamin Spock made an interesting pair. The soft-spoken and pensive Spock in his Brooks Brothers suits and starched shirts contrasted neatly with the outspokenly aggressive Hobson. Most were unaware that Hobson had been diagnosed with terminal cancer in 1971, but he campaigned as though he were in perfect health. At the top of the People's Party platform was a statement of militant opposition to the war in Vietnam, and although the candidates complained bitterly to the Federal Communications Commission that network television news had unfairly ignored their campaign, Spock managed to appear on several news programs during the campaign. Spock and Hobson, financed by a meager forty-thousand-dollar campaign budget, campaigned on a platform which included free medical care, abortion rights, legalized marijuana, a guaranteed minimum income, and an immediate military withdrawal from Vietnam. They were, however, perhaps at their most visible when they attempted to hand out anti-war literature at a military base in California from which they had been barred from entry. Their ensuing lawsuit—albeit unsuccessful—succeeded in bringing the ticket limited visibility. Still, the Spock-Hobson ticket was on the ballot in eleven states and managed to tally over seventy thousand votes, most of which came from California. Hobson's last political campaign—conducted from his wheelchair—came in 1974 when he was elected to the Washington, D.C. City Council, the city's first home-rule legislative body in the twentieth century. He died of cancer in 1977.

The People's Party continued its close association with African American candidates in 1976 when it selected Margaret Wright, a fifty-four-year-old grandmother and self-described socialist from Los Angeles, California as its presidential nominee. The party originally nominated another Californian, Maggie Kuhn, for vice president, but Kuhn was eventually replaced with Dr. Benjamin Spock who agreed at the last moment to be Wright's running mate. Wright had a long history of involvement in the black community of East Los Angeles, particularly as a crusader for community controlled public schools. She had been active in the Black Panther Party in the 1960s, but she was also an outspoken feminist who could be sharply critical of the role of black males in the quest for gender equality. "I was chosen," Wright pointed out, "because I am black, a woman, and I've been discriminated against." She was running, she said, in language with which many other radical black candidates would agree, because there was very little difference between the Republicans and the Democrats.

Echoing the 1972 party platform, she favored full employment, free health care, welfare reform, amnesty for draft dodgers and deserters, and the decriminalization of victimless crimes. In foreign affairs, Wright was outspoken in her support of black liberationist movements in South Africa and in her condemnation of Zionism. Wright was on the ballot in ten states, but, owing to her tight budget of twenty thousand dollars, she campaigned mostly in California where she received the lion's share of her 49,000 votes. Because her party dissolved amid a factional dispute shortly after the 1976 election, Margaret Wright was the last presidential candidate the People's Party fielded, though the Peace and Freedom Party continued to run candidates in California. Wright gained some non-political notoriety in 1980 when she appeared in the award winning documentary film, "The Making of Rosie the Riveter," playing herself.

An interesting variation on Peace and Freedom Party presidential candidates is Ron Daniels, who won the party's nomination in 1992 in unusual fashion. Daniels had had an important role in racial politics in the United States for more than a decade. He had the background of a black nationalist who was instrumental in attempting to create an all-black political party. Such an organization, the National Black Independent Party, actually appeared briefly in 1980—with Daniels as one of its officers—but quickly dissolved in the wake of Ronald Reagan's election in 1980. Daniels joined Jesse Jackson's Rainbow Coalition as its chief executive officer in an effort to launch an insurgent movement of left-leaning blacks in the Democratic Party. He was also deputy director of Jackson's 1988 presidential campaign. By 1992, Daniels was once again an independent, this time in California's Peace and Freedom Party. In fact, Daniels was a member of Peace and Freedom's central committee in 1992 at the same moment that outside forces, notably in the person of the aggressively successful Lenora Fulani (whose role as an independent organizer in the New Alliance Party is chronicled in Chapter 8 of this volume), were threatening to seize the party's nomination process.

Exercising unusual, though legal, powers, the party's Central Committee substituted Daniels for Fulani even though she had actually won the delegate count, prompting an uproar at the convention, especially among Fulani delegates. Daniels was Peace and Freedom's legal nominee, but he and the party's Central Committee had ironically won at the expense of the kind of independence—indeed, one led by a black woman—that they were on record as supporting in principle. Fulani may have had the last laugh, however, when she actually won more votes nationally—she tallied over 70,000, Daniels had only about 25,000—and appeared on more state ballots (Fulani was on the ballot in thirty-nine states, Daniels could be found on only nine) by far than did Daniels.

One of the obvious reasons that Lenora Fulani was more successful than other black independent presidential candidates is that she and her New Alliance Party were so well organized and knowledgeable about how to qualify for ballot status in every state—something never accomplished by a black independent before 1988—and comparatively well financed. But the New Alliance also suffered from a dubious and somewhat mysterious reputation. Many of its left-wing critics, and they were legion, were convinced that the New Alliance was little more than a personality cult that revolved around the white, Stanford-trained, Ph.D. psychologist Fred Newman, whose clinics in New York City and elsewhere funded his forays into politics. Fulani, a psychologist herself, was for many years Newman's most trusted adviser and acolyte who helped give New Alliance a veneer of black leadership. The party made its first entry into politics in the early 1980s by recruiting candidates from the ranks of aspiring black politicians—many from Harlem—who were attracted to the New Alliance promise of financial support and its appearance of black leadership. Al Sharpton, for example, was among those young African Americans who were wooed by New Alliance until he chose a more opportunistic path to public prominence.

Dennis Serrette, a forty-four-year-old Harlem-based labor activist, however, found New Alliance less resistible. Serrette was born in 1940 and raised in a Harlem welfare family of eleven children; he joined the labor movement in his late teens. Convinced that organized labor was an effective vehicle for promoting civil rights, Serrette threw himself into the center of New York labor politics. By late 1970 he was a vice president of the Communications Workers of America and a leading voice in New York labor disputes. He held the distinction of leading the longest strike in the history of the New York Telephone Company for seven months during 1971–72 and now, in his early forties, was the acknowledged founder of the Coalition of Black Unionists and the National Black Communications Coalition and openly a socialist. Serrette was recruited personally by Lenora Fulani who saw in him the kind of activist with whom she could promote the New Alliance as a logical and legitimate choice for African American voters who sought a legitimate black independent candidate, especially in light of Jesse Jackson's failure to win the Democratic nomination in 1984.

Serrette, in fact, had been a supporter of Jackson's primary campaign, and in some ways he admired the potential of the Jackson for President movement. For Serrette, Jackson's allegiance to the Democratic Party was a mistake. As he saw it, Democrats were exploiting Jackson's blackness to attract black votes, but they would never support his Rainbow Coalition. There was, he thought, not much difference between Walter Mondale and Ronald Reagan. Simply put, Serrette made it clear that working within either major party was misguided; only an independent candidacy could bring about the changes black people needed. In fact, it was never his intention or anticipation to win the election, but rather to begin the process of drawing voters away from Republicans and Democrats and to build a new black-led party that would nominate Jackson in 1988.

Serrette and his running mate, a former school teacher and one-time independent candidate for governor of New York, ran their campaign out of a small apartment on the Upper West Side of Manhattan. His $200,000 campaign was comparatively large for black independents and the New Alliance operatives had found a way to get his name—under various party labels—on the ballots of thirty states, more than any previous black candidate. His platform, which he summarized as "people before profits," was predictably leftist. He favored full employment, increased public housing, and a system of national health care, which could be paid for by drastic cuts in Defense Department spending. His foreign policy would have included sharp cuts in Pentagon weapons systems and a renewal of arms-control talks. He condemned most of American policy in Central America, including the Reagan administration's support for the regime of President Jose Napoleon Duarte in El Salvador. Perhaps because he sensed a new kind of enthusiasm from black voters, especially for black candidates, Serrette predicted confidently that he would attract six million voters nationwide, many of them from the South. Despite his optimism about the outcome of the election of 1984, however, the results fell embarrassingly short of his six million vote projection. In fact, his final tally was only 21,919 votes.

Serrette's candidacy also revealed that ideological and philosophical schisms within independent parties could be important components in their failure. Within weeks of the end of the election of 1984, rumors were circulating that Serrette had turned against his New Alliance supporters, and had actually disavowed the party. And indeed, in the next year, an article signed by Serrette appeared in several left-wing publications which condemned the New Alliance Party, Fred Newman, and Lenora Fulani in devastatingly bold language. New Alliance, he argued, was masquerading as a black-led party to increase the power and influence of the legendary Fred Newman and Fulani. It was not black-led and, despite its rhetoric, was not particularly progressive either. Rather, he saw New Alliance as a kind of personality cult under the control of Newman's pseudo-scientific brand of psycho-therapy that was designed to advance an insidious cause that had virtually nothing to do with black liberation, political or otherwise. Serrette urged his supporters to spurn Newman, Fulani, and New Alliance and to return to the true cause of political organizing for the greater good. Fulani politely denied the charges of cultism, and simply pointed out the obvious: that Serrette's departure from New Alliance had been amicable and uneventful. Serrette continued his charges against New Alliance for several years thereafter, and doubtless weakened it in the minds of some black voters, but Lenora Fulani would soon show that her party's better days lay ahead.

Less successful in terms of votes won and ballot exposure, but nonetheless reflective of an important component of black independency are Marxist groups who have used the electoral process not to actually win elections, but instead to advance their reputation and appeal among black voters, particularly the young. The Workers World Party (WWP) may be the best example of this kind of organization which works tirelessly in many ways to keep its ideological agenda in plain view, even though, as the *New York Times* once put it, they were "spectacularly unlikely" to win elections. The Workers World Party traces its historical roots to the Trotskyist Socialist Workers Party, but it broke with the SWP in the early 1950s over several doctrinal issues, including the Soviet invasion of Hungary. For several years its activities were confined mostly to Buffalo, New York, but expanded its activities through several front organizations during the Vietnam War protests in the 1960s.

Unlike most Trotskyite organizations, the WWP had no clear ties to any international revolutionary movement, but it did support a worldwide revolution against capitalism and was in favor of liberating oppressed peoples everywhere, including those in the United States. Its many critics, on the right as well as the left, pointed out that despite its Trotskyist origins, the WWP often defended repressive regimes like those of Kim Jong Il in North Korea and Slobodan Milosevic in Yugoslavia. It was primarily action-oriented, however, and was recently most visible in mounting large anti-war protests, sometimes numbering tens of thousands of participants, through such front groups as Act Now Against the War and Racism and Troops Out Now. But in addition to its Marxist rhetoric and anti-imperialist protests, WWP also supported more practical issues which sometimes resonated with black voters: affirmative action, universal health care, abolition of the death penalty, and guaranteed income. The WWP first entered electoral politics in 1980 and others fielded a presidential candidate—frequently an African American—in every election since.

Larry Holmes was the first African American candidate for the WWP. Holmes was the party's vice presidential nominee in 1980 and its presidential candidate in 1984 and 1988. In some ways he is emblematic of the party's history. He was born in Roxbury, near Boston, Massachusetts in 1952 and moved with his three siblings and single mother to Harlem when he was six. While a student at Hunter College in 1971 he was drafted and served in the military for a year and a half in the Vietnam War. He quickly grew disenchanted with American policy there and turned into a GI war resister who served a short term in an army prison before he was dishonorably discharged for, among other things, attempting to create an American Servicemen's Union. Holmes joined the WWP and in the 1970s made a reputation as a skilled organizer of both anti-war and anti-racist demonstrations for the WWP. He also had a quick ascent up the party's hierarchy, and was shortly a member of the ruling secretariat, a group from which virtually all of the WWP candidates would be drawn. In 1980, although he was only twenty-eight, Holmes was on the first WWP ticket as vice president. Both Holmes and his white running mate, Deirdre Griswold, campaigned for almost a year. In California they entered the Peace and Freedom Party's primary, but lost overwhelmingly to Benjamin Spock and his black running mate Julius Hobson. In fact, the WWP ticket finished last with only 1,232 votes out of a total of 9,092 cast. But they were on the ballot in thirteen states and received approximately 15,000 votes while spending only $150,000 in campaign funds. In 1984, Holmes was at the top of the WWP ticket which announced publicly that it would support Jesse Jackson's efforts to win the Democratic Party's nomination, but when Jackson failed in his bid, Holmes and his running mate Gloria La Riva were only able to win 17,935 votes of their own. They ran on the slogan, "Jobs, Equality, Socialism, Not War," and a platform of guaranteed jobs, food, education, and health care. Both Holmes and La Riva insisted that the class struggle in the United States was imminent and they were quick to condemn American imperialism in Latin America. Their campaign war chest was no larger than the tiny one in 1980, but they were able to get on the ballot in sixteen states, an indication that their organization and political savvy had improved modestly. Neither Holmes nor La Riva were the required age of thirty-five to be president, so in two states, Ohio and Rhode Island, Holmes's wife, Gravielle Holmes, replaced her husband on the ballot.

La Riva and Holmes ran again in 1988 on essentially the same platform, but with a smaller campaign fund. The results—barely 7,000 votes—were embarrassingly disappointing in an election where Lenora Fulani won over 200,000 votes and was on the ballot in all fifty states. La Riva and Holmes switched places on the WWP ticket in 1992, but their electoral fortunes were clearly in political free fall. The 1992 campaign was on the ballot in New Mexico only where it drew a meager 181 votes. Holmes has remained a loyal WWP member who continues to organize impressive demonstrations and maintain a high profile for the WWP with such front groups as Millions for Mumia which is attempting to exonerate the African American journalist, Mumia Abu-Jamal, who was convicted of killing a Philadelphia policeman in the early 1980s and who has languished on death row for two decades. Holmes also organizes frequent demonstrations against the American military presence in Iraq.

Just before the 2008 presidential election Holmes took pains to explain the dramatic success of Barack Obama as a major party candidate in an editorial in his party's newsletter, *Workers World*. He was careful to note that Obama's Republican opponents and even some of those in his own party were largely motivated by racism, but Holmes was equally clear in his condemnation of Obama as a tool of the capitalist and imperialist power structure. He also observed what he thought was a fundamental difference between the Jesse Jackson campaigns of the 1980s and that of Obama in 2008. For Holmes, it seems, the Jackson candidacy was the more legitimate because it emanated from the masses, while Obama's was the result of the support of reactionary elites who were desperately trying to reestablish American imperialistic hegemony around the world. Black people and other progressive elements in the electorate would be well advised, he argued, to support black candidates who could help check the popularity of Obama among oppressive capitalists. Not surprisingly, he urged support for the presidential candidacy of Cynthia McKinney (who is discussed at length in Chapter 10), the former six-term black congresswoman from Georgia whom the WWP (and the Green Party) had nominated for the 2008 campaign.

In many ways, Monica Moorehead, the WWP's nominee in both 1996 and 2000 is difficult to distinguish, in rhetoric and philosophy at least, from Larry Holmes. Moorehead, born in Tuscaloosa, Alabama in 1952, got her first exposure to race activism during the civil rights movement of the 1960s when she was affiliated with the Black Panther Party. After college, she joined the WWP in 1972 and quickly became one of its highest-profile leaders, an axiomatic precondition for representing the WWP in elections. In the early 1990s, she became a frequent contributor to the party's official newspaper, *Workers World,* and virtually all of the WWP's official views carry her imprimatur. When, in her 2000 campaign, Moorehead asked the rhetorical question, "Why do communists run in capitalist elections?" she might as well have been speaking for all leftist independent candidates. When she answered her own questions by saying that it was enough just to let oppressed people know that there did exist a revolutionary alternative, she was articulating the motivation of radical candidates everywhere.

Getting the message out can be difficult for any independents unless they can find ways to seize media attention in some dramatic way. Few would repeat the tactics of Joan Jett Blakk on the floor of the Democratic National Convention in 1992, but Monica Moorehead and La Riva came close when they confronted Bill Clinton at his birthday bash in the New York Sheraton Hotel, demanding to know why he had signed a bill that put thousands off welfare. Before the Secret Service could drag her away she demanded to know "how can you eat cake when you've condemned a million more children to poverty?" Two months later they stunned the moderator of a C-Span televised debate between representatives of the National Law

Party, the Libertarian Party, and the National Taxpayers Party. The WWP had not been invited, and Moorehead interrupted the proceedings by screaming "I am a socialist and I represent millions of workers who are suffering from layoffs and low wages. . . . I am the only African American woman running a serious campaign on behalf of poor and working people."

For twelve minutes she held the floor and summarized her platform of guaranteed jobs, free health and child care, gay rights, and affirmative action. The next day news of the event was dispatched to several newspapers in an Associated Press story entitled "Moorehead Disrupts Debate!" and soon media outlets were calling for interviews with the WWP candidate. WWP protestors also dogged Hillary Clinton when she attempted to campaign for her husband, and other party activists attempted to embarrass the Bob Dole campaign as well. To some extent Moorehead's confrontational strategy worked. She was on the ballot in twelve states in 1996 and got approximately 29,000 votes, more than any WWP candidate in history. In 2000, she was on only four state ballots, and her total support amounted to a mere 4,795 votes. Her second campaign, though cheaper, was largely confined to college campuses where her radical message often found eager listeners. But she still got a bit of publicity in Florida when C-Span and even the television talk show host, Jay Leno, noted that her vote count there was approximately the margin between the Al Gore and George W. Bush campaigns in one of the closest presidential elections in recent history. Dubbed the "Monica factor" in a less than serious article by the liberal white documentary filmmaker Michael Moore, Moorehead's tiny turnout brought her some welcome attention.

The WWP 2004 candidate was John Parker, a young African American, who, like the other WWP candidates, was a solid organizational insider who had given years of service to its revolutionary cause. A former schoolteacher, Parker claimed to have led his first union drive at eighteen at a small steel plant in New Jersey. Parker moved to California in the 1990s to represent the organizing efforts of the WWP, especially in organizing non-union workers and in leading anti-war youth rallies. His running mate was Teresa Gutierrez of New York. The Parker/Gutierrez campaign worked vigorously in seventeen states and twenty-four cities to generate enthusiasm for its radical platform of anti-imperialism, gay rights, affirmative action, working-class solidarity, and expanded social services. It was conventional WWP rhetoric, but the party could only muster a miniscule turnout of 1,541 votes. In a post-election pep talk, Parker insisted the campaign was not about vote totals, but about spreading the message of revolution to oppressed peoples. "Real change happens through class struggle," Parker insisted, "not elections." But clearly the WWP efforts had been undermined by the defection of a faction led by former WWP stalwart, Gloria La Riva. Thus, despite Parker's optimistic assessment, the WWP had its worst electoral year on record in 2004, a fact which may help explain why they chose to endorse Cynthia McKinney of the Green Party in 2008 rather than run their own slate of candidates.

An even smaller, but highly disciplined offshoot from the Socialist Workers Party is the Workers League which shares much of the WWP's agenda, but insists that it represents a more authentically international Marxist agenda. It has historically close ties to groups in Europe and the United Kingdom, though recent arcane doctrinal differences have weakened those links. In the United States the League—which changed its name to the Socialist Equality Party in 1996—is legendary for its ruthless legal and doctrinal battles with the Socialist Workers Party and others with which it disagrees. The Workers League was founded in the United States in the mid-1960s, but it did not run its first candidates for office until the early 1980s, when at least two of them, Edward Winn and Helen Halyard, were African Americans. The Workers League has been headquartered for two decades in Detroit, Michigan where it apparently aspires to organize workers in the automobile manufacturing and related industries and where it frequently runs candidates for local and state offices. In 1984 and 1988, Ed Winn, a former New York City transit worker, was the party's nominee for president, and in both years Helen Halyard, a Brooklyn native, who would later be the party's assistant national secretary, was on the ticket in two states as vice president. Both Winn/Halyard campaigns attacked the attempts by Jesse Jackson to win the Democratic nomination as counter-revolutionary and dangerous to the worldwide anti-capitalist movement. They also advocated the abolition of the military budget, the disbanding of the CIA and the FBI, and the cancellation of NATO. Both candidates made it clear that their goal was not to be elected, but to win supporters for the abolition of capitalism. In 1984 Winn and Halyard won 10,801 votes in six states, and increased their support in 1988 to 18,693. Halyard, who actively attacks other radical groups—including the WWP—on the Socialist Equality Party's website, was at the top of the ticket in 1992 when the Workers League received only 3,050 votes.

Independent black candidates—especially radical ones—have few alternatives for electoral success in the United States. As Professor Omar Ali suggested in a recent study, a two-party system of the American type has every incentive to discourage challenges from independent candidates. They have done an effective job of it by making it difficult to get on more than a handful of state ballots without an extensive and expensive organization and by virtually excluding independent candidacies from qualifying for federal campaign funds. Moreover, the national news media routinely ignores independents unless they use outrageous campaign tactics which sometimes attract short-term attention, but almost inevitably lead to longer-term ridicule. Black independents who operate very long on the fringes of mainstream politics are usually members of radical or leftist groups who have abandoned any hope of winning an election in favor of advertising their revolutionary agendas or those for whom political intrigue has become a way of life. The experience of these candidates stands in stark contrast to the recent electoral success of Barack Obama who doubtless learned from them valuable lessons about the necessity of establishing a highly efficient political organization and the need to appeal to a broadly based and moderate group of supporters, many of whom were white. Larry Holmes and other black fringe candidates dismissed Obama's campaign slogan, "The Audacity of Hope," as empty rhetoric and the candidate himself as the tool of white capitalist exploitation, but they could not deny that he had mastered the frustrating reality of American consensus politics.

Further Reading

Alexander, Robert Jackson. *International Trotskyism, 1929–1985: A Documented Analysis of the Movement.* Raleigh, NC: Duke University Press, 1991.

Ali, Omar H. *In the Balance of Power: Independent Black Politics and Third Party Movements in the United States.* Athens: Ohio University Press, 2008.

Bennetts, Leslie. "Goal of Workers World Candidate is to Spread the Socialist Message." *New York Times* (August 28, 1980), section B, page 8.

Clements, James (ed.). *The Encyclopedia of Third Parties in America.* Armonk, NY: Sharpe Reference, 2000.

Fankel, Glen. "Organizers of Antiwar Movement Plan to Go Beyond Protests." *Washington Post* (March 3, 2003).

Freeman, Jo. *We Will Be Heard: Women's Struggle for Political Power in the United States.* Lanham, MD: Rowman and Littlefield, 2008.

Gerney, Elizabeth "Julius Hobson Sr., Activist, Dies at 54." *Washington Post* (March 24, 1977).

Goldberg, Marsha. "The Moorehead-La Riva Factor: Using Election to Build the Struggle." *Workers World* (November 23, 2000). Home page online. Available from http://www.workers.org/ww/2000/campaign123.php. (Accessed May 7, 2009).

Goodman, Walter. "Under Various Parties, Presidential Candidate Runs in 33 States." *New York Times* (October 20, 1984), page 8.

——. "A Small Workers Party Aims Fire at Capitalism." *New York Times* (October 10, 1984), section A, page 21.

Gottlieb, Martin. "Minor Candidates Fund-Raising Success Turns Spotlight on Party." *New York Times* (December 31, 1991), page A16.

Greene, Marcia Slacum. "Presidential Candidate Beats the Clock." *Washington Post* (August 23, 1984), page DC12.

Griswold, Deirdre. "Workers World Party Selects Candidates." *Workers World*. Home page online. Available from http://www.workers.org/ww/2004/wwelect0603.php. (Accessed February 16, 2009).

Guide to U.S. Elections. Washington, DC: Congressional Quarterly Press, 2005.

Holmes, Larry. "The Black Radical Congress." *Workers World*. Home page online. Available from http://www.hartford-hwp.com/archives/45a/227.html. (Accessed February 23, 2009).

——. "Obama—An Analysis," *Workers World*. Home page online. Available from http://www.workers.org/2008/us/obama_0605/. (Accessed March 7, 2009).

——. "Obama's Speech in Denver." *Workers World*. Home page online. Available from http://workers.org/2008/us/obama_8911/. (Accessed May 7, 2009).

Jeffreys, Joe E. "Joan Jett Blakk for President: Cross Dressing at the Democratic Convention." *TDL* (August, 1993), 186–195.

Karvoski, Ed, Jr. *A Funny Time to be Gay: Gay and Lesbian Comedy Routines From Trailblazers to Today's Headlines.* New York: Fireside Press, 1997.

Keehnen, Owen. "Kisses for My President: An Interview with Queer Nation Presidential Candidate Joan Jett Blakk." Queer Cultural Center, 1996. Home page online. Available from http://queerculturalcenter.org/Pages/keehnen/Blakk.html. (Accessed May 7, 2009).

Kumbala, Tendayi. "The Other Presidential Candidates." *Los Angeles Times* (October 27, 1976), section I, page 21.

Maier, Thomas. *Dr. Spock: An American Life.* New York: Basic Books, 2003.

"Minor Candidates Broaden the Spectrum," *Los Angeles Times* (October 31, 1976), section VIII, page 3.

Moore, Michael. "Blame Monica!" MichaelMoore.com. Available from http://www.michaelmoore.com/words/message/index.php?messageD. (Accessed February 16, 2009).

Moorehead, Monica. "The State of the Workers & How to Improve It. *Workers World*. Home Page online. Available from http://www.workers.org/ww/1996/fileout53.html. (Accessed February 16, 2009).

Perez, David. "Breaking Through: Moorehead Crashes Debate." *Workers World*. Home page online. Available from http://www.workers.org/ww/1997/campaign.html. (Accessed February 16, 2009).

Pratt, Minnie Bruce. "Candidates Spread Message of Revolutionary Hope." *Workers World*. Home page online. Available from http://www.workers.org./ww/2004/wwcampaign1118php. (Accessed May 7, 2009).

Scheibe, John. "28 Candidates Seek 5 Education Board Posts." *Los Angeles Times* (April 4, 1971), page E6.

Serrette, Dennis L. "Inside the New Alliance Party." *Political Research Associates*. Home page online. Available from http://www.publiceye.org/newman/critics/Serrette.html. (Accessed March 3, 2009).

Sigerman, Harriet (ed.). *Columbia Documentary History of American Women Since 1941.* New York: Columbia University Press, 2003.

Smith, Sam. "Place: From 'Multitudes: An Unauthorized Memoir.'" Progressive Review Index. Available from http://www.prorev.com/mmplace.htm. (Accessed February 23, 2009).

Socialist Equality Party. "Contributions to the ISSE/SEP Conference: Jerome White and

Helen Halyard," World Socialist Web Site. Home page online. Available from http://www.wsws.org/articles/2007/apr2007/isse-a11.shtm1. (Accessed March 5, 2009).

Thavarajah, Ajit K. "Third-Party Candidate Speaks of Social Issues, Injustices." *Michigan Daily Online* (October 10, 1996). Available at http://www.pub.umich.edu/daily/1996/oct/10-16-96/news/news6.html. (Accessed February 16, 2009).

Representative Barbara Jordan of Texas presenting her keynote address at the Democratic National Convention on July 12, 1976. Jordan, although not formally nominated, received delegate votes for both president and vice president. (Courtesy of the Library of Congress, LC-U9-32937-32A/33.)

CHAPTER 10

Black Politicians

Paving the Way

HANES WALTON, JR., JOSEPHINE A. V. ALLEN,
SHERMAN C. PUCKETT, AND DONALD R. DESKINS, JR.

African American presidential candidates have used a highly diverse and ever expanding number of political vehicles to obtain the highest elected office in the nation. Barred from legal suffrage rights in most states until the passage of the Fifteenth Amendment in February 1870, the African American electorate could not influence and/or impact the outcome of any presidential election even in terms of being a "balance of power" force. After the passage of this amendment, such a possibility was extremely probable until the Era of Disenfranchisement, 1890–1901.

Prior to the passage of the Voting Rights Act of 1965 and its subsequent renewals, northern migration once again restored African Americans to the status of a "balance of power" force in presidential electoral outcomes, but only in the northern and Midwestern states. In the southern states of the old Confederacy during this period from 1890 to 1965, the African American voter and vote were systematically suppressed and reduced in local, state, and national elections. After the VRA, these voters became a factor in the southern states like their counterparts in northern and Midwestern states. African Americans could impact and influence presidential elections. Given the suppressed voter and vote, only half of the national electorate could vote for a black candidate, thus no major political party would nominate, even at the vice presidential level, an African American.

But the failure of major political parties to nominate African American candidates was not just limited to the majors, this was also the policy of the so-called *significant* third/minor parties as well, i.e. those that got at least 5 percent or higher of the popular vote. In this category were the nation's first third party, the Anti-Masonic Party in 1832, as well as the Free-Soil Party in 1848, the Populist Party in 1892, the Progressive Party in 1912 headed by former President Theodore Roosevelt, and the Progressive Party in 1924 headed by Senator Robert LaFollette, through to H. Ross Perot's parties in 1992 and 1996, the United We Stand and the Reform Party, respectively. While this group of *significant* third/minor parties can be considered the more "progressive" ones, the others which were less than progressive on race like the American "Know Nothing" Party of 1856, the Constitutional Union Party of 1860, and the George Wallace American Independent Party of 1968 did not even consider nominating an African American candidate for their presidential tickets. This indicates that at certain times in American presidential election history, potential African American candidates had to look to other types of political vehicles to run for the presidency.

However, it is not just the failure of the major parties and the significant third/minor parties to nominate an African American simply because of a geographically limited electorate. There were also structural impediments in the nomination procedures. The initial nominating procedure adopted by the early political parties from 1788 to 1832 was known as "King Caucus." It allowed *only* members of Congress of that political party to select the party's nominee. Thus, with no members of Congress during this period and with only limited voting rights, African American candidates had literally no chance of being nominated and consequently, none were nominated.

A second nominating procedure, the national party convention, an Anti-Masonic Party innovation, emerged in September 1831, but it was not adopted by the Democratic Party until May 1832. Party elites and bosses along with delegates to these national conventions determined the party nominee. The national conventions' selection of presidential candidates reigned supreme from 1832 until 1968. From 1972 to the present, presidential primaries and caucuses became the third and current presidential nominating procedure. During the entire period of the nominating convention procedure 1832 until 1968, some 136 years, literally none of the major parties, Democrats or National Republicans, Whigs or Democrats, Democrats or Republicans ever nominated an African American candidate for the presidential or vice presidential positions. Thus, African American presidential hopefuls had to choose other types of political vehicles, and they did.

African American presidential candidates seeking major party nominations had to await the arrival of the third nomination procedure, the primaries and caucuses in 1972, and it should come as no surprise that in that first year, Congresswoman Shirley Chisholm (D. N.Y.) became the first of her race to run for a major party nomination. Thus, in the end, the parties' failure to nominate was not only embedded in a limited African American electorate but also in two of the three party nominating procedures. These two variables reinforced each other and pushed African American presidential candidates to use other means to get to 1600 Pennsylvania Avenue.

Such political vehicles included small and fringe third/minor parties, independent candidacies, African American political parties—both the separate and satellite ones—economic protest parties, and nomination at the national conventions of the major political parties via delegates seeking to reform the candidate selection processes, to gain support for their political platforms, and to get commitments of support for issues and public policies essential and critical to the African American community. Of these limited political vehicles, the small Liberty Party, organized in 1840, was the first political party to have African American delegates to attend its national convention. Two planks in the party platform addressed issues pertinent to the African American community. However, even this small anti-slavery political party never nominated an African American to its ticket despite the fact that it competed in every presidential election from 1840 until 1860, some six national contests.

As for African American political parties of the satellite category, there are the well-known Mississippi Freedom Democratic Party (MFDP), which had several African Americans among its presidential electors; the National Democratic Party of Alabama (NDPA), which had African Americans among its presidential electors; and the lesser known but earlier South Carolina Progressive Democratic Party (SCPDP). In terms of Republican satellite parties, one finds the Black and Tan Republican Party in Texas in 1920 with an entire slate of African American presidential electors and the Black and Tan Republican Party of Mississippi with its slate of African American presidential electors for every election from 1928 until 1956.

Moving from the satellite political vehicles to the separate political parties, one finds such organizations as the National Liberty Party in 1904, the Independent Afro-American party in 1960, and the United Citizens Party of South Carolina that is still in existence and currently allowing third/minor party candidates to be listed under their name on the South Carolina presidential ballot. Finally, African American presidential hopefuls have found themselves on the ballots of Communist and Socialist Party tickets. Although the Socialist Party in 1912 got 6 percent of the vote, making it one of the significant third parties in American party history, no subsequent socialist or communist party has ever made it back into this significant category since 1912, despite a number of African American presidential candidates running under these political banners.

At this point, we are left with one other category of political vehicles for African American presidential hopefuls, the Democratic National Conventions and the Republican National Conventions. However, there were structural barriers that hindered African American delegate participation at these national conventions which in turn hampered the possibility of nominations from this procedure. Although the Democrats held their first national convention in 1832, the first regular African American delegates did not appear until 1936. An alternate African American delegate, selected in 1924, was quickly replaced with a regular white one. The Republican Party, on the other hand, held its first national convention in 1856. The first regular African American delegation did not appear until 1868 and has appeared unabated since then until the present. African American senator Blanche K. Bruce became one of the nine individuals nominated for the vice presidential spot in 1880 at the Republican National Convention. He won enough delegate votes to capture fifth place in the initial balloting. Upon losing, he withdrew his name. Eight years later, at the Republican National Convention in 1888, both he and Frederick Douglass were nominated. Again, both men withdrew their names when they did not secure a high place in the initial balloting. These two different nomination events at the 1880 and 1888 Republican National Conventions bring us to the purpose and objective of this chapter because they are pioneering milestones in the African American political experience. These two nominations were the very first African American nominations by a major political party.

One of the many groups of individuals seeking the American presidency was significantly not just civil rights leaders and/or protest leaders, but African American politicians. This chapter will identify, analyze, and evaluate ten such individuals. While the majority (eight of the ten) were elected officials, the two non-elected, Channing Phillips and Alan Keyes, were constant candidates for elected offices. In sum, this chapter will focus on these ten candidates at both the national conventions and in the primaries and caucuses to capture the major parties' nominations for the White House.

It is important to note that these ten individuals have specific party affiliations. One ran on the Green Party ticket in 2008, one ran for the Republican Party nomination in 1992, 1996, 2000, and 2008, and eight ran for the Democratic Party nomination between 1968 and 2004. The large number of African American Democratic partisans and elected officials in this group of ten should come as no surprise simply because this was the way that the African American electorate was voting at those moments in time. However, in the final analysis, this chapter will not be limited to Democrats. Instead, it will cover both of the major parties, Republican and Democratic, as well as one of the rising new third parties. And since some of these candidates ran multiple times, like Keyes and Dellums, we will have an opportunity to compare and contrast their campaigns.

More importantly, this chapter will include an evaluation and assessment of two of the current nominating procedures, first the national convention followed by the state primary and caucus in order to determine the strengths and weakness of both procedures in terms of their being viable political vehicles for African American presidential candidates. Primary and caucus voting data will be used in this analysis as well as national convention delegate voting data to create an empirical portrait and assessment of these two different political vehicles. At this moment, nothing in the current academic and scholarly literature addresses this political dilemma and problem. With these empirically based insights, the basic groundwork for future candidates will be established. These empirical findings will be this work's major contribution to the literature.

The Rise of African American Politicians as Protest Presidential Candidates

African American protest leaders became political party activists because of both the need to abolish slavery and the failure of the major political parties in the 1830s, 1840s, and early 1850s as they ignored, avoided, sidestepped, denied, dismissed, and excluded the slavery issue from their political platforms and agendas. These were the strategies and tactics of the Whig Party, which eventually caused its demise and collapse. The Democratic Party, on the other hand, accepted and vigorously supported slavery and the slave institution until they were defeated by their strong endorsement of this issue, prior to and during the Civil War, which resulted in the northern-based Republican Party victory in the 1860 and 1864 presidential elections.

The birth of African American protest leaders' transformation into political party activists began when a schism appeared between the moral abolitionists and the political abolitionists. This first group of abolitionists, led by William Lloyd Garrison, sought only moral means to defeat slavery and its associated institutions. They eschewed political activity as immoral means and tactics. However, the political abolitionists argued that the institutions of slavery were too entrenched and too strong to simply be routed by moral suasion. Their political power had to be counteracted by opposing political power and this led the group of political abolitionists to form the Liberty Party on April 1, 1840, the first of many anti-slavery parties in the nation. Leaders of this group were James Birney, the party's first presidential candidate, Gerrit Smith, and Lewis Tappan. Leading African American protest leaders like Frederick Douglass, Henry Highland Garnet, J. W. Logeum, and William W. Brown supported this and other anti-slavery third parties. Thus, with this third/minor party, protest leaders now had a political vehicle to become politically active in and with. This eventually led some of these political party activists to initially think about becoming presidential candidates in order to agitate and protest against slavery and the slave institutions.

They also wanted to agitate and protest against the major political parties for ignoring and avoiding this critical issue in the political process.

Prior to the Civil War, none of the African American political party activists accepted a presidential nomination. They would become participants in the Republican National Convention because that party allowed them to be voting delegates beginning in 1868 to the present. The other incentive was the abandonment of Southern African American civil and political rights during and after Reconstruction (1866–76) that ended with the political Compromise of 1877 when incoming Republican president Rutherford B. Hayes turned "home rule" back over to white Southerners and promised that the Federal Government would pursue a "hands-off" policy toward the entire region. African American Republican politicians had to protest, or at least, pretend to do so, and one way to do that was to seek and/or accept nominations from the national convention floor. And in gaining such nominations they became visible examples of the plight of their brethren in the South.

Rarely did these brief and fleeting moments in the nomination spotlight translate into meaningful political promises, much less protective public policies. But these nominations did come in 1880 and 1888, the years in which white supremacy was in full flowering and implementation. Civil liberties, civil rights, and protesters' lives were lost in great abundance. Therefore, the Republican National Conventions attempted and made limited nominations of African American politicians allowing these nominees to become a form of political theater and thereby exemplify a small degree of party protest. It was two things at once, a brief nomination, and a brief protest of the political party and the nation. The other major party, the Democrats, did not even engage in this type of political theater until after the rise of the primary and caucus nominating procedure in 1972. Yet a few of the third/minor parties did engage in this political theater like the Republicans. And by the time that these nominations were finally made by both major and/or third/minor parties, the political motive beyond personal ambition was the need to demand geographical and organizational reform in regard to race and racial discrimination.

The Ten Black Politicians and their Political Party Nominations for President

Thus, we began our empirical analysis by organizing the African American politicians via partisanship categories: (1) Republican, (2) Democratic, and (3) third/minor parties. Such an organizational structure allows both a chronological ordering and a comparative evaluation of the same party candidates, i.e. Democrats vs. Democrats, Republicans vs. Republicans and third parties vs. third parties. And this will allow a later sequence in which we can contrast the different parties with each other.

Secondly, this categorization via partisanship also allows the reader to see and understand the differences between the two different types of nomination procedures used by the major political parties. Hence, the reader can observe African American presidential candidates in the major parties acquiring the nomination: (1) at the Republican and Democratic National Conventions, or (2) via the presidential primaries and caucuses. The first procedure, which predates the primary and caucus procedure, requires the political party elites, political brokers, and kingmakers in smoke-filled backrooms to select the candidates, whereas the second procedure, the primaries and caucuses, especially after 1972, relies upon the party electorate to make the decision about the eventual nominee. Although this latter procedure does not eliminate the elites completely, it does allow some marginalization and minimizing of their power and influence. As Senator Obama's 2008 race shows, one can win without the political elites' uniform or unanimous approval.

Lastly, and perhaps more importantly, one can, with this party-based categorization, see the roles of both the African American convention delegates and the African American electorate. At one point in time, the African American electorate was significantly and very strongly aligned with one of the major political parties. For a time they fell away but eventually realigned with another major political party. Hence, the question can now be raised and empirically answered in regard to the relationship of these African American presidential candidates to the party alignment of the African American electorate. Probing this relationship as one of the possible or potential determinants in the rise of these African American presidential candidates in major parties has not yet found its way into the study of this political phenomenon but clearly it should have due to the very long struggle in both the nation's and African Americans' history to acquire and exercise the right to vote. Given that there is a link from reformism to these candidacies it is now essential to explore in an empirical manner this possible relationship and connection.

The African American Republican Politicians for the Party's Presidential Nomination

Table 10.1 lists all of the African American Republican candidates who have sought the party's nomination across time. Thus, it should come as no surprise that the initial major party in which African American presidential candidates would surface is the Republican Party. Nor should it be striking that the initial African American presidential candidate should be a member of Congress, the only U.S. Senator at the time who had served a full term, Blanche K. Bruce, and that he would be a candidate for the vice presidency. In addition, he would resurface in 1888 with a second nomination for the same position. However, in this second bid for the nomination, he would be

Table 10.1 Republican Party African American Candidates for President or Vice President of the United States, 1880–2008

Year	Candidate	Office Sought	Candidate Number of Ballots	Number of States Won	Candidate Primary Votes	Total Primary Votes	Total General Election Votes	Number of Convention Votes	Total Number of Delegates
1880	Blanche K. Bruce	Vice President					9,213,184	8	756
1888	Blanche K. Bruce	Vice President					11,379,868	11	820
1888	Frederick Douglass	President					11,379,868	1	820
1968	Edward Brooke	President				4,473,251	73,203,097	1	1,333
1992	Alan Keyes	President				12,590,305	104,418,840	1	2,185
1996	Alan Keyes	President	36	0	471,716	15,313,343	96,272,382	1	1,975
2000	Alan Keyes	President	40	0	914,548	19,279,218	105,400,734	6	4,335
2008	Alan Keyes	President	28	0	58,977	21,185,030	128,916,353		2,380

competing with the leading African American protest leader in the nation, Frederick Douglass. Each time Bruce, the former elected politician, would garner many more delegate votes than Douglass, the non-elected leader. One, by virtue of his previous governmental positions, had more top-level political experiences that the former protest leader. Nevertheless, this did not help in their effort to secure the nomination because while Bruce got a little over 1 percent of the delegate vote, Douglass, the very first African American to be nominated for president, got less than 1 percent of the vote.

Following these two pioneering presidential candidates, one sees another African American U.S. senator, and the first popularly elected one, Edward Brooke, being placed in nomination for vice president and garnering less than 1 percent of the delegate vote. His appearance came exactly eighty years after the Douglass and Bruce efforts. Much later, the most recent candidate Alan Keyes surfaced some twenty-four years after Brooke. The most unique feature about the non-elected Keyes is that not only has he been a candidate for the U.S. Senate three times, but he has also sought the party nomination for president four times, in 1992, 1996, 2000, and 2008, without success. Finally, in 2008 after withdrawing from the Republican primary and caucus races, without any close victories, he became the presidential candidate on the America's Independent Party ticket.

If the Republican African American presidential candidates before Keyes, Bruce, Douglass, and Brooke, sought to reform the party on the basis of race, Keyes sought to reform it via ideology, i.e. that of conservatism. Despite their diverging reform efforts, none of these four candidates had very much success in acquiring the nomination and even less in attaining their reform goals. The empirical data reveals that the primary and caucus races for Keyes have found some voter support, a high of 3.1 percent in 1996, which translated only into very minor delegate support, one vote in 1996. This is the same delegate voter support that Douglass and Brooke got in their nomination bids. Bruce is still the highest-supported of all of the Republican presidential candidates and that occurred in 1888 for the vice presidential position.

In linking the African American electorate to the appearances of these Republican presidential candidates, it is strongest during the period from 1868 until about 1900. This is when African Americans were still trying to exercise their newly won Fifteenth Amendment voting rights. One of the key manifestations of this was the election from the eleven states of the old Confederacy as delegates to the party's national conventions as well as to both houses of Congress. Moreover, the delegate votes that Bruce and Douglass received never exceeded the number of African American delegates present at these Republican National Conventions. Nor did their delegates ever equal the total number of African American delegates, which suggests the possibility that not all of these delegates voted for the candidates of their own race.

Therefore, the empirical data suggest that these initial national convention candidacies were not very well organized or planned prior to the convention. None of these candidates from the historical record had campaign and/or floor managers. Thus, they were essentially spontaneous, ad hoc, and doomed to fail.

The African American Democratic Politicians for the Party's Presidential Nomination

Given the pro-slavery and pro-segregation ideology of the Southern wing of the Democratic Party as well as the dominance of this wing inside the party elite circles and the accommodation of the other wings to this position, African American delegates did not make it to any Democratic Party National Convention until 1936. This was two years after the first African American Democratic congressman Arthur Mitchell had been elected from Chicago in 1934. Furthermore, since the African American electorate in the South had been disenfranchised and suppressed, said delegates had to come from northern and Midwestern big industrial urban centers and such delegates were selected and/or determined by the big city political bosses and machines. They were not independent at all. Even Congressman Mitchell either had to toe the line submitted by the bosses or be removed from office, which is precisely what happened to him in 1942 when he was summarily replaced by William Dawson. In the final analysis, the early African American northern convention delegates, because of their reliance upon party bosses and machines, could not force the party elites at the national conventions to undertake reforms with regard to race. That had to await the coming of the *Smith v. Allwright* Supreme Court decision in 1944 that ended the white primaries in the South and allowed the African American electorate to enfranchise itself and become a force in party politics. This enfranchisement process hit full stride with the passage of the Voting Rights Act of 1965.

In 1972, Congresswoman Shirley Chisholm, who dubbed herself "unbossed and unbought," broke through the old barriers and pointed the way for Jackson, Sharpton, Moseley-Braun, and Obama. At the same time that Chisholm unleashed pioneering primary and caucus challenges, Congressman Walter Fauntroy launched a national convention "favorite son" strategy. A "favorite son" strategy is a national convention technique whereby a popular state or district congressperson runs in his or her own state primary and wins. Then, he or she will parlay this primary victory into a bargaining chip at the national conventions by swapping his or her state or district's delegates with one of the party's frontrunners for some public policy concessions, political patronage, platform inserts, and/or campaign contributions. In this case, Chisholm, who had more delegates (152 or 5 percent) at the convention, simply had more to offer than Fauntroy. Nevertheless, Fauntroy's strategy is well-known and used in national convention politics. A little-known fact is that when Chisholm eventually released her delegates, she was nominated from the floor of the convention for the vice presidential spot and got some twenty votes (0.7 percent). While with the Republican Party it was a two-step deal, with the Democrats in 1972 it occurred in a seamless fashion.

At the very next presidential election, Congresswoman Barbara Jordan delivered a much-respected and rousing keynote address which got her both a presidential and a vice presidential nod. Congressman Ronald Dellums also received a vice presidential nomination at that convention, with Jordan receiving some twenty-eight delegate votes and Dellums some twenty delegate votes. In this instance, Jordan won more vice presidential votes than Chisholm did during the previous national convention. However, Chisholm would get a second vice presidential nod during Jesse Jackson's 1984 run and garnered some thirty-nine delegate votes (1 percent). As a consequence of these two vice presidential nominations in 1972 and 1984, Chisholm holds the record at this moment in time. Her closest competitor is Jordan with one nomination for each office. Table 10.2 provides all of the empirical data on these and other African American Democratic presidential candidates.

In 1992, the "favorite son strategy" was employed by Congressman Louis Stokes in Ohio. He was only able to attain three delegates from the state, while the majority of African American delegates went to the eventual Democratic nominee, William Jefferson Clinton, who did not need these three delegate votes. Along with Stokes in 1992 were African American physician Lenora Fulani and the first elected African American governor, L. Douglas Wilder. Although Wilder withdrew before the initial Iowa caucus, Wilder's name remained on the ballot in two states and he got several popular votes anyway. He bowed out of the 1992 presidential race simply because he could not raise the requisite finances.

After the 1992 efforts, no other African American Democratic presidential candidates would appear until 2004, more than a full decade later. African American protest leader, the Reverend Al Sharpton, who had run twice for the U.S. Senate in New York and once for the office of mayor in New York City, announced that he was running to establish himself as the new leader of the African American community, thereby replacing Reverend Jackson. Fearing that Sharpton would cause a white backlash as Jackson had in his 1984 and 1988 runs, some members of the party elite asked former senator Carol Moseley-Braun to enter the primaries and caucuses as a counter-weight to Sharpton. She did enter, but before the Iowa caucus, she withdrew. However, her name remained on the ballot in some fourteen states and she, like Governor Wilder, received some popular votes anyway. An unknown candidate Huda Muhammad also entered the race but barely

Table 10.2 Democratic Party African American Candidates for President or Vice President of the

Year	Candidate	Office Sought	Candidate Number of Ballots	Number of States Won	Candidate Primary Votes
1968	Channing Phillips	President			
1968	Julian Bond	Vice President			
1972	Shirley Chisholm	President	14	3	430,703
1972	Walter Fauntroy	President	1	0	21,217
1972	Shirley Chisholm	Vice President			
1976	Barbara Jordan	Vice President			
1976	Barbara Jordan	President			
1976	Ronald Dellums	President			
1980	Ronald Dellums	President			
1984	Jesse Jackson	President	28	2	3,282,380
1984	Shirley Chisholm	Vice President			
1988	Jesse Jackson	President	36	9	6,685,699
1992	Douglas Wilder	President	2	0	240
1992	Lenora Fulani	President	1	0	402
1992	Louis Stokes	President	1	0	29,983
2004	Al Sharpton	President	24	0	385,082
2004	Carol Moseley-Braun	President	14	0	103,205
2004	Mildred Glover	President	2	0	4,050
2008	Barack Obama	President	59	29	18,011,878

surfaced as a vote getter. In fact, all of the candidates in 2004 hardly made a dent at the national convention.

A unique feature and candidate in the 2004 race was Mildred Glover, former Georgia state legislator (1974–80), city council candidate (1973), mayoral candidate (1981), and gubernatorial candidate (1982). Glover, a graduate of Savannah State College, obtained a doctorate in Education from the University of Georgia in 1970 after which she moved to Atlanta and became a political activist and elected official. Running in 1973 for the city council, she lost in a runoff to James Bond, the brother of SNCC activist and Georgia state legislator, Julian Bond. One year later, in 1974, Julian Bond resigned his Georgia House seat to run for a state Senate seat. Glover immediately ran for the vacated Bond House seat and won. She then served four terms in the state legislature. After 1980, when the redistricting of the Georgia legislature changed the boundaries of her district, she stepped down. However, she continued to run for a host of local and state offices. By 2004, she entered the Democratic presidential primary getting on the ballot in two states and receiving a few votes. Her near single state race was the continuation of similar efforts by a few African American presidential

United States, 1968–2008

Total Primary Votes	Candidate General Election Votes	Total General Election Votes	Candidate Number of Delegates	Number of Convention Votes	Total Number of Delegates
7,522,696		73,203,097		68	2,622
7,522,696		73,203,097		48.5	2,622
15,993,965		77,743,403	28	152	3,016
15,993,965		77,743,403		1	3,016
15,993,965		77,743,403		20	3,016
15,574,598		81,526,042		28	3,008
15,574,598		81,526,042		1	3,008
15,574,598		81,526,042		20	3,008
19,514,244		86,508,792		3	3,331
18,009,192		92,650,564	466		3,933
18,009,192		92,650,564		39	3,933
22,961,936		91,588,082	1,219		4,162
20,239,385		104,418,840			4,276
20,239,385		104,418,840			4,276
20,239,385		104,418,840	3		4,276
16,182,439		122,267,553	26	0	4,353
16,182,439		122,267,553			4,353
16,182,439		122,267,553			4,353
37,990,062	68,041,419	128,916,353	2,201	3,188.5	4,234

candidates who appeared on the ballot in only one state dating back at least to 1988. These candidates never made it to the national convention and they did not win any delegates to have any impact whatsoever.

Four years later, the process which began in 1972 would bear fruit after thirty-six years when U.S. senator Barack Obama won the Democratic Party nomination for president in August and went on to win the general election over Senator John McCain on November 4 to become the first of his race to win the White House. In this historic race, Obama faced several African American presidential candidates on their party tickets, most notably his Republican challenger in the 2004 Senate race, Alan Keyes.

The African American Third Party Candidates for President in 2008

By this point, it should have become increasingly clear that not all of the past African American politicians who became presidential candidates have run for only a major party's nomination. They have also attempted to win the White House via third/minor political parties. Looking at these candidates in the 2008 election cycle, one finds some five individuals as listed in Table 10.3. In this table, the most prominent candidate is the former Democratic congress-woman from Georgia, Cynthia McKinney. After losing her reelection bid, McKinney accepted the Green Party nomination for president and competed with the Obama/Biden, and McCain/Palin tickets for the presidency. She came in fifth. It was, to say the least, a very poor showing compared to previous Green Party presidential efforts, particularly the one made by Ralph Nader.

Besides McKinney, there was the perennial Obama challenger, Alan Keyes. In 2008, Keyes launched another quest for the Republican Party nom-ination. He entered several of the primaries and caucuses but this candidacy faltered like all of his previous attempts. This time, his campaign faltered very badly and he was soon eliminated from most of the pre-primary Republican debates. Soon, he withdrew from the quest to capture the Republican nomination and accepted the nomination of the America's Independent Party. As this party's presidential candidate, Keyes received little more than 46,000 votes, fewer than he had as a Republican primary candidate. Clearly, it was not a breakthrough performance. McKinney captured nearly three and a half times more votes than he did.

James Harris was the Socialist Workers Party presidential candidate in five states because the party's main presidential candidate Roger Calero was born in Nicaragua and was banned from the ballot in these states by state law. Under the U.S. Constitution you must be a native-born American to qualify for the office. In those five states, Harris received 2,347 votes.

Also among the African American presidential candidates in 2008 were two individuals seeking the vice presidential spot. Eugene Puryear, running on the combined Socialism and Liberation Party ticket saw that ticket win 7,392 votes in twelve states. Needless to say, he performed even less well than the Green and American Independent third parties but still the party did not come in last. That would come to the Socialist Party where Stewart Alexander was in the second spot on the party's ticket. This party captured a bit more than 6,000 votes and registered no real challenge to the Obama/Biden ticket. In point of fact, even if one adds up the entire third-party vote and gives it to the McCain/Palin ticket it would not change the total outcome at all. Although there are several states where the total third-party vote would shift the election to McCain/Palin, it still would not change the winner of the election, Obama/Biden.

Overall, the total vote for the third parties with African American presi-dential candidates comes to 219,227 which is less than a quarter of a million votes out of the nearly 129 million votes cast. This is not a notable share of the votes nor could it be when one of the six African American candidates in this 2008 race had a solid chance to win the presidency. To say the least, this was a bad political environment for third party African American presidential candidates in this historic election.

Table 10.3 Third-Party African American Candidates for President or Vice President of the United States, 2008

Year	Candidate	Political Party	Office Sought	Candidate General Election Votes	Total General Election Votes
2008	Alan Keyes	America's Independent Party	President	46,308	128,916,353
2008	Cynthia McKinney	Green Party	President	159,175	128,916,353
2008	Stewart Alexander	Socialist Party	Vice President	6,352	128,916,353
2008	James Harris	Socialist Workers Party	President	2,347	128,916,353
2008	Eugene Puryear	Socialism and Liberation Party	Vice President	7,392	128,916,353

Black Politicians' Presidential Campaign Strategies and Electoral Outcomes

At the Republican National Conventions, African American presidential candidates had their greatest success between 1880 and 1888, despite a plethora and continual flow and presence of African American convention delegates. Protest about party reform came not from protest presidential candidates but from delegates who served on the key convention committees and issued minority reports and/or verbalized their frustration, displeasure, and anguish. Since the advent of the power of the primary and caucus procedure, only one African American, Keyes, has tried to capture the nomination and his failure led him to exit the party and join a third party as a new political vehicle. To put it bluntly, past conventions before 1900 were better to these African American presidential candidacies than contemporary conventions. Although African Americans became participants and delegates to the Republican National Conventions first, this party may be the last political party to nominate one of these candidates. What effect the new African American Republican Party chair will have on the presence and success of potential African American presidential candidates only the future can tell. Michael Steele's initial pronouncement of goals and objectives for the party did not list diversity among candidates as being part of his political agenda.

Turning to the Democratic National Convention where African American participants and delegates arrived decades after they did in the Republican convention, although, when they did arrive, the Southern white delegates were totally against them and their presence, it is the Democrats who have elected the first African American president. To be sure, African American presidential candidates and hopefuls had to await the arrival of the third convention procedure, the primary and caucus technique, where self-starting candidates can put together a winning coalition and raise enough money to secure the nomination. This is yet to surface among the Republicans. However, one must understand it is not just the presence of the candidates that is crucial, but also the involvement of the African American electorate along with the Latino and Asian electorates, to say nothing of women, young people, and white men. Clearly, while the presence of a compelling candidate is important, it is not the only prerequisite.

Lastly, there is the political context variable, like the outgoing incumbent administration, the nature of the economy, foreign affairs, the other major party's candidates and the media. All of these variables matter in shaping the electoral outcome around a compelling and attractive candidate. Many of these factors might change in terms of degrees of impact and influence; they will still be variables of some consequence. And they will exist despite the nature of the candidate.

Summary and Conclusions

The power of the state primary and caucus procedure has proven to be enormous in capturing the nomination for president prior to the national party conventions. It, together with the incorporation of modern technological advances such as the Internet, e-mail, blogs, text messaging, Facebook, Twitter, and YouTube, have signaled a new era in American politics. This contemporary era is one which promises to open up the previously closed circles of the powerful political elites and to make widespread access and participation by all American voters possible. This is especially true for those who were previously alienated from electoral politics as well as for those who were not allowed to participate due to enormous structural barriers. The promise of greater transparency in governance will encourage and facilitate the empowerment process among the wider American electorate of all socio-economic means and philosophical or ideological positions.

There is one variable that was in the process of shaping itself as the first few months of the Obama presidential administration began. Much has been made of the fact that an Obama presidential candidacy has been about deracializing his public policy agenda and public comments. His defenders will argue that he had to do this in order to win. Past presidential campaigns that have been race-based, like Jackson and Sharpton and many of the third parties, end up being losing campaigns. Such candidates cannot win their party's nomination or the general election. Thus, the key to victory has been to expand the base and the issues. Hence, one has to transcend race and become post-racial, if that is possible. It is important to become more inclusive and appeal to the wider electorate on the issues that are most critical.

If Obama, and one of his mentors, Mayor Harold Washington, taught us anything, it is that a winning formula and coalition must be biracial or multiracial and that it is quite possible. However, the unknown question at this point is whether one can transcend the age-old problems that plague the urban centers of America where the most concentrated enclaves of African American voters reside. Can these new biracial politicians and/or post-racial politicians transcend the "urban problems"? The Obama administration will have a socializing effect on the African American community. If his policies are like those of Associate Supreme Court Justice Clarence Thomas or Ward Connerly, will the voter turnout in the African American community be as high for him or for the next "Obama" type candidates? This question is critical because these second- and third-cycle candidates will not have the driving force of being the first any more. The African American community is experiencing that phenomenon at this time with Obama.

High turnout rates have been the key to success for this presidential pioneer because he would not win a majority of the majority electorate. Few are talking about this important reality in the heady days of victory. Moreover, we have seen shades of this reality in Chicago, and New York, where disunity in the African American electorate translated into a string of losing candidates and the top prize moving on to other contenders. High turnout becomes a critical variable which depends upon the prospect for solving nearly intractable urban problems. Failures in service delivery on these points can cause failures in turnout in subsequent elections. We will know more about this variable once the first Obama administration has run its course.

There is one other point to make from comparing the tables relating the progress of African American politicians. Numerous vehicles of involvement have been attempted by African Americans in their quest of legitimacy and inclusion in the national political process, from participation in various third/minor parties to participation in the mainstream major parties. Comparing experiences within the major parties reveals the insight that the Democratic Party has promoted itself as being the party of diversity, with the enactment of the Voting Rights Act of 1965 and the subsequent reversal of political fortunes in the Old Confederate South. Just seven years after the 1965 Voting Rights Act an African American woman sought the office of president and won three state primary elections. From there other African American presidential aspirants competed and won other Democratic state primaries until Barack Obama won a majority of the state primaries and ultimately attained the presidency. Contrast this achievement made possible by participation in the Democratic Party with that of African Americans in the Republican Party: that party facilitated their emancipation from slavery one hundred years before the Voting Rights Act but has yet to field an African American candidate who has won a single Republican presidential state primary.

Rare was the prediction even a generation ago that matters of race would recede into the background of national concerns long enough to enable an African American to become president of the United States. However, through numerous attempts, using various vehicles for national participation, Democratic Party African American politicians have competed and won by emphasizing diversity in their contribution to leadership on the world stage. Only time will tell whether America has turned this page permanently and whether it will bring diversity to both of the major political parties.

Further Reading

Beatty, Bess. *A Revolution Gone Backwards: The Black Response to National Politics, 1876–1896.* New York: Greenwood Press, 1987.

Chisholm, Shirley. *Unbought and Unbossed.* Boston: Houghton Mifflin, 1970.

Eldersveld, Samuel J. *Political Parties in American Society.* 2nd ed. New York: Bedford/St. Martin's, 2000.

Ifill, Gwen. *The Breakthrough: Politics and Race in the Age of Obama.* New York: Doubleday, 2009.

McClain, Paula, and Steven C. Tauber. "An African American Presidential Candidate: The Failed Presidential Campaign of Governor L. Douglas Wilder." In Hanes Walton, Jr. (ed.), *African American Power and Politics: The Political Context Variable.* New York: Columbia University Press, 1997: 294–304.

Mendell, David. *Obama: From Promise to Power.* New York: Amistad, 2007.

Obama, Barack. *The Audacity of Hope: Thoughts on Reclaiming the American Dream.* New York: Crown Publishers, 2006.

Stone, Pauline. "Ambition Theory and the Black Politician." *Western Political Quarterly* (March, 1980).

Todd, Chuck, and Sheldon Gawiser. *How Barack Obama Won.* New York: Vintage Books, 2009.

Walters, Ronald. *Black Presidential Politics in America: A Strategic Approach.* Albany: State University Press of New York, 1988.

Walton, Jr., Hanes. *The Negro in Third Party Politics.* Philadelphia: Dorrance & Co., 1969.

———. "Black Female Presidential Candidates." In Hanes Walton, Jr. (ed.) *Black Politics and Black Political Behavior: A Linkage Analysis* Westport, CT: Praeger, 1994: 251–276.

———. "The First Black Female Gubernatorial Candidate in Georgia: State Representative Mildred Glover." In Hanes Walton, Jr. (ed.) *Black Politics and Black Political Behavior: A Linkage Analysis*, 235–250. Westport, CT: Praeger, 1994.

———. "African Americans and the Clinton Presidency: Political Appointments as Social Justice." In Hanes Walton, Jr. (ed.), *African American Power and Politics: The Political Context Variable*, 313–322. New York: Columbia University Press, 1997.

Walton, Jr., Hanes, and Ronald Clark. "Black Presidential Candidates: Past and Present." *New South* (Spring, 1972).

Walton, Jr., Hanes, and C. Vernon Gray. "Black Politics at National Republican and Democratic Conventions: 1868–1972." *Phylon* (September, 1975).

Walton, Jr., Hanes, and Robert Smith. *American Politics and the African American Quest for Universal Freedom.* 5th ed. New York: Longman, 2009.

Walton, Jr., Hanes, and Lester Spence. "African American Presidential Convention and Nominating Politics: Alan Keyes in the 1996 Republican Primaries and Convention." *National Political Science Review* (1999).

Walton, Jr., Hanes, Sharon Wright, and Frank Pryor. "Texas African American Republicans: The Electoral Revolt in the 1920 Presidential and Gubernatorial Election." *National Conference of Black Political Scientists Newsletter* 16 (Spring, 2002): 1–6.

Walton, Jr., Hanes, Josephine A. V. Allen, Sherman Puckett, and Donald R. Deskins, Jr. "Barack Obama: The Making of the President 2008." *The Black Collegian* (January, 2009): 7–12.

———. "The Red and Blue State Divide in Black and White: The Historic 2008 Election of President Barack Obama." *The Black Scholar* 38.4 (2009): 19–30.

Walton, Jr., Hanes, Josephine A.V. Allen, Sherman Puckett, Donald R. Deskins, Jr., and Billie Dee Tate. "The Literature on African American Presidential Candidates." *Journal of Race & Policy* 4 (Spring/Summer, 2008): 103–123.

A close-up view of General Colin Powell, chairman of the Joint Chiefs of Staff, as he tours military facilities during Operation Desert Shield. (Courtesy of the Department of Defense, DF-ST-91–06284, 9/13/1990 by SrA Rodney Kerns.)

CHAPTER **11**

Colin Powell
The Candidate Who Wasn't

CARY D. WINTZ

When Barack Obama walked out on that stage in the Denver Stadium to formally accept the Democratic Party's nomination for president of the United
States, it seemed to many that a seismic shift in American politics had
reshaped the landscape, and had radically altered the paradigm of the pre-
ceding two centuries. A little less than six months later the new era born during the Denver convention came of age on a blustery winter day with the
inauguration in Washington. The impossible had happened; the unbeliev-
able had occurred; an African American was the president of the United
States. In the excitement of election night as it became obvious that Obama
would win, a poignant reminder of those who had attempted the race before
was a tearful Jesse Jackson in the crowd gathered in Chicago to celebrate the
victory. It is not surprising that the black men and women who made earlier
runs for the nomination were largely forgotten. At the moment their efforts
seemed insignificant compared with the Obama campaign machine. The
Obamamania that swept the nation in 2008 relegated, at least temporarily,
those earlier efforts to the background. However, was Obama really that
distinctive? Was the Obama campaign unique? Could not all of this have
happened earlier?

In early November, thirteen years before Obama won his historic victory,
another African American seemed poised to seize the ultimate political
prize. In many ways the political events of 1995 anticipate and provide a prel-
ude to the Obama campaign. The potential candidate, Colin Powell, was not

187

a typical African American politician. He did not approach the presidency from a background of civil rights and political activism; indeed, he had never sought nor held elected office. His rise to political power had no direct connection to the African American community or to African American politicians or electoral politics. He did not achieve power by representing an African American community or a predominantly black electoral district. Powell rose to power in a national institution, the U.S. Army. He entered politics at the national level through appointment to and service in the executive branch of government. He attained public acclaim and popularity as an architect of American victory in the Gulf War. He approached the 1996 presidential race as a distinguished soldier and public servant whose achievements in these fields were unprecedented for an African American, and impressive for anyone.

Powell also attracted enthusiastic support. As with Obama, the prospect of his candidacy excited many Americans who saw Powell as challenging not only American racial mores, but the rigid and moribund two-party political system that dominated politics at the end of the twentieth century. Among those most excited by the prospect of a Powell presidential challenge were the media and their political pundits. Coincidentally a number embraced Powell as a symbol of "hope and change" who would rescue American politics from the domination of two political parties which seemed mired in tired old ideas, and from candidates tainted by their association with the political system. Colin Powell appeared as a new type of candidate respected for his career and leadership, of modest demeanor but strong and decisive, and a man whose political positions, to the degree they were known, tied him to neither political party. The fact that his political affiliations were unknown, that he truly seemed more of a statesman than a politician, and that he seemed far removed from the lust for office that characterized most politicians, separated him from the field of presidential aspirants.

Childhood and Education

Colin Powell was born in Harlem April 5, 1937, the second of two children. His parents each immigrated to New York from Jamaica. Luther Powell arrived in New York in 1920. After several menial jobs, he found work in a warehouse in the Garment District. Eventually he became a shipping clerk, then the foreman of the shipping department. Maud Ariel McCoy moved to New York as a teenager, joining her mother, who had immigrated a number of years earlier. After she married Luther Powell, she worked as a seamstress in the Garment District.

In 1941 the Powells and their two children moved to a four-bedroom apartment at 52 Kelly Street in the South Bronx. Their neighborhood, which years later would be the burned-out setting for the gritty Paul Newman film, *Fort Apache, The Bronx*, was still functional during Powell's childhood. It was poor, and there was crime, and it was racially mixed—Jewish, Irish, Polish, blacks, Puerto Ricans, and West Indians. Powell recalled that "Banana Kelly," the area he grew up in, maintained a "rough-edged racial tolerance" and that most of the families there were "intact and secure."

While race was clear, Powell's Jamaican heritage muddied the picture. A culture defined by rum, calypso, Anglican religion, and the adults constantly talking about going back home distinguished his world from that of other African Americans, especially those with Southern and Baptist roots. The ethnic jumble of his surroundings, where everyone was a minority, shielded young Powell from the ugliness of prejudice common in America at this time. In recalling when he first felt a racial identity and the sense that he belonged to a minority, Powell insisted that it was not in his South Bronx neighborhood: "I was eventually to taste the poison of bigotry, but much later, and far from Banana Kelly."

The one negative in Powell's childhood was his academic weakness. In contrast to his older sister who excelled in school, Colin ran into academic trouble when he entered the fourth grade. He was placed in "bottom form" among fourth-grade children assessed by his teachers as "a little slow." Powell asserted that he "lacked drive, not ability and that he was a happy-go-lucky kid, amenable, amiable, and aimless." Colin's academic troubles were of great concern to his family, and continued through junior high and high school. Powell did not fail courses; he was simply a "C" student, academically undistinguished. Nevertheless, he graduated from high school and, surprisingly, he was admitted to City College of New York.

Powell entered CCNY in the spring semester of 1954. His major, selected by his mother after a family council, was engineering. Powell's lack of interest and aptitude in math and science was not a consideration; engineers got good jobs—that was all that mattered. Powell did all right his first semester, but a mechanical drawing course the following summer ended his study of engineering. Powell switched his major to geology, a science, but one with less mathematics than the others. His parents were troubled by the switch. Once again Colin had demonstrated his lack of direction. However, in the 1954 fall semester he made a decision that altered his life when he signed up for the Reserve Officer Training Corps (ROTC). ROTC, not geology, became the focus of his college life. And, ROTC was something he excelled in.

In attempting to explain his attraction to ROTC Powell noted that he had spent his childhood during World War II and his high school years during the Korean War. He also recalled his feelings when he first donned his ROTC uniform: "I put the uniform on and looked in the mirror. I liked what I saw."

The uniform gave him a sense of belonging, and of being distinctive, "something I had never experienced all the while I was growing up." He also mentioned an attraction to the order and discipline as well as the camaraderie of the military. Whatever the reason was, ROTC reordered his life. His academic courses were secondary. And, he was excellent in ROTC courses and the drills, demonstrating the focus and direction that had earlier eluded him; most importantly he discovered that he had the ability to lead. In his junior year the drill team he led won first place in the city-wide ROTC competition. That summer at ROTC summer camp at Fort Bragg, he was named the Best Cadet of Company D, and runner-up as Best Cadet of the entire camp. That fall he was the cadet colonel, head of the CCNY ROTC, as well as company commander of the Pershing Rifles. Still a "C" student in his academic classes, he earned straight As in his ROTC courses.

On June 9, 1958 at a ceremony at CCNY, Colin Powell was sworn in as a second lieutenant in the U.S. Army. The following day, he graduated from CCNY with his BS degree in geology. Powell noted that he viewed his college degree as an "incidental dividend" of his four and a half years at college. Nevertheless, Powell acknowledged that even as a mediocre student, his CCNY education provided him with the skills to "think, write, and communicate effectively," and made him competitive with those educated at more elite universities.

Soldiering

Shortly after graduation Powell left New York for officer basic training at Fort Benning, Georgia. This was Powell's first sojourn in the South and it occurred as the civil rights wars were heating up. Before he left CCNY, his ROTC commander cautioned Powell to be careful in the South and to refrain from challenging the racism of the region. While Fort Benning was reflective of the new, post-segregation army, once he left the base he encountered the full weight of racism and discrimination for the first time. His response was to focus on his military career, and not let the indignities he had to endure throw him off track, no matter how provoked, or make him show how angry he was. As he put it, "I was not going to let bigotry make me a victim. . . . I occasionally felt hurt; I felt anger; but most of all I felt challenged. I'll show you!" And, in his military training he did. He was one of the top ten in his officer basic class. He then went through Ranger school, followed by airborne training. Five months after leaving home, he returned on leave as an "airborne ranger," one of the elite of the American infantry.

Powell's career path in the military was impressive. His first posting was as a platoon commander in Germany, on the front line of the cold war. One of his first efficiency reports identified him as having unlimited potential for a military career, and recommending that he be "developed on an accelerated basis." In 1962 he was sent to Vietnam as an advisor to the South Vietnamese army, another sign that he was on the army's fast track. In Vietnam he learned his next stop would be infantry officers' advanced training, and a prediction he would receive an early promotion to major. That prognosis proved true. He became a major in 1966 after less than eight years in the army. Promotion to major is a significant transition, moving young officers from company grade to field grade. Typically it requires ten or eleven years to reach that rank.

One aspect of military life that Powell undoubtedly did not anticipate was that in the modern army the amount of time spent in combat or command was much less than the amount of time spent in training courses and the classroom. Since entering the army in 1958 he had taken the officers' course, ranger school, and airborne training before his first posting in Germany. Before going to Vietnam he spent time at the Unconventional Warfare Center at Fort Bragg studying French Colonial history, Communist political tactics, and basic Vietnamese; after returning from a little less than a year in Vietnam, he had advanced airborne ranger training and infantry officer advanced training at Fort Benning. Then he joined the faculty of the infantry school at Fort Benning. The formerly mediocre student performed very well in his military education, graduating at or near the top of his class. In 1967 he was selected for command and general staff school at Fort Leavenworth, the equivalent of graduate school for the army. Only about half the majors were selected to attend. Once again Powell excelled in his studies. He was the top infantry graduate and the second ranked overall.

While he was at Leavenworth, Powell began planning for graduate work at a non-military university. In the fall of 1969, just back from his second tour of Vietnam, Powell began classes for his MBA at George Washington University. It was here that his weak academic background caught up with Powell. He had to take the courses he had avoided at CCNY in calculus, statistics, and economics, as well as courses in computer programming and business. The extra courses added a semester to his program. Nevertheless, after two years he graduated with his MBA, earning As in all courses except computer logic. He also was promoted to lieutenant colonel.

In 1971, with his MBA in hand, Powell was ready to continue his military career. As a military officer, his major objective was to assume command of a military unit. To this point, he had not been very successful in pursuing this goal. He had two brief stints as a company commander while he was a lieutenant, and during his first tour of Vietnam he had been the de facto commander of a battalion of South Vietnamese troops, but not officially. The problem was that Powell increasingly was offered or assigned political jobs. Beginning in 1971 his career vacillated between political assignments and military command. Most of his time would be consumed by the former, although he did achieve command positions. In 1973 he assumed command of the 1st battalion of the Eighth Army in Korea. Then after graduating from the National War College and promotion to colonel, he took command of a brigade of the 101st Airborne Division.

Other military commands and promotions followed. In 1979, at the age of forty-two, Powell became the youngest brigadier general in the army. For most new brigadier generals, that is their last promotion. Powell continued to advance, ultimately achieving the top rank, a four star general. Of all his military commands, perhaps the most satisfying was the assignment to Germany in 1986 as commander of V Corps, one of the two armies that comprised the U.S. commitment to the defense of Western Europe. The assignment was especially poignant for it returned Powell to the site of his initial army posting in 1958. It also reflected the degree to which African Americans had been integrated throughout the army following the desegregation during the Truman administration. While Colin Powell commanded one of the American armies in Europe, Lieutenant General Andy Chambers, also an African American, commanded VII Corps, the other army in Europe. This coincidence, and the fact that no one seemed to take special note of it, illustrated in Powell's mind how far the army had come from its days of rigid segregation. Powell put it simply, "the military has done a tremendous job in integrating its forces," but he also observed "I wish that there were other activities in our society and in our nation that were as open as the military to upward mobility, to achievement, to allowing them in."

The Politics of the Military

As Powell's career progressed, he frequently was pulled out of military command and placed in political and administrative positions. It was these experiences which increasingly involved Powell in politics. As a military officer, Powell tended to keep his political affiliations to himself. As a child, a portrait of Franklin Delano Roosevelt hung in his home, and his parents voted Democratic, at least until his father broke ranks and voted for Eisenhower. Powell cast his first vote for Kennedy in the 1960 election. Four years later he voted for Johnson, because he had pushed through the 1964 Civil Rights Act. In 1980 he voted for Reagan. His political appointments brought him into both Republican and Democratic administrations and, at least publicly, he maintained a nonpartisan stance through much of his career. As he put it, in 1993, "active duty military officers have no business talking about partisan political matters. So, nobody knows what party I belong to or don't belong to or may belong to."

Powell's first foray into Washington politics occurred immediately after he completed his MBA in July 1971 when he was assigned to the Pentagon.

He became involved with the group of reformers who were charged with designing the army of the future in the post-Vietnam era. In 1972 Powell left this assignment when he was selected as a White House Fellow. During his fellowship year, he opted to work in the Office of Management and Budget. Powell chose this seemingly unexciting assignment because he had learned that the OMB, which had authority over every department's budget, was the most powerful and least understood agency in the government. The choice was wise, and also fortuitous, because it introduced Powell to two men who would play an important role in his political future, Frank Carlucci and Caspar Weinberger. Essentially Powell spent the year studying how power worked within the Washington bureaucracy.

A field command followed the White House Fellowship, but Powell was again summoned to Washington where he worked as military advisor for several high-level officials, including Deputy Secretary of Defense Charles Duncan. Again he was schooled in the politics and power of the military system. When Duncan became secretary of energy, Powell moved with him to the Energy Department. While at Energy, Powell first attracted media attention when in September 1979 *Newsweek* identified him as one of Duncan's "whiz kids" who would wage "the moral equivalent of war" against the energy crisis. After a brief time at Energy, Powell returned to the Defense Department and remained there during the last unfortunate days of the Carter years, including the failed attempt to rescue the American hostages in Iran, and the Soviet invasion of Afghanistan. In 1980 he cast his vote for Reagan.

Reagan's election in 1980 reunited Powell with Caspar Weinberger, who was now secretary of defense, and Deputy Secretary Frank Carlucci. He became senior military assistant for Carlucci. Powell, though, was anxious to get back to military command. The problem he faced was that he was too good at the politics of the Defense Department. He had become adept at moving the Pentagon bureaucracy. As his political skills developed so did his reputation as an effective administrator and political operative within the Pentagon's bureaucracy. Additional opportunities appeared but they conflicted with his desire to get back to his military career. For example, he was offered the position of secretary of the army, contingent on resigning from the army. He turned the offer down and began pressuring Carlucci to let him return to a military command. Finally in 1981 after three years in the Departments of Defense and Energy Powell got his wish, first as assistant division commander at Fort Carson, Colorado, then as deputy commanding general of Combined Arms Combat Development Activity at Fort Leavenworth.

Less than two years later, Powell was back at the Pentagon as senior military assistant to the secretary of defense, Caspar Weinberger. Powell's duties ranged from providing Weinberger military advice, controlling the calendar and access to the secretary, and accompanying him on overseas trips. On his watch the marines' barracks at the Beirut airport was bombed by terrorists, and the United States invaded Grenada. These events influenced Powell as he developed his own concepts of policy and command. The Beirut debacle convinced Powell of the seriousness of placing American troops in harm's way. The marines were in Lebanon, not to carry out a mission, but to provide a "presence." Powell concluded that

> foreign policy cannot be paralyzed by the prospect of casualties. But lives must not be risked until we can face a parent or a spouse or a child with a clear answer of why a member of that family had to die. To provide a "symbol" or a "presence" is not good enough.

The Grenada invasion alerted Powell to another problem. The invasion was a joint operation combining navy, marine, and army forces. It should have been quick and easy, but it took a week to pacify the small island. The problem was a lack of communication and cooperation among the various forces involved, fractured command, and micromanagement from Washington. The post-Vietnam efforts to reform the military and establish a seamless military structure had not yet borne fruit. Powell also helped prepare Weinberger for the initial testimony before Congress on Reagan's Strategic Defense Initiative. The most troubling issue that Powell and Weinberger were involved with was the legal (but according to Powell, "ill-advised") aspects of what later became known as the Iran-Contra scandal. Under authorization from the White House, they arranged the sale of military equipment to the Iranians during the last months that Powell worked with Weinberger. In March 1986 Powell finally received his next military command, and after nearly three years of service, left the secretary of defense's office.

After only five months as commander of V Corps in Germany, Powell received a summons back to Washington that he could not refuse. The Iran-Contra scandal had erupted and it decimated the National Security Council. Robert McFarlane, national security advisor, and Colonel Oliver North, his military assistant, conceptualized and implemented the guns for hostages phase of the program, and then used funds from the sale of weapons to Iran to fund the Contra movement in Nicaragua. Reagan removed McFarlane, made Frank Carlucci the new national security advisor, and personally asked Colin Powell to serve Carlucci as deputy to help clean up the mess. On January 2, 1987 Powell moved into a small office in the West Wing of the White House. He and Carlucci revamped the procedures in the National Security Office to prevent rogue operations from reoccurring. The following November Carlucci became the secretary of defense and Powell became the national security advisor and head of the National Security Council.

The significance of this appointment cannot be understated. As Powell observed,

> I had the job that . . . Henry Kissinger . . . had held. I was no longer some-
> one's aide or number two. I would be working directly with the Presi-
> dent, the Vice President and the Secretaries of State and Defense. . . I
> was now expected to give him [the President] my own national security
> judgments.

Among the issues that Powell contended with during his tenure as national security advisor, the most historic was the series of meetings and negotiations between Reagan and Gorbachev that marked the thawing of the cold war and the beginning of the end of the Soviet Union.

As Powell entered the final year of the Reagan administration he became aware of an exchange of notes between Senator Ted Stevens and Vice President Bush. Senator Stevens suggested that Bush should consider Powell as a potential running mate in the coming presidential election. While this suggestion was never acted on and Bush did not raise the issue with Powell, it indicated the level to which he had risen in political circles. And, in the months ahead, Stevens would not be the only person to consider Powell as a vice presidential candidate. As the election campaign heated up in early 1988, Reagan's chief of staff Howard Baker included Powell on a short list of potential vice presidents in response to a press question. Baker may have done this seriously or he may have dropped Powell's name to counter the Jesse Jackson phenomenon in the Democratic Party, but it elicited several columns by pundits speculating about placing Powell on the ticket. For example Tom Wicker, writing in the *New York Times*, suggested that the selection of Powell as a running mate would be a bold stroke for Bush. In August during the Republican convention there was still some speculation about Powell as a candidate, but that was put to rest by the selection of Dan Quayle. Immediately following the election Bush met with Powell, asked him to remain in the administration, and proposed several positions he could fill, including remaining as national security advisor. Instead Powell took an army command. He became the head of FORSCOM which placed him in charge of all army forces in the United States. He also received a promotion to the top army rank.

Before he could complete a year as FORSCOM commander, Powell was back in Washington, this time as the nominee to serve as the chairman of the Joint Chiefs of Staff. Secretary of Defense Dick Cheney had made the nomination, and President Bush had concurred. The position of chair of the Joint Chiefs of Staff had been revised in 1986, three years before Powell took the office. Previously the role was simply a chair. The Chiefs of Staff discussed the issue and came to a conclusion; the chair carried their decision to the secretary of defense and the president. The revision had significantly increased the power and authority of the chairman, who was designated by the revised act as the principal military advisor to both the secretary of defense and the president and became the supervisor of the sixteen hundred staff personnel who served the joint chiefs. The chair would consult with the Chiefs of Staff, but it was the chair who decided what course of action to recommend. Powell was the first chair to come into the office under the new law. Powell was confirmed by the Senate on September 20, 1989, becoming the youngest person to hold the position, the first African American, and the first to rise from the ranks of ROTC.

During his tenure as chair of the Joint Chiefs of Staff, Powell confronted three major challenges. The first was the invasion of Panama designed to bring to an end the regime of the criminal dictator Manuel Noriega. This was the first use of military force that Powell directed, and it was an effective operation. The second challenge involved responding to the changes wrought by the slow collapse of the Soviet Union and the impact this would have on American military planning and preparations. Powell anticipated the withdrawal of the Soviet military from Eastern Europe, and prepared a plan for redesigning the American military for the needs of a post-Soviet world. On Christmas Day 1991, when the Soviet Union officially dissolved, Powell pushed to sell his vision of a smaller, but more flexible force that could address the new international realities. The third and most significant challenge involved the American response to the Iraqi invasion of Kuwait, and the resulting American-led Gulf War. American success in this operation transformed Powell from a relatively unknown bureaucrat into something of a celebrity, and it made him extremely popular among the American people. His televised briefings made him the voice and the face of the war. It also fueled speculation about his political future, and caused Powell himself to entertain thoughts about the presidency.

Vice President Powell?

The Gulf War significantly altered Powell's life and his future prospects. Politically, and in the public consciousness, it moved him from the background to the forefront. Much of this was a change in perception. Powell had been a major member of the administration in the Reagan and Bush years, first as national security advisor then as chairman of the Joint Chiefs of Staff. But it was the Gulf War that made him a public figure. Sometimes this new status was troublesome. In 1991 Powell was featured prominently in Bob Woodward's new book, *The Commanders*, which discussed decision-making in the Pentagon, largely focusing on the Panama Campaign and Desert Storm.

In preparing the book Woodward had interviewed Powell extensively, along with other administrative figures, and Powell spoke openly and frankly with Woodward about the decision-making process that led to war. When the book appeared Powell was shocked that he was presented as opposing military action in the Gulf and as a reluctant warrior. President Bush stood by his embarrassed military advisor. To silence any speculation about Powell's position in the administration he reappointed the general to a second term as chair of the Joint Chiefs of Staff four months early. In the public announcement of the reappointment, Bush, with Powell at his side, praised the general for his advice and leadership in both the Panama and Iraq conflicts, and told the reporters that in the case of Iraq "it was Colin Powell more than anyone else, who deserves the credit . . . after all options, in my view, were exhausted, for drawing the line in the sand." Ironically, *The Commanders* increased Powell's stature among the public. It depicted Powell as an independent agent rather than just an administrative yes-man, and it portrayed him as a prudent leader who chose war only as a last resort.

Colin Powell's increasingly high profile did not go unnoticed by political operatives. In the aftermath of the Gulf War the national polls showed Powell with an approval rating above 80 percent. As Powell's popularity soared both political parties began to wonder about his future political plans, and more importantly, his political affiliation. Throughout his career, Powell had remained non-committal regarding his political identity. Political speculation about a Powell political campaign began even before the war. In November 1990 during the build-up to the Gulf War, *Parade Magazine* speculated about a Bush-Powell ticket in 1992. Following the war in the summer of 1991 political writer Joe Klein wrote an article on Powell for *New York* magazine in which he praised the general's leadership qualities and his dynamic presence and observed that he was a "master politician" that should attract the attention of both parties. Klein especially urged the Democrats to take note that Powell was registered as an independent.

The first direct approach from the Democrats came in December 1991. Congressman (and former marine) Ron Dellums visited Powell in his Pentagon office. Dellums, whom Powell knew socially, got right to the point. He told Powell that he had been speaking with the top people in the Democratic Party, and that Powell could be their "fondest dream" or "worst nightmare." If Powell would agree to a place on the ticket as vice president, the Democrats could not lose; if, however, he ran as the Republican vice presidential candidate, he would split the black vote and the Democrats could not win. Dellums pushed Powell to commit himself—run as a Democrat, run as a Republican, or remain neutral. Powell's response was typical. He said that although he was flattered by the question, as a military officer on active duty he could not answer it. Powell believed that Dellums left satisfied that he would remain neutral in the coming election.

Dellums's visit did not end Democratic efforts to bring Powell into the party and onto the ticket. In May 1992, Vernon Jordan, a close personal friend of the Powells and a close advisor to the Clinton campaign, visited Powell in his home to discuss his political options. Jordan told Powell that his polling data was off the charts, and asked if he was interested in joining Clinton on the Democratic ticket. Powell again rejected the offer, noting that he was not ready to retire from the military, he was not sure of his political affiliation, and finally he would not run against George Bush.

There was also some chatter in Republican circles about a Bush-Powell ticket in 1992. By May 1992 Bush's poll numbers had dropped to 40 percent, and many saw Vice President Dan Quayle's unpopularity as part of the problem. Private polling data showed that Powell would be a help to the ticket. Bush campaign manager Fred Malek, who had been Powell's mentor back when he had interned at the Office of Management and Budget, was rumored to be the man pushing the Powell candidacy. Richard Armitage, another old friend, set about trying to convince Powell to accept the position if offered. Knowing the difficulty Powell had to saying no to the president, it is likely that Powell would have taken the nomination if Bush had asked him to. However, Bush remained loyal to Quayle, and the offer never came.

Powell served in the Clinton administration as chairman of the Joint Chiefs of Staff until his retirement on September 30, 1993. His few months with the new president were anything but uneventful. He was involved in the effort to address the issue of gays in the military through the "don't ask, don't tell" policy, a less than satisfactory compromise hammered out between the president, who had made a campaign promise to end discrimination against gays in the military, and the generals who resisted the change.

Powell reentered civilian life having served in the army thirty-five years, three months, and twenty-one days. Retirement did not end public service. Although his primary goal in becoming a private citizen was to address the financial needs of his family, he soon was asked by the president to participate in public activities. One of the more pleasant of these was President Clinton's request that he join the U.S. delegation to the inauguration of Nelson Mandela. A more serious assignment involved accompanying former president Carter on a mission to Haiti to negotiate the peaceful U.S. invasion of that nation.

In December 1994, following the Republican victories in the off-year elections, Vernon Jordan again brought Powell the news that the President wanted to speak with him about a position in the administration. The next day, at a White House meeting, Clinton asked Powell if he would be willing to serve as secretary of state. Powell turned down the offer for several reasons. First, he was still settling into private life, and was not ready to return to public service. Secondly, there was no crisis that he felt obligated to help resolve—there was just a vacancy that needed to be filled. Thirdly, he felt that foreign policy under Clinton lacked clear direction and form—a situation with which he felt uncomfortable. As Powell recalled, "if the nation had faced an immediate crisis, it would have been impossible to say no." Since this was not the case, Powell declined the offer.

Powell for President: The 1996 Campaign

When Powell retired in 1993 his major concern was to supplement the relatively modest income a retired general brought to his family. To this end he entered the speakers' circuit. In addition to generating revenue, this activity brought him face to face with audiences across the country and kept him in the public eye. His second major objective was to write his memoirs. Random House gave him a reported $6 million advance, and he went to work with a co-author Joseph Persico. Powell, a gifted story teller with a remarkable memory for detail and an abundant supply of notes, told the stories of his life and career to Persico and a tape-recorder. Persico transformed the transcriptions of the tapes into chapters which Powell reviewed. Like the speaking tour, the book provided a significant source of income as well as an opportunity to present himself and his beliefs to the American public. It was during this time, in late 1993 and throughout 1994, that Powell confronted questions and inquiries about his political plans—especially whether he intended to run for president. While Powell generally deflected these questions, privately he began to assess the potential for the race.

One question concerned when and through which party he would seek the nomination. Powell had carefully avoided committing himself to one party or another. He also had expressed interest in a third party as an option. In part Clinton's offer of the secretary of state position forced a decision on these questions. Clinton approached Powell in the aftermath of serious Democratic defeats in the 1994 congressional elections. Having Powell in his cabinet would bring order to his foreign and defense policy, but it would also diminish the possibility that Powell might challenge him in the 1996 elections. By rejecting the offer, Powell left open the possibility of entering the 1996 race, and also pretty much ended the possibility that he would run as a Democrat. Meanwhile the Republican front runner Senator Bob Dole also wanted to neutralize a Powell challenge by bringing the general onto the ticket as vice president. A Dole supporter, former senator Warren Rudman, approached Powell with a proposal. If Powell joined the ticket Dole would agree to serve only one four-year term, allowing Powell to run in 2000 and 2004.

By early 1995 the pressure on Powell to run was intense. Informal "Powell for President" groups sprang up across the country, and a more formal presidential exploration committee was emerging. At a March speech to students at Trinity University in San Antonio, Powell responded to a question about whether he intended to run by observing that while he lacked a strong passion to run, he was not ruling out the possibility. On his speaking tours he began to meet with potential supporters and funders for a presidential campaign. And the media began to push the Powell campaign. As the campaign intensified a political war-room of sorts was set up in the Powell home, and a core of Powell supporters emerged to provide some direction to the effort.

By the summer of 1995 the prospect of a Powell candidacy dominated political news. Newspaper editorials and op-ed opinion pieces examined and reexamined every aspect of a Powell run for the presidency, as did the television news shows. A consistent theme was that if Powell ran he would alter the American political landscape and he would have a very good chance of winning. The discussions in print and broadcast media focused on Powell as a symbol of change and hope. Powell appeared as an alternative to normal politics, which in 1995 consisted of an incumbent president, wounded by scandal and challenged by a tired, aging Republican who had failed to win the nomination in two previous attempts. Discontent with both parties had been growing for years, as evidenced by the large number of Americans who identified themselves as independents. As *Time* magazine reported in the feature article in its July 10, 1995 issue (which placed the general's face on the cover behind the headline, "Will He Run?"), Powell had a better opportunity than anyone in modern American political history to "become President of the U.S. on his own terms, and thus redefine the public debate in a profound and lasting way." Columnist Anthony Lewis in the *New York Times* wrote that at a time when society seemed to be out of control and individuals behaved as if they owed nothing to the community, Powell "projects the sense of duty and order that we miss."

Other African Americans before Powell had campaigned for the presidency, but Powell differed from past candidates in two critical ways. First, no other African American approached a presidential campaign with as much experience in the executive branch of government. Over a twenty-five year period he had served in a variety of posts—White House Fellow, intern with the Office of Management and Budget, military advisor to the deputy secretary of defense, senior military assistant to the secretary of defense, assistant to the national security advisor, national security advisor, and chairman of the Joint Chiefs of Staff. He had served in the Pentagon and/or the White House during every administration from Richard Nixon to Bill Clinton (except for Gerald Ford), and he worked closely with three presidents: Reagan, Bush, and Clinton. He was better versed in politics and administration than any other African American presidential candidate.

Secondly, as Powell pondered the presidency, he had but one objective—to win. As he stated, "I would not enter [the race] to make a statement but to win. I understand the battlefield and I know what winning takes." Powell's determination to win was supported by polling data. Early in the process polls taken in June 1995 indicated that Powell polled significantly higher than President Clinton. An ABC News poll, conducted June 6–8, asked how respondents would vote in an election with Clinton running as a Democrat and Powell as a Republican; the results gave Powell an 8 point lead, 47 percent to 39 percent for Clinton. On August 30 a Newsweek poll showed Powell with a 9 point lead, 46 percent to 37 percent. Midway through his highly publicized book tour, Powell's lead in a CNN-USA Today poll, conducted by Gallup, increased to 14 points (53 percent to 39 percent). Finally, on November 8, the day Powell shut down his campaign, he still held a 10 point lead in an ABC News poll (52 percent to 42 percent). Unlike any other African American candidate, Powell, at least according to the polls, not only had a chance to win the election, but he maintained a lead over the incumbent as long as he seemed to be in the race. Furthermore additional polling data suggested that this support continued through the spring and summer of 1996.

Powell also differed from other black presidential candidates in the route that he took to his political career. He did not emerge from a background of civil rights or radical political activism as did most other black presidential aspirants. He came to politics from the military. His professional background held more in common with that of Dwight Eisenhower than Jesse Jackson. Like Eisenhower Powell pursued a military career, rose to the top rank in the army, served as chair of the Joint Chiefs of Staff, garnered huge popular support as a war commander, had no known party identity, was pursued as a candidate by both Republicans and Democrats, and had never held elected office when he considered running for the presidency.

Powell's approach to the campaign was also unique. It centered on the publication of his memoirs, *My American Journey*, and the book tour that followed. Although Powell did not set out to write his memoirs as a political document that is what the book evolved into. Throughout the book, there are episodes and explanations that positioned Powell for a presidential campaign. First was the issue of race. Powell connected himself to the African American tradition in several ways. First in discussing his youth he described a summer job in a factory where, unlike his white colleagues, he was handed a broom and spent three months sweeping. In a story that paralleled Booker T. Washington's iconic "entrance exam" at Tuskegee, Powell passed the broom test, and in subsequent summers was given greater responsibility. In other sections of the memoirs Powell addressed his racial experience, from the multi-ethnic neighborhood he grew up in, to the indignities of segregation and the fear of racial violence he endured in the South as a young soldier, to his praise of those who challenged discrimination in the streets and the courts, and to his own strategy to defeat racism through hard work and achievement. The book also effectively served as a political résumé, both establishing his credentials for the job and also presenting an image of himself as both competent and human, and as an African American who transcended race through the military and public service. Finally in an epilogue added just before the book went to press, and after the presidential speculation was well underway, Powell issued his campaign statement, a nine-page discussion of his political beliefs and political philosophy.

If the book served as his campaign biography, then the book tour was the campaign. For about four weeks Powell got a taste of the campaign trail as he crisscrossed the nation (and visited London), meeting enthusiastic and adoring crowds who purchased the book, stood in line for the autograph, but mostly came to be in the presence of Colin Powell. The media covered these book signings as though they were campaign stops; in the press conference that was a part of each event, the inevitable question was "will he run?" As the book tour progressed Powell was edging closer to a decision—and those close to him expected that he would run, and run as a Republican. All Powell promised was that he would announce his decision after the book tour ended. Powell was certainly impressed by the size and the adoration of the crowds, and as the tour progressed his doubts about running faded.

When the tour ended, Powell gathered at home with his friends, advisors, and family to make his decision. While the press speculated about the impact of a Powell candidacy, the candidate himself vacillated, one day determined to run, two days later in doubt. Away from the crowds of the book tour his enthusiasm waned. However, in late October he drafted a speech announcing his candidacy. He would run because the American people wanted change and a smaller government, but one still responsive to their needs. On November 1 the decision to run seemed to be made, but two days later Powell reversed that decision and told his wife Alma that he would not run. The next day he worked on a second speech, a more difficult explanation of why he would not run. These last minute vacillations were impacted by the assassination of Israeli prime minister Yitzhak Rabin on November 4 by a radical right-wing opponent of his efforts to secure peace with the Palestinians. Televised coverage of the tragic events reminded Powell of the uncertain turns of politics, and reinforced Alma Powell's fears of assassination. There followed one more moment of indecision when Powell questioned whether he was making a mistake, but the decision held. He would not run.

On November 8 Colin Powell met with the press and announced his decision not to seek the presidency of the United States. As an explanation, he stated that he lacked the "passion and commitment" for a political life, and that "such a life requires a calling that I do not yet hear." This brought to an end a phenomenal but brief, and never official, presidential campaign. However, it did not completely shut the door to future political involvement, or a future campaign for the presidency. As he noted, politics required a calling that he did not *yet* hear. He also noted that the decision to withdraw was the right decision "at this time." Powell would never act on this escape clause; he would not again seek elected office.

Powell made another announcement at that November 8 news conference. He announced that he had registered that day as a Republican and that he intended to speak out about candidates and issues. His goal, he announced, was to "help the party of Lincoln move once again close to the spirit of Lincoln."

Powell's decision was purely a personal and family decision. He was under no political pressure to withdraw. Although he would have faced attacks from the Republican right wing, and from Democrats, including some black Democrats, he also had the support of a number of prominent Republicans including the party leadership. Powell chose not to run for his own reasons and those of his family. His closest friends indicated that Alma Powell, who never wanted the campaign, was a factor, and obviously favored the decision, but she had indicated her willingness to support and even work for her husband if he chose to run.

Could Colin Powell have won the presidency in 1996? We will never know. The early November polls indicate that he certainly had a good chance—and certainly a better chance than any previous African American presidential candidate. However, November 1995 polls do not elect presidents. Powell faced two serious challenges—the primaries and caucuses that would select the Republican nominee where he would face the conservative wing of the Republican Party, and the general election where he would confront the always formidable Clinton machine. Also unanswered was the question of how the mostly Democratic African American leadership would respond to a Powell candidacy. Jesse Jackson and others had been critical of the prospect of a Powell candidacy, especially questioning whether he was black enough. One fact that is obvious is that Powell's massive popularity that cut across racial and ethnic lines increased the likelihood that an African American candidate could be a successful candidate for the presidency.

After 1996

Colin Powell did not retire from public life following his decision not to seek the presidency in November 1995. He was again considered for the vice presidency on the Dole ticket. Most Republicans saw it as the dream team that could defeat Clinton. However, when the two men met in June 1996, Powell preempted the invitation by indicating that he had no interest in the office. He did, however, endorse Dole and he made a major address at the Republican National Convention. When George W. Bush began organizing his campaign team in 1998 Powell was not involved. However, Powell assumed an advisory role after Bush had locked up the nomination, and became the new president's secretary of state in 2001. Powell served in this capacity for Bush's first term, and was part of the team that sold the nation on the necessity for the Iraqi War, a role that Powell later regretted.

Shortly before the election of 2008, Colin Powell announced his support for Barack Obama. Powell did not join the Obama administration. Instead he became a vocal participant in the struggle to redefine the Republican Party following its defeats in 2008. Powell's message was consistent with the beliefs he held throughout his career. Republicans should be inclusive not exclusive, they should reject extremism, and return to their moderate roots.

Further Reading

Clines, Francis X. "The Powell Decision: The Announcement; Powell Rules Out '96 Race; Cites Concerns for Family and His Lack of 'a Calling.'" *New York Times* (November 9, 1995).

DeYoung, Karen. *Soldier: The Life of Colin Powell.* New York: Alfred A. Knopf, 2006.

Greenstein, Fred I. "Colin Powell's American Journey and the Eisenhower Precedent: A Review Essay." *Political Science Quarterly* 110 (Winter 1995–96): 625–629.

Lewis, Anthony. "Abroad at Home: The Authentic Quality." *New York Times* (September 18, 1995).

Lusane, Clarence. *Colin Powell and Condoleezza Rice: Foreign Policy, Race, and the New American Century.* Westport, CT: Praeger, 2006.

Means, Howard. *Colin Powell: A Biography.* New York: Ballantine Books, 1993.

Powell, Colin L. *My American Journey.* With Joseph E. Persico. New York: Random House, 1995.

Roth, David, *Sacred Honor: Colin Powell: The Inside Account of His Life and Triumphs.* San Francisco: HarperSanFrancisco, 1993.

Shaw, Lisa, ed. *In His Own Words: Colin Powell.* New York: The Berkley Publishing Company, 1995.

Stacks, John F. "The Powell Factor." *Time,* July 10, 1995.

Steins, Richard. *Colin Powell: A Biography.* Westport, CT: Greenwood Press, 2003.

Thelwell, Ekwueme Michael. "'He Coulda Bin A Contendah': The Curious, Unprecedented, Enigmatic Political Career of General Colin L. Powell, U.S.A. Ret." *The Massachusetts Review* 37 (Winter 1996): 581–615.

Wicker, Tom. "In the Nation: A Balance for Bush." *New York Times,* July 29, 1988.

Woodward, Bob. *The Commanders.* New York: Simon and Schuster, 2002.

The official White House portrait of President Barack H. Obama, January 2009.

CHAPTER 12

Barack Hussein Obama
An Inspiration of Hope, an Agent for Change

PAUL FINKELMAN

Barack Hussein Obama, Jr. is the most successful black politician in American history. His election as president in November 2008 is historic in numerous ways. He is the first president: raised outside the forty-eight contiguous states (Hawaii); of African ancestry; with Muslim ancestry; with a parent who was not a U.S. citizen. And of course, he is the first non-white president. He is the nation's first African American president. Obama's career and election illustrate the statement he made when introducing his first Supreme Court nominee, "No dream is beyond reach in the United States of America."

Early Life

Obama's background is both unusual and in some ways quintessentially American. His mother, Ann Dunham, who was white, traced her ancestry to England and Ireland. She was born in Kansas and graduated from high school in suburban Seattle, Washington and then studied at the University of Hawaii. The migration of the Dunham family reflects the steady movement of people from east to west which has always been a central aspect of American history. His father, Barack Hussein Obama, Sr., was a visiting student from Kenya. Obama's parents were students at the University of Hawaii when they were married after Dunham became pregnant with the future president. At the time Obama's father was still legally married to, but legally separated from, a woman in Kenya. Barack was born in 1961 and a year later his father went to Harvard for graduate school, leaving his son and wife in Hawaii. In 1964 Dunham divorced Obama, Sr. and Barack (who as a child went by the name Barry) saw his father only once more, in 1972, when he was eleven. Although his father was Muslim, Obama was raised entirely by his mother and her parents, and despite claims of fringe opponents of Obama, he was not raised Muslim and is not a Muslim. As a boy he briefly attended a Catholic school in Indonesia, was introduced to numerous religious heritages by his anthropologist mother while growing up in Hawaii, and for most of his adult life he attended Unitarian Churches.

This background makes Obama unusual among American presidents—all other presidents have been white men of British, Irish, Dutch, or German background. On his mother's side he is also English-Irish, but of course on his father's side he is African. However, except for his African heritage and his skin color, Obama is in many ways very much like other presidents. Like all other presidents except John F. Kennedy, Obama is Protestant. Indeed, his family background reflects the cultural and ethnic diversity of America. After his election the Irish singing group the Corrigan Brothers produced a music video entitled *There's No More Irish Than Barack Obama*, with signs in the video spelling his name "O'Bama" and noting his great-great-great grandfather came from the Irish village of Moneygall. Like so many other American Presidents—from Jackson to Buchanan to Kennedy to Reagan—the Irish claim Obama as their own. This underscores the political viability of his diversity and the universality of his appeal.

Obama's many geographic relocations also suggest how he represents modern America. He was born in Hawaii, studied in California, New York, and Massachusetts, and built his political base in Illinois. He's African, English, Irish, Hawaiian, Midwestern, Californian, and Northeastern. He's black and he's white. He's Protestant with a Moslem connection. In his political campaigns he further expanded his reach, with the Jewish David Axelrod as his chief strategist for his 2004 senate campaign and his 2008 presidential campaign. After securing the Democratic nomination he chose a Roman Catholic running mate (the first ever to be elected to that office), and after his election chose Rahm Emanuel, an Orthodox Jew with an Israeli-born father, as his chief of staff. Others in his inner circle include African Americans and white Protestant Americans. He is, and has become, "everyman"—the perfect candidate and, through the varied backgrounds of his advisors, running mate, and cabinet—the perfect representative of the most diverse and open society in the world.

In 1967 Obama's mother married Lolo Soetoro, an Indonesian with whom she had a second child, Maya Soetoro, who grew up mostly in Hawaii, studied at the Universities of Hawaii and Columbia before returning to Hawaii where she became a history teacher and an author of children's books. Barack remained in Indonesia with his mother and sister from 1967 until 1971, when he returned to Hawaii where he won a scholarship to the prestigious Punahou School. He was mostly raised by his maternal grandparents while his mother returned to Indonesia to pursue anthropological research. In 1979 Barry Obama left Hawaii for Occidental College in California, where he was known as "Barry the Bomber" for his long-range shots on the school's basketball team. After two years he transferred to Columbia University in New York City, where he graduated in 1983 as Barack Obama. By this time he had immersed himself in African American literature and thought, and shaped his own identity as a black American. However, his early life and complex heritage had also shaped his racial identity and his sense of self. He was half-African and half-white; he had been schooled in Jakarta and Honolulu and then in California and New York; he had been mostly raised by his white, Midwestern grandparents in Hawaii (the nation's only majority-minority state); he had a half sister who was half-white and half-Indonesian; he had a Kenyan father he had never really known and a mother who was often absent. Barry Obama had become Barack Obama by choice. He would soon immerse himself in community politics of a mostly African American world, but at the same time, he brought an understanding of white America, Asian American culture, and the complexity of race that could be matched by very few Americans.

Community Organizer and Harvard Law Student

After college Obama worked in the corporate world when he could not find a job in a public interest setting. In 1985, however, he moved to Chicago to work with steelworkers facing unemployment in the declining rustbelt. He then worked with a variety of community organizations, on asbestos and lead paint abatement, and other issues involving environmental concerns. Scholars and activists dispute how important Obama was in these activities, but it is clear he was hard-working and helped achieve some successes. He also failed miserably in an attempt to bring the black clergy in Chicago together as a united force for social change.

In 1988 Obama left Chicago for Harvard Law School, where he impressed the faculty and his fellow students with his energy, work ethic, and his common sense. He was a research assistant for the school's famous constitutional law specialist, Laurence Tribe, and became the first African American elected president of the *Harvard Law Review*, which is probably the single most important honor at the law school. The presidency of the *Harvard Law Review* is usually a stepping stone to a federal clerkship—often a Supreme Court clerkship—a high-paying job with a law firm, or a teaching job at an elite law school. The fame from this accomplishment did lead to a book contract, and in 1994 Obama published *Dreams of My Father*. (The book would be reprinted with a new introduction in 2004 as Obama campaigned for the U.S. Senate.) But, Obama did not follow the usual route from the presidency of the *Harvard Law Review* to a clerkship and then either a lucrative law firm job or a prestigious academic position. Rather, in 1991 he returned to Chicago, running a voter registration campaign that helped Bill Clinton carry Illinois in 1992. He then worked in the public interest firm of Miner, Barnhill & Galland while also teaching constitutional law at the University of Chicago. In 1992 Obama married Michelle Robinson, who was also a Harvard Law graduate. Unlike Obama, who was a relative newcomer to Chicago, Michelle Robinson had deep roots in Chicago's black community. Indeed, she had once been a babysitter for Jesse Jackson, Jr., who would eventually serve in Congress and become a key supporter of Obama in his presidential campaign. At the time they married Michelle worked in the corporate world and in public service. Thus, she helped her husband connect to white political, legal, and business leaders, while at the same helping him make connections to the city's black leadership.

Early Political Career: From the Illinois Senate to the U.S. Senate

In 1996 Obama launched his political career, winning a seat in the Illinois Senate from a racially integrated South Side district that included one of Chicago's wealthiest neighborhoods (Hyde Park), its greatest intellectual institution (the University of Chicago), its most important civil rights organization (the headquarters of Rev. Jesse Jackson's Operation Breadbasket), and some of the city's poorest and most dangerous slums.

Obama's road to this seat was a combination of luck, hard work, and his willingness and ability to play hardball politics in a city famous for ruthless campaigns. In early 1995 the incumbent state senator, Alice Palmer announced her intention to seek an open seat in the House of Representatives (caused by the resignation of Mel Reynolds after a sex scandal). The special election was scheduled for November 1995. Obama then announced that he would seek Palmer's state senate seat. Palmer did not oppose Obama, and appeared to endorse him, although supporters of Palmer and Obama later disagreed about this. In any event, Obama vigorously campaigned for the nomination, gathering signatures for his nominating petitions and going door-to-door throughout the district. Meanwhile, Palmer was unable to gain any significant traction in her congressional campaign, and in the special election in late November ran a distant third to Jesse Jackson, Jr., who easily won the seat. After some indecision, Palmer announced she would indeed seek another term in the state senate, but had only a few days to gather signatures to get on the ballot for the March 1996 primary. By this time Obama had secured many more signatures than he needed, including many supporters of Palmer who signed Obama's petitions because Palmer had emphatically announced she would not seek the seat. After losing the congressional race Palmer demanded that Obama withdraw from the race, which he refused to do.

When the nominating petitions were submitted to the board of election, Obama sent a team of very skilled lawyers and supporters to challenge the signatures on the petitions of Palmer and two others who were seeking the nomination. Obama had worked hard to register voters for Clinton and he understood the rules of the game and intricacies of election law. His team successfully challenged the nominating petitions of all of his Democratic primary opponents, including the incumbent Palmer. Critics of Obama would later denounce him for ending Palmer's thirty-year career as a community activist and state legislator by trickery. But there were no tricks. Palmer and his other opponents had hired people to gather signatures and many of those who signed were not in fact registered voters or did not reside in the district. Obama played by the rules—and more importantly—knew how to play by the rules. Equally important, even in this first campaign he had the self-confidence (and intelligence) to surround himself with very smart people who could get the job done. This victory also illustrated that in addition to his enormous personal skills and his Ivy League education, Obama understood the rough and tumble nature of urban politics. He knew how to fight tough and use the rules of the game to his advantage.

Obama ran unopposed in the Democratic primary and easily won the general election in this heavily Democratic district. Obama would later say he "liked Alice Palmer," and clearly respected her long dedication to progressive politics; he also believed that once she pulled out of the race he was free to seek the seat. Palmer apparently never forgave Obama for not stepping aside so she could hold her seat. In 2008 Palmer supported Hillary Clinton's candidacy in the Democratic primaries.

In the Illinois Senate Obama quickly emerged as a new kind of black politician. Although he had been a community organizer and was a political progressive, he had not come out of the civil rights movement and he carried none of the scars of older black politicians who had lived through de jure and de facto segregation. He was better educated than almost anyone else in the state legislature—black or white. He was a skilled negotiator, and he soon emerged as a hard-working new legislator. He had great rhetorical skills, but he was not flamboyant. Indeed, since his community organizing days in the

1980s, he had been known as "No-drama Obama." Thus, in the state senate he was able to work with Republicans and downstaters, as well as his fellow Chicago Democrats.

In 2000, Obama challenged Bobby Rush, the four-term incumbent U.S. representative, from his South Side district. Rush was a former Black Panther leader who had deep roots in the community and connections to President Bill Clinton, who endorsed his reelection. During the campaign Rush derided Obama for his youth and emphasized his lack of political experience and life experience. He also took shots at his Ivy League credentials, which contrasted with Rush's inner city roots and "school of hard knocks" education. In his quest for the presidency his opponents would raise similar issues. Rush did not question Obama's right to represent the mostly black district, but another primary opponent (who also lost) accused Obama of being a "white man in black face." Some black activists and intellectuals would make a similar argument when Obama sought the presidency. In the poor black neighborhoods of Obama's congressional district such claims had some resonance. Obama was not an "African American" in the traditional sense but an American who was literally half-African. He had been raised in a state that has one of the lowest percentages of blacks and had been educated in elite private schools with few black classmates. Obama had no first-hand knowledge of growing up in a black community, or even being raised by black parents. Thus, there was some truth to the claim in South Side Chicago that he was truly an outsider. However, as Obama eventually moved to a larger political stage this aspect of his background would work in his favor. For most non-African Americans Obama emerged as a black man who could appeal to all people without regard to race, ethnicity, or social class.

In the Democratic primary Rush crushed Obama, carrying about 65 percent of the votes. Obama carried a majority of the white vote, which illustrated his appeal across racial lines. He overwhelmingly lost the black vote to the popular Rush, although probably not because of Obama's mixed race background, his unusual upbringing, or his educational credentials. Rather, he lost to an experienced popular incumbent who had served his district well. Rush's constituents liked him and had no reason to turn him out for a newcomer. In retrospect Obama's campaign against Rush did not hurt his career, but it surely showed a lack of good political judgment. Without very compelling reasons, it never makes much sense to run in a primary against a popular incumbent.

Obama briefly considered leaving politics after this devastating loss, but instead built new alliances and focused on the 2004 senatorial election. In moving towards this campaign Obama learned from his loss to Rush. In a sense, the change of direction illustrates the way Obama was a fundamentally new kind of black politician. Raised among whites in the most racially diverse state in the nation, Obama was as comfortable with whites as he was with blacks. Raised away from a segregated world, he understood segregation and racism, but at the same time understood the possibility—because he had seen it in Hawaii—of a less racially charged world where people were in fact not judged by the color of their skin.

Unlike other black politicians, Obama did not start with a base in the black community. He was not like Chicago's first black mayor, Harold Washington, who began with a huge base in the black community and then built alliances with whites to win a slim majority in the mayoral election. Obama's failed run for Congress showed he was capable of gaining strong support among whites, just as his successful election to the state legislature showed he could carry the black community when not running against a popular "race" candidate. This put Obama in a strong position to run for statewide office as a black candidate who could be more successful with white voters than almost any other black in the history of the nation, while at the same time successfully attracting support in the black community. This made a run for the U.S. Senate seem plausible, even though he had never held office outside of the state legislature.

Obama's run for the Senate benefitted from skill, hard work, and luck. He learned much from his defeat in his race to unseat Bobby Rush, and worked hard to gain support among Chicago's black politicians. In 1992 Carol Moseley-Braun had won the Illinois seat and become the first black woman ever elected to the U.S. Senate. She was narrowly defeated in 1998 by a moderate millionaire Republican, Peter Fitzgerald. Fitzgerald was not particularly popular. He owed his victory to a poor campaign by Moseley-Braun, his enormous wealth, and the appearance of scandal on the part of Moseley-Braun. The incumbent was also weakened because she had visited Nigeria's brutal dictator, General Sani Abacha. If Moseley-Braun seemed vulnerable in 1998, Fitzgerald seemed equally vulnerable when Obama announced his candidacy. In the end, Fitzgerald decided not to run for reelection because he had little support in his party or in the state. This created an open seat, which gave Obama a greater chance for victory.

By 2004 Obama had also gained more recognition in the state, as the Democrats took control of the state senate and Obama became chair of the Health and Human Service Committee. Working with civil libertarians and the police—and getting along with both—Obama guided a law through the state legislature to require the video-taping of all police interrogations and confessions in capital cases. This law strengthened the hand of the police in using such evidence while at the same time preventing coerced confessions. "No-drama Obama" quietly worked with people on both sides of an issue to create a valuable piece of legislation. He was simultaneously the defender of the rule of law, a civil libertarian, and a supporter of more effective law enforcement.

In the primary campaign two better-known white candidates had the early lead. The early favorite, millionaire Blair Hull, saw his support evaporate when his divorce records indicated spousal abuse, while the other leading opponent, career politician Dan Hayes, simply could not match Obama's charisma, rhetorical skills, or his fund-raising among well-heeled white liberals in Chicago and its suburbs. Obama also scored well by denouncing the Iraq War as a huge mistake—as a "dumb war." Obama was hardly a radical, but he successfully appealed to the growing opposition to a war which was not going well. The rising death toll in Iraq correlated to rising support for Obama. Obama also benefitted from being the "new kid on the block"—a fresh face and a superbly articulate voice. As the only black in the contest, he was also able to draw on the large African American community in Chicago, even though he did not campaign as a "black" candidate. In the primary he won only thirteen counties, but these included Cook and its suburbs, as well as the university communities outside of metropolitan Chicago. The endorsement of the daughter of the late senator Paul Simon helped him downstate. Thus, he won 53 percent of the primary vote.

Obama initially faced a formidable Republican opponent, a wealthy businessman Jack Ryan. But in the middle of the campaign Ryan was caught in a sex scandal and was forced off the ticket. A desperate Republican Party turned to Alan Keyes, an extremely conservative black political activist with a Ph.D. from Harvard. Keyes was a skilled debater but no match for Obama's charisma or speaking ability. Keyes was ideologically to the right of most Republicans, and pushed an anti-gay, anti-choice agenda in a state that had become increasingly liberal on these social issues. Keyes even attacked the family of Vice President Dick Cheney because his daughter was gay. Such shrill cultural issues had little traction as the voters in Illinois weighed the two candidates and the real issues—especially the Iraq War—that the nation faced. Keyes, a resident of Maryland when the state Republican committee asked him to run—had never actually lived in Illinois and thus his candidacy defused any lingering doubts that the native of Hawaii with a Kenyan father could successfully represent the state. Compared to Keyes, Obama, who had first moved to the state nearly twenty years earlier, was a bona fide citizen of the Land of Lincoln.

During the campaign Keyes argued that Obama was not really "black," because he was not the descendant of slaves. This argument doubly backfired. Coming from a black ultra-conservative whose hostility to civil rights legislation, affirmative action, and the needs of the poor made him seem like a traitor to his race, this argument had almost no traction in the black community. Few African Americans in Illinois were impressed by the racial attacks from Keyes, who most blacks thought was a traitor to his race and utterly indifferent to the economic needs or to the desire for racial justice. But, to the extent that whites in Illinois believed Keyes on this issue, they may have been more inclined to vote for Obama because he was clearly not a traditional African American candidate. Keyes also alluded to the fact that Obama's father was a Muslim, and claimed that Obama was not a Christian. Similar attacks on Obama would be made when he ran for president but, except among fringe groups, they would not be taken seriously. Indeed, Obama may have been lucky that both these claims, which were connected to his ancestry, were first raised by a candidate (Keyes) who was an extremist even within his own party and who was also black.

By the time the polls closed in November 2004 Obama had won an unprecedented victory, carrying 70 percent of the vote. Unlike the primary, where he only won thirteen counties, in the general election Obama won 92 of the state's 102 counties and beat Keyes by more than 2,000,000 votes. This was one of the most spectacular senate victories in modern politics. Clearly, Obama was a candidate who could appeal to people of all races and backgrounds. After this victory he was not the black senator from Illinois, rather, he was one of the most popular candidates in the history of the state, who happened to be black.

Toward a National Presence and a Presidential Campaign

Shortly after entering politics in the 1990s Obama began to talk with his closest confidants, including his brother-in-law Craig Robinson, about someday running for the presidency. For a man who was only a state senator, this seems audacious if not outrageously arrogant. Yet, it is likely that Obama's early articulation of this long-term goal—to be president—was not much different than others who sought the office such as Bill Clinton, or another once-obscure Illinois state legislator, Abraham Lincoln. In many ways the parallels to Lincoln and Clinton are obvious. All three grew up poor—on the edge of poverty. Clinton and Obama grew up without a father present; Lincoln with a father he came to despise. Obama was mostly raised by his grandparents; Lincoln was mostly raised by his step-mother. All worked hard to gain solid educations—Lincoln informally on the frontier; Clinton and Obama through scholarships to elite schools. All three were attorneys. The Obama–Lincoln parallels are intriguing. Both made their careers in the same adopted state, Illinois. When they sought the presidency neither had any executive experience and almost no national legislative experience. Lincoln served a little longer in the Illinois legislature than Obama, and Obama had served just three years in the United States Senate compared to Lincoln's one two-year term in the House of Representatives. Opponents of both men sneered at their lack of experience. Indeed, Obama was the least experienced person elected president since Lincoln, and arguably (along with Wendell Willkie who ran in 1940) the least experienced person to be nominated for the presidency since Lincoln.

Obama's first opportunity for national exposure came at the Democratic National Convention in 2004, which nominated John Kerry. Looking for a fresh face and a new voice to kick off the campaign against the incumbent George W. Bush, the party asked the handsome, charismatic, and articulate Obama to give the keynote speech. It was a gamble to put a virtually unknown state senator in that national spotlight. But, Obama had some powerful allies—including Harvard Law School's Laurence Tribe and the enormously talented Democratic political consultant, David Axelrod, who was his senatorial campaign manager.

The gamble paid off, as Obama gave the speech of a lifetime. Throughout the speech he wove a series of themes that exemplified the complexity of American society and culture: his deep American roots through his mother, his immigrant background through his father; the poverty of his father and his mother and their relentless and successful struggle to achieve for themselves and their children; his opposition to President Bush's increasingly failed war policy in Iraq and his strong support for the troops fighting that war. In this speech Obama faced down the conservative shibboleths that had placed Democrats on the defensive for decades.

In contrast to the racially charged rhetoric of past campaigns, Obama refused to make race or inequality an issue: he faced the race issue but defused it, noting that "Tonight is a particular honor for me because, let's face it, my presence on this stage is pretty unlikely." But, he did not focus on his "unlikeliness" as a speaker or a party leader. Instead, he embraced his commonality with all Americans. Moreover, he tied his unlikeliness on the podium not to his race but to his immigrant background and the poverty of his parents—his father who herded goats in Africa, his mother who raised him as a struggling single parent.

While opposing the Iraq War, he embraced patriotism and military strength—drawing on his grandfather who had "signed up for duty" immediately after Pearl Harbor, and "joined Patton's army, marched across Europe" while "back home" his "grandmother raised a baby and went to work on a bomber assembly line." Through his maternal grandparents the black "skinny kid with a funny name," as Obama humorously described himself, was as American as apple pie. He represented the real America as much or more than the wealthy Bush with his blue-blood pedigree.

In this speech Obama appealed to the deepest cultural values of Americans and challenged the Republican cultural wars on their own terms. He openly rejected the idea that there were real differences between "red" and "blue" states, noting that:

> The pundits like to slice and dice our country into red states and blue states: red states for Republicans, blue states for Democrats. But I've got news for them, too. We worship an awesome God in the blue states, and we don't like federal agents poking around our libraries in the red states. We coach little league in the blue states and, yes, we've got some gay friends in the red states.

Obama deftly focused on race by denying that race was the critical issue in the campaign, declaring "There's not a black America and white America and Latino America and Asian America; there's the United States of America." At the same time, he quoted the Declaration of Independence, "We hold these truths to be self-evident, that all men are created equal . . . that they are endowed by their Creator with certain inalienable rights, that among these are life, liberty and the pursuit of happiness." He reminded Americans that at the core of the nation's core values—"the true genius of America,"—was

> a faith in simple dreams, an insistence on small miracles; that we can tuck in our children at night and know that they are fed and clothed and safe from harm; that we can say what we think, write what we think, without hearing a sudden knock on the door; that we can have an idea and start our own business without paying a bribe; that we can partici- pate in the political process without fear of retribution, and that our votes will be counted—at least most of the time.

Obama ended his speech with an appeal to core values of patriotism: "We are one people, all of us pledging allegiance to the stars and stripes, all of us defending the United States of America." Challenging the Republicans' claim to the vote of religious Americans, Obama argued for a religious basis for a community that cares about all people: "it is that fundamental belief— I am my brother's keeper, I am my sister's keeper—that makes this country work." Again, rejecting the politics of race or class—the politics of divi- sion—he stressed that it was national unity that "allows us to pursue our individual dreams, yet still come together as a single American family: 'E pluribus unum,' out of many, one." Refusing to directly attack the nega- tivism of the Bush administration, he appealed to what Lincoln had called "Our better angels," asserting:

> Hope in the face of difficulty, hope in the face of uncertainty, the audac- ity of hope: In the end, that is God's greatest gift to us, the bedrock of

this nation, a belief in things not seen, a belief that there are better days ahead.

The speech was a resounding success. It was clearly the best speech of the convention and one of the most memorable speeches of any political convention. The speech also contrasted with Jesse Jackson's "Keep Hope Alive," speech, which was a masterful sermon preached by a skilled clergyman using politics to further his agenda of social equality and social justice. Jackson's 1988 speech was a call to arms for a greater attention to fairness and equality, but for all its power, it was a civil rights speech echoing the rhetoric of Martin Luther King, and ill-suited for a national political campaign. It may have inspired those who agreed with Jackson and thrilled many Democrats, but it was unlikely to reach moderates, the undecided, and those who were not focused on civil rights. Indeed, it was the speech of a defeated candidate, who urged his follower to "keep hope alive."

Obama's speech was different. It was not a speech about civil rights, although he placed civil rights on the national agenda. Rather, it was a speech that called for national unity and inclusion. It was a speech which tried to capture the flag and the mantle of patriotism for the Democratic Party. It did not criticize the nation, or sermonize the faithful. Rather, it celebrated the nation, acknowledged the great civil rights advances of the last half century, and urged the party and the nation to move forward to reclaim the heritage of America. Obama ended by predicting that with a Democratic victory "this country will reclaim its promise, and out of this long political darkness a brighter day will come." It would not come in 2004, as the Kerry ticket lost, but the speech suggested that with the right man at the top of the ticket, the party might do just that. The media quickly recognized Obama's charisma and his potential as a presidential candidate. The speech thrust Obama onto the national stage as a future star of the Democratic Party.

Obama's electoral success in Illinois in November confirmed this. John Kerry narrowly lost the presidential election as his campaign failed to gain traction or respond to vicious attacks on his character and war record in Vietnam. Other Democrats, including the party's senate leader Tom Daschle, also lost. But in Illinois, Obama won in an unprecedented landslide. When he reached Washington in January 2005 the new junior senator was clearly a celebrity with great potential.

From Senator Obama to Presidential Candidate Obama

First-term senators rarely have much impact on legislation or politics. With the Democrats in the minority and Obama at the bottom of the seniority list, he had relatively little power. Yet, following the path he developed in Illinois, Obama successfully cooperated, where possible, with Republicans, working closely with Richard Lugar, the moderate Republican senator from Indiana and even, on occasion, with hard-line conservatives, such as Tom Coburn of Oklahoma. Generally, he voted as a strong liberal, favoring social welfare policies while attacking the Bush administration on the war in Iraq. But, "No-drama Obama" continued to demonstrate his ability to work with the opposition.

Obama also distinguished himself from his fellow senators in another way. In 2006 he published his second book, *The Audacity of Hope*. The book was a combination of political philosophy, policy prescriptions for changing America, and personal self-revelation. The book had enough technical detail to illustrate that Obama was serious and thoughtful about the complexities of government, taxes, social security, and similar issues. But at the same time, the book showed Obama was not merely a boring policy wonk or a technocrat. He could explain things simply but not simplistically. Able to parse Supreme Court decisions with the best elite law professors, Obama could also reduce a sophisticated constitutional issue to a level that a citizen untrained in the law could understand:

> The simplest statute—a requirement, say, that companies provide bathroom breaks to their hourly workers—can become the subject of wildly different interpretations, depending on whom you are talking to: the congressman who sponsored the provision, the staffer who drafted it, the department head whose job it is to enforce it, the lawyer whose client finds it inconvenient, or the judge who may be called upon to apply it.

The book was more than an autobiography or a policy statement by a young senator: it was the preview of a presidential campaign. His chapter on "Faith" began with a frank discussion of the politics of abortion. Obama was clearly pro-choice, but wanted to reach out to those who disagreed with him. As he stressed in his book and his presidential campaign, both sides of the argument could come together to work to reduce the need for abortions. Similarly, Obama stressed his own religious faith in the book. For decades Republicans had worked the social issues of abortion, gay rights, and religion to their benefit. In *The Audacity of Hope* Obama confronted these issues and moved to defuse them. By expressing his own faith, he made himself, and his party, more acceptable to evangelical Christians. This was simply a longer, more articulate version of his assertion in his 2004 speech at the Democratic convention that Democrats in the blue states "worship an awesome God."

In the 2006 midterm elections Obama campaigned throughout the nation for house, senate, and gubernatorial candidates, helping give Democrats control of Congress, building up good will in the party, expanding his own name recognition, and raising significant sums for any future campaign he might undertake. By the end of 2006 he had over $4.5 million in his own political action committee.

The publication of *The Audacity of Hope* set the stage for Obama's announcement on January 17, 2007 that he would seek the presidency, with "a different kind of politics." Obama faced an uphill battle for the nomination. The leading candidate, Senator Hillary Rodham Clinton, had a huge campaign fund, great name recognition, and what appeared a powerful asset in being able to call on her husband, former president Bill Clinton, to campaign for her. Clinton had strong support in the black community, because of her husband's strong civil rights record and his advocacy of racial justice. Senator Clinton also had a strong base among Democratic women, who felt it was their turn to have a candidate. In addition to defeating Clinton, Obama would also have to campaign against John Edwards, the handsome and wealthy former senator from North Carolina who had run for vice president with John Kerry in 2004. Edwards presumably had a strong base in the South, which had produced the only successful Democratic presidential candidates (Johnson, Carter, and Clinton) in the last four decades. Democratic women and many African Americans could be expected to rally to Clinton while Democrats, hungry for a victory, saw the brilliant stump speaker Edwards as the candidate most likely to carry the nation.

While Clinton had a natural base among party regulars and women, and Edwards presumably had a base in the South, it was not clear whether Obama had a base at all. At the beginning of his campaign many blacks were reluctant to support Obama on the theory that he could never win, and therefore they should support Clinton in return for her husband's civil rights record, or support the more populist Edwards because he was the only candidate focusing on economic inequality. Some black political leaders also seemed to resent Obama because he had not struggled and fought for civil rights as they had. Obama was of the next generation, and older black leaders were reluctant to see themselves displaced by the new and untested senator from Illinois. Some blacks may have also bought into the criticism that Obama was not a legitimate representative of black Americans because he was half-white, raised in Hawaii, and had a Kenyan father.

Once the campaign began, Obama quickly surprised skeptics. In four critical areas he out-campaigned Clinton. First, as the underdog he ran harder than any of his opponents. Clinton had been the front runner for so long that her advisors just assumed she would win the nomination. She lost the Iowa caucuses, running third behind Obama and Edwards, and after that never caught up. In many states Obama simply out-campaigned her. Clinton's overconfidence—some would say arrogance or hubris—alienated many voters and pushed independents towards Obama. She and her husband expected African Americans to turn out in large numbers for her, and they were deeply shocked and angry when the vast majority of blacks in South Carolina supported Obama. The Clintons were also surprised when substantial numbers of college-educated women supported Obama. While Clinton campaigned hard, especially after her shocking loss in Iowa, her campaign never seemed to quite click.

Second, Obama quickly emerged as a great stump speaker and a deeply likeable campaigner. He was a better speaker than Clinton and appeared more sincere and open than Edwards. As a new face, with some fresh ideas, Obama simply was more attractive and exciting than the older, better-known candidates. Obama energized people, especially young people, in a way that no candidate had done since Bobby Kennedy ran in 1968. As John McCain's chief strategist would say a few months after Obama took office, "This was, in my view, the unfinished Bobby Kennedy campaign— the idealism, the passion, the inspiration he gave to people, it was organic and it was real and it wasn't manufactured at a tactical level in the campaign" (quoted in *Newsweek*, May 4, 2009, page 17). The Kennedy comparison was aided relatively early on in the campaign, when on January 27, 2008, Caroline Kennedy, the daughter of slain president John F. Kennedy, endorsed Obama in a *New York Times* op-ed, saying he would be "a president like my father."

Obama's team understood, far better than Clinton's team, the strategy necessary to gain the nomination. Each state had different rules for how convention delegates would be allocated. Every state required a different kind of campaign, with a different strategy. For all their experience in national politics, Clinton and her advisors never seemed to understand that. Thus, Senator Clinton expressed surprise after the Texas primary that winning the popular vote did not guarantee her a majority of the convention delegates, which were chosen through a complicated process that began with precinct caucuses. Obama supporters flooded those caucuses in Texas as they had done in Iowa and elsewhere. Similarly, in Pennsylvania the Clinton campaign failed to recruit candidates to run as convention delegates throughout the state. Equally important, Obama vigorously campaigned in small states and traditionally Republican states, carrying many of them, or as in Texas and Indiana, just narrowly losing them. With each primary victory in places like Iowa, Virginia, Montana, Idaho, Utah, Colorado, Oregon, and Georgia, Obama demonstrated his appeal across geography, race, and class. From the beginning of the campaign Obama had enormous momentum, which he never lost.

Finally, and most surprising of all, Obama was able to raise more money than Clinton, who started with much greater resources. Obama built a huge network of contributors through the internet. They were able to contribute small amounts with a click of a mouse and continue to support the campaign throughout the primaries and later in the general election. Obama's fundraising turned out to be the most massive grassroots political funding in history. By the end of April 2008 Obama had raised over $270 million dollars. More significantly, he raised this money through contributions from more than 1.5 million individual donors contributing on average only $175 each. By June 30, 2008 Obama had raised an astounding $335 million from individual donors. Clinton had raised a total of $252 million, with only $207 million coming from individuals. Clinton also raised more than a million from political action committees, and used over $13 million of her own money. Obama raised just $1,500 from PACs and contributed no personal money to the campaign. Obama's campaign was not based on "fat cats" contributing the maximum amount; it was based on huge numbers of small donors giving well below the maximum allowed under the law. This was a popular campaign, funded literally by millions of people who were enamored of Obama's style, positions, and his mantra of hope and change from the Bush administration.

After Iowa Clinton and Obama battled head-to-head in a number of primaries, with Clinton winning New Hampshire and Obama coming back to take South Carolina. On Super Tuesday Obama carried more states than Clinton and they more or less split the delegates up for grabs. But such an outcome was in truth a huge victory for Obama. He proved he could go head-to-head with the front runner and best her in many states. Moreover, Obama showed enormous strength in the West and the South, which is where Democrats had to win if they were to take the White House in 2008. Clinton did well in the Northeast and California, but these were places that were certain to go Democratic no matter which candidate gained the nomination. Moreover, most of Clinton's victories were close. On Super Tuesday she won more than 55 percent of the vote in only five states, while Obama carried twelve states by more than that amount. Only in her husband's home state of Arkansas did Clinton get more than 60 percent of the vote, but Obama carried nine states with more than 60 percent of the vote. After Super Tuesday, Obama won ten states in a row.

The greatest threat to Obama's campaign in the end came not from his opponents, but from his former preacher, the Rev. Jeremiah Wright, a proponent of black liberation theology, who had on tape claimed that the attacks of 9/11 were the "chickens" of American foreign policy "coming home to roost" and had been recorded declaring "God damn America." Obama defused the controversy on March 18, with a brilliant speech in Philadelphia about the problem of race and American culture. He refused to "disown" Wright, while at the same time rejecting his rhetoric, anti-American anger, his "incendiary language," and his "views that denigrate both the greatness and goodness of our nation; that rightly offend white and black alike." This was the first campaign speech in American history that confronted race head on in a complex and thoughtful way.

The controversy probably helped Obama in three ways. First, it gave him a forum to once again discuss race with the entire nation listening. He frankly confronted the dilemma of race in the United States. He was able to talk about segregation, racism, and poverty, while at the same time extolling the progress the nation had made in the last half century. He noted that Rev. Wright's "profound mistake" was "not that he spoke about racism in our society," but that

> he spoke as if our society was static; as if no progress has been made; as if this country—a country that has made it possible for one of his own members to run for the highest office in the land . . . is still irrevocably bound to a tragic past.

Thus, Obama was able to discuss race and the need for change and progress without seeming radical or threatening. He used the speech to reiterate his support for unity and cooperative change. The Wright incident provided Obama with yet another forum to denounce "a politics that breeds division, and conflict, and cynicism."

He also used the speech to frankly discuss the place of race in his own campaign. He noted that "at various stages in the campaign, some commentators have deemed me either 'too black' or 'not black enough.'" He pointed out that "the press has scoured every exit poll for the latest evidence of racial polarization." He used the Wright incident to denounce this search for racial polarization, echoing his 2004 convention speech that "There's not a black America and white America and Latino America and Asian America; there's the United States of America."

The speech also gave Obama the opportunity—again with all of the nation's media listening—to underscore his own religious values. He spoke of how Wright had "helped introduce me to my Christian faith," and how this faith was tied to his own agenda of reaching out to the dispossessed in America. Obama's refusal to reject Wright—while rejecting his inflammatory rhetoric—was probably useful in shoring up the inroads Obama was making among evangelicals in the "red states." In the general election this would help Obama carry both Virginia and Indiana, states that had not voted Democratic since 1964, and North Carolina, which had not voted Democratic since 1976.

By the end of the spring it was clear Obama had the nomination in hand, although Senator Clinton refused to concede till shortly before the Democratic convention. His victory was not only a result of skillful campaigning and brilliant fund-raising. Obama also won on the key issue of the moment: the Iraq War. Obama had denounced the war from the beginning. Clinton had initially supported it, and throughout her campaign she waffled on where she really stood. In many ways this represented the "old politics" that Obama was also running against. Obama stood for change—his campaign slogan was "Change You Can Believe In." Clinton stood in part for the past.

With the economy teetering toward free fall and the Iraq War turning into an increasingly bloody conflict with no chance of ending soon, Obama's mantra of Change was enough for most Americans. He was aided in the general election by John McCain's choice of Sarah Palin as a running mate. Inexperienced, shrill, and far more conservative than her running mate or most Americans, Palin stood in contrast to Obama's choice of a long-time Washington insider, Joe Biden. McCain increasingly moved to the right in his campaign, backing away from issues such as immigration reform or even his opposition to torture, that made him at first appear to be a different kind of Republican.

Significantly, General Colin Powell, a moderate Republican who had been secretary of state in the Bush administration, endorsed Obama a few weeks before the election. Powell was a long-time friend of McCain, who was a decorated veteran of the Vietnam War. Powell did not endorse Obama because they were both black. Indeed, Powell had been a stalwart supporter of a black presence in the Republican Party. Rather, Powell rejected McCain for his divisive and dishonest campaign, his choice of Palin as a running mate, and because of Obama's strength. Powell frankly doubted that McCain could handle the economic crisis facing the nation. He declared that McCain's campaign was "over the top" in its negativity, and that Sarah Palin was not fit to be a heartbeat away from the presidency. In his endorsement Powell denounced Republicans for insinuating that Obama was Muslim: "Well, the correct answer is, he is not a Muslim, he's a Christian. He's always been a Christian." But then General Powell made a strong plea for religious freedom:

> But the really right answer is, what if he is? Is there something wrong with being a Muslim in this country? The answer's no, that's not America. Is there something wrong with some seven-year-old Muslim-American kid believing that he or she could be president? Yet, I have heard senior members of my own party drop the suggestion, "He's a

Muslim and he might be associated with terrorists." This is not the way we should be doing it in America.

Powell's endorsement was not solely based on McCain and Palin. Implicitly, Powell, a war hero and former four star general, acknowledged that Obama was prepared to lead America during wartime, as well as deal with the nation's growing economic crisis. Most importantly, Powell realized, as by this time a majority of Americans had, that Obama had set the right tone for the campaign and the nation. On NBC's Meet the Press General Powell declared:

> I come to the conclusion that, because of his ability to inspire, because of the inclusive nature of his campaign, because he is reaching out all across America, because of who he is and his rhetorical abilities—and you have to take that into account—as well as his substance—he has both style and substance—he has met the standard of being a successful president, being an exceptional president.

Powell's endorsement was the final crowning of Obama as the next president. Sixteen days later the nation would confirm this as Obama won an impressive victory, winning 53 percent of the popular vote and 365 electoral votes to McCain's 173. Obama swept the Northeast, carried Virginia, North Carolina, and Florida in the South, carried the entire Pacific Coast except Alaska, and every midwestern state except Missouri. He also carried Colorado and New Mexico. He lost Missouri by less than 4,000 votes and Montana by less than 13,000 votes.

Obama ran better than any Democrat since the Civil War except Franklin D. Roosevelt and Lyndon Johnson. Obama won 78 percent of the Jewish vote and 95 percent of the black vote. Fifty-six percent of all women voted for him, in contrast to Bill Clinton and Al Gore, who won 54 percent of all women. Clearly, defeating Hillary Clinton did not hurt him with women. McCain's choice of Sarah Palin as a running mate probably helped Obama, because many women saw the choice as cynical, opportunistic, and indeed insulting to women because Palin was so clearly unqualified to be on the ticket. Obama captured a majority of Hispanic voters and non-Hispanic Roman Catholics. He won more than two-thirds of voters under thirty.

America's First Black President

Obama's election marks a turning point in American history. As noted at the beginning of this chapter, he is the first African American to be elected to the nation's highest office. Although elected with strong black support, he was never the "black candidate" but was always the candidate who happened to be black. Unlike conservative blacks, such as Justice Clarence Thomas or his senatorial opponent in 2004, Alan Keyes, Obama did not reject issues that were of most concern to blacks. On the contrary he confronted racism and the heritage of segregation as well as the culture of poverty that plagues minority communities. He also gave more than lip service to issues of diversity. Under Obama Eric Holder became the first black attorney general of the United States. His original cabinet had seven women, including Secretary of State Hillary Rodham Clinton. In all there were four African Americans, three Asian Americans and two Hispanics in the cabinet. Unlike Bush, who only appointed members of his own party, Obama brought Republicans into the cabinet as well. This reflects the openness of his administration, and his belief in real change. His administration is likely to be the most integrated, diverse, and politically complex in the nation's history. His first nomination to the U.S. Supreme Court, Sonia Sotomayor, is the first Hispanic justice and only the third woman to sit on the Court.

As he entered office, issues of race and diversity were not, however, the central problems Obama faced. He inherited two wars from President Bush, as well as a legacy of torture in Guantanamo, and an uncertain legal status of men captured in Afghanistan, the United States, and elsewhere in connection with the war on terror. The economy was in shambles. Unemployment was higher than at any other time since the Great Depression while the stock market had lost more value than at any other time since the Great Depression. Obama noted these problems at the beginning of his inaugural address:

> That we are in the midst of crisis is now well understood. Our nation is at war against a far-reaching network of violence and hatred. Our economy is badly weakened, a consequence of greed and irresponsibility on the part of some but also our collective failure to make hard choices and prepare the nation for a new age.

The crisis was clear: "Homes have been lost, jobs shed, businesses shuttered. Our health care is too costly, our schools fail too many, and each day brings further evidence that the ways we use energy strengthen our adversaries and threaten our planet."

His inaugural address was filled with references to historic moments—Gettysburg and Normandy; the sacrifices of previous generations, and the need to develop new technologies and new programs to both turn the economy around and plan for the future. He also acknowledged the nation's past failures, even as he used them to illustrate the nation's great strength: "we have tasted the bitter swill of civil war and segregation and emerged from that dark chapter stronger and more united."

In setting out his agenda, Obama marked a new era. Since Ronald Reagan politicians in both parties had been afraid of activist government, mirroring Reagan's claim that government was not the solution, it was the problem. But, nearly three decades of mostly Republican government had brought the economy to a standstill, thrown millions out of work, and displaced millions more from their homes. Savings, retirement funds, and housing values had disappeared almost overnight as the Bush administration came to an end, while America's reputation abroad had been destroyed by the administration's use of torture and its unwise and failed military adventures. Obama offered plans to rebuild America's infrastructure, finally create a health care system that could serve all Americans, and revitalize the economy. Not since Lyndon Johnson had a president begun with such a long and detailed list of goals and plans.

Ending his inaugural with a reference to the struggle for Independence and the fundamental need to preserve liberty for all, Obama also both reiterated his historic moment, reminding the nation of its heritage of racism and how far it had progressed:

This is the meaning of our liberty and our creed, why men and women and children of every race and every faith can join in celebration across this magnificent mall. And why a man whose father less than 60 years ago might not have been served at a local restaurant can now stand before you to take a most sacred oath.

However his administration turns out, the new president inaugurated a new age and a new politics as he took the oath of office. Obama's election surely changed America, just as it symbolized how much America has changed.

Further Reading

Dougherty, Steve. *Hopes and Dreams: The Story of Barack Obama.* New York: Black Dog & Leventhal, 2007.

Mendell, David. *Obama: From Promise to Power.* New York: HarperCollins, 2007.

Niven, Steven J. *Barack Obama: A Pocket Biography of Our 44th President.* New York: Oxford University Press, 2009.

Obama, Barack. *Dreams of My Father: A Story of Race and Inheritance.* New York: Three Rivers Press, 1994, 2004.

——. Keynote Speech, Democratic National Convention, 2004, available at: http://www.washingtonpost.com/wp-dyn/articles/A19751-2004Jul27.html.

——. *The Audacity of Hope: Thoughts on Reclaiming the American Dream.* New York: Crown Publishers, 2006.

——. *Change We Can Believe In: Barack Obama's Plan to Renew America's Promise.* New York: Three Rivers Press, 2008.

African Americans and the Presidency
A Selected Bibliography

BRUCE A. GLASRUD AND CARY D. WINTZ

Ali, Omar H. "Independent Black Voices from the Late 19th Century: Black Populists and the Struggle against the Southern Democracy." *Souls* 7.2 (2005): 4–18.

——. *In the Balance of Power: Independent Black Politics and Third-Party Movements in the United States*. Athens: Ohio University Press, 2008.

Allen, Robert L. *Reluctant Reformers: Racism and Social Reform Movements in the United States*. Washington, DC: Howard University Press, 1983.

Bailey, Harry A., Jr., ed. *Negro Politics in America*. Columbus, Ohio: Charles E. Merrill Books, 1967.

Barber, Floyd, ed. *The Black Power Revolt: A Collection of Essays*. Boston: Porter Sargent Press, 1968.

Barker, Lucius Jefferson, and Mack H. Jones, eds. *African Americans and the American Political System*. 3rd ed. New York: Prentice Hall, 1994.

Barker, Lucius J., Mack H. Jones, and Katherine Tate, eds. *African Americans and the American Political System*. 4th ed. Upper Saddle River, NJ: Prentice Hall, 1999.

Bass, Charlotta. *Forty Years: Memoirs from the Pages of a Great Newspaper*. Los Angeles: Charlotta Bass, 1960.

Beatty, Bess. *A Revolution Gone Backwards: The Black Response to National Politics, 1876–1896*. New York: Greenwood Press, 1987.

Bell, Howard H. "National Negro Conventions of the Middle 1840s: Moral Suasion vs. Political Action." *Journal of Negro History* 42.4 (1957): 247–260.

——. *A Survey of the Negro Convention Movement, 1830–1861*. Reprint. New York: Arno Press, 1970.

Brooke, Edward W. *Bridging the Divide: My Life*. Piscataway, NJ: Rutgers University Press, 2007.

Brown, Elaine. *A Taste of Power: A Black Woman's Story*. New York: Anchor Books, 1993.

Brown, Willie. *Basic Brown: My Life and Our Times.* New York: Simon and Schuster, 2008.

Buni, Andrew. *The Negro in Virginia Politics, 1902–1965.* Charlottesville: University Press of Virginia, 1967.

Bush, Rod, ed. *The New Black Vote: Politics and Power in Four American Cities.* San Francisco: Synthesis Publications, 1984.

Callahan, Linda Florence. "A Fantasy-Theme Analysis of the Political Rhetoric of the Reverend Jesse Louis Jackson, The First Serious Black Candidate for the Office of President of the United States." Ph.D. dissertation, Ohio State University, 1987.

Carmichael, Stokely S., and Charles V. Hamilton. *Black Power: The Politics of Liberation in America.* New York: Random House, 1968.

Chisholm, Shirley. *Unbought and Unbossed.* Boston: Houghton Mifflin, 1970.

———. *The Good Fight.* New York: Harper & Row, 1973.

Christopher, Maurine. *Black Americans in Congress.* New York: Thomas Y. Crowell Company, 1976.

Clay, William L. *Just Permanent Interests: Black Americans in Congress, 1870–1991.* New York: Amistad Press, 1992.

Clemente, Frank, and Frank Watkins, eds. *Keep Hope Alive: Jesse Jackson's 1988 Presidential Campaign.* Boston: South End Press, 1989.

Clines, Francis X. "The Powell Decision." *New York Times.* November 9, 1995.

Committee on House Administration of the U.S. House of Representatives. *Black Americans in Congress, 1870–2007.* Washington, DC, 2008.

Cook, Samuel D. "The Tragic Myth of Black Power." *New South* (Summer 1966): 58–64.

Cruse, Harold. "The Black Political Process—Myth or Reality: A Theoretical Analysis." *Afro-American Communicator* 1.1 (1979): 1–13.

Daniels, Ron. "The National Black Political Assembly: Building Independent Black Politics in the 1980s." *The Black Scholar* 11 (March/April 1980): 32–42.

Davidson, Chandler, and Bernard Grofman, eds. *Quiet Revolution in the South: The Impact of the Voting Rights Act, 1965–1990.* Princeton, NJ: Princeton University Press, 1994.

Davis, Angela. *Angela Davis—An Autobiography.* New York: Random House, 1974.

———. *Women, Race & Class.* New York: Random House, 1981.

Davis, Benjamin. *Communist Councilman from Harlem.* New York: International Publishers, 1969.

Dawson, Michael C. *Behind the Mule: Race and Class in African-American Politics.* Princeton, NJ: Princeton University Press, 1994.

Dellums, Ronald V. *Lying Down with the Lions: A Public Life from the Streets of Oakland to the Halls of Power.* Boston: Beacon Press, 2000.

Duckett, Alfred. *Changing of the Guard: The New Breed of Black Politicians.* New York: Coward, McCann & Geoghegan, 1972.

Dymally, Mervyn. *The Black Politician: His Struggle for Power.* Belmont, Calif.: Duxbury Press, 1971.

Elliot, Jeffrey M. *Black Voices in American Politics.* San Diego: Harcourt Brace Jovanovich, 1986.

Foner, Eric, "Politics and Prejudice: The Free Soil Party and the Negro, 1849–1852." *Journal of Negro History* 50 (October 1965): 239–258.

Foner, Philip S., and James S. Allen. *American Communism and Black Americans: A Documentary History, 1919–1929.* Philadelphia: Temple University Press, 1987.

Frady, Marshall. *Jesse: The Life and Pilgrimage of Jesse Jackson.* New York: Random House, 1996.

Freer, Regina. "L. A. Race Woman: Charlotta Bass and the Complexities of Black Political Development in Los Angeles." *American Quarterly* 56: 607–632.

Fulani, Lenora B. *The Making of a Fringe Candidate, 1992.* New York: Castillo International, 1992.

Gibbons, Arnold. *Race, Politics, and the White Media: The Jesse Jackson Campaigns.* Lanham, MD: University Press of America, 1993.

Gill, Laverne McCain. *African American Women in Congress: Forming and Transforming History.* New Brunswick, NJ: Rutgers University Press, 1997.

Gillette, William. *The Right to Vote: Politics and the Passage of the Fifteenth Amendment.* Baltimore: The Johns Hopkins Press, 1965.

Gilmore, Glenda Elizabeth. *Defying Dixie: The Radical Roots of Civil Rights, 1919–1950.* New York: W. W. Norton, 2008.

Glasrud, Bruce A. "Blacks and Texas Politics during the Twenties." *Red River Valley Historical Review* 7 (Spring 1982): 39–53.

——. "Obama's Victory—a Texas Connection." *Gilmer Mirror* (January 11, 2009).

Gomes, Robert, and Linda Williams, eds. *From Exclusion to Inclusion: The Long Struggle for African American Political Power.* Westport, CT: Greenwood Press, 1992.

Gong, May May, "National Black Independent Political Party Sabotaged by Democrats." *Socialist Action* (February 1989).

Gosnell, Harold F. *Negro Politicians: The Rise of Negro Politics in Chicago.* 1935. Chicago: University of Chicago Press, 1967.

Gross, Bella. "The First National Negro Convention." *Journal of Negro History* 31 (1966): 435–443.

Henderson, Lenneal J., Jr., ed. *Black Political Life in the United States.* San Francisco: Chandler Publishing, 1973.

Henry, Charles. *Jesse Jackson: The Search for Common Ground.* Oakland, CA: Black Scholar Press, 1991.

Holden, Matthew. *The Politics of the Black "Nation."* New York: Chandler, 1973.

Holmes, Warren N. *The National Black Independent Party: Political Insurgency or Ideological Convergence?* New York: Routledge, 1999.

Horton, Gerald. *Communist Front? The Civil Rights Congress, 1946–1956.* Rutherford, N.J.: Fairleigh Dickinson Press, 1988.

Hughes, Alvin C. "The National Negro Congress Movement." Ph.D. dissertation, Ohio State University, 1982.

Hutchinson, Earl Ofari. *Blacks and Reds: Race and Class in Conflict, 1919–1990.* East Lansing: Michigan State University Press, 1995.

Ifill, Gwen. *The Breakthrough: Politics and Race in the Age of Obama.* New York: Doubleday, 2009.

Jackson, Jesse, Jr., and Frank Watkins. *A More Perfect Union: Advancing New American Rights.* New York: Welcome Rain, 2001.

James, Winston. "Being Red and Black in Jim Crow America: On the Ideology and Travails of Afro-America's Socialist Pioneers, 1877–1930." *Souls* 1.4 (1999): 45–63.

Jenkins, Elaine Brown. *Jumping Double Dutch: A New Agenda for Blacks and the Republican Party.* Silver Spring, Md.: Beckham House Publishers, 1996.

Johnson, Cedric. *Revolutionaries to Race Leaders: Black Power and the Making of African American Politics.* St. Paul: University of Minnesota Press, 2007.

Jordan, Barbara. *Barbara Jordan: A Self-Portrait*. New York: Doubleday, 1979.

Key, V. O. *Southern Politics in State and Nation*. New ed. Knoxville: University of Tennessee Press, 1984.

Kleppner Paul. *Chicago Divided: The Making of a Black Mayor*. DeKalb: Northern Illinois University Press, 1985.

Kurlander, Gabrielle, and Jacqueline Salit, eds. *Independent Black Leadership in America: Minister Louis Farrakhan, Dr. Lenora Fulani, Reverend Al Sharpton*. New York: Castillo International Publications, 1990.

Ladd, Everett Carl, Jr. *Negro Political Leadership in the South*. Ithaca: Cornell University Press, 1966; New York: Atheneum, 1969.

Lewinson, Paul. *Race, Class, and Party: A History of Negro Suffrage and White Politics in the South*. New York: Grosset & Dunlap, 1965.

Loewenstein, Gaither, and Lyttleton T. Sanders. "Bloc Voting, Rainbow Coalitions, and the Jackson Presidential Candidacy." *Journal of Black Studies* 18 (September 1987): 86–96.

Lusane, Clarence. *African Americans at the Crossroads: The Restructuring of Black Leadership and the 1992 Elections*. Boston: South End Press, 1994.

Mabry, Marcus. *Twice as Good: Condoleeza Rice and Her Path to Power*. New York: Modern Times, 2007.

McAdam, Doug. *Political Process and the Development of Black Insurgency, 1930–1970*. Chicago: University of Chicago Press, 1982.

McFeely, William S. *Frederick Douglass*. New York: W. W. Norton, 1995.

Marable, Manning. *Black American Politics: From the Washington Marches to Jesse Jackson*. London: Thetford Press, 1985.

——. *Race, Reform, and Rebellion: The Second Reconstruction in Black America, 1945–1990*. 2nd ed. Jackson: University Press of Mississippi, 1991.

Matthews, Donald R., and James W. Prothro. *Negroes and the New Southern Politics*. New York: Harcourt, Brace & World, 1966.

Maxwell, William J. *New Negro Old Left: African-American Writing and Communism Between the Wars*. New York: Columbia University Press, 1999.

Moon, Henry L. *Balance of Power: The Negro Vote*. New York: Doubleday, 1948.

Morris, Lorenzo, ed. *The Social and Political Implications of the 1984 Jesse Jackson Presidential Campaign*. New York: Praeger Publishers, 1990.

Neary, John. *Julian Bond: Black Rebel*. New York: Morrow, 1971.

Obama, Barack. *Dreams from My Father*. New York: Three Rivers Press, 1995.

——. *The Audacity of Hope: Thoughts on Reclaiming the American Dream*. New York: Crown, 2006.

Packer, George. "The New Liberalism." *The New Yorker* (November 17, 2008): 1–7.

Pease, Jane H., and William H. Pease. "Black Power—The Debate in 1840." *Phylon* 29 (1968): 19–26.

——. "The Negro Convention Movement." In *Key Issues in the Afro-American Experience*, ed. Nathan I. Huggins, Martin Kilson, and Daniel M. Fox, 191–205. New York: Harcourt Brace Jovanovich, 1971.

Powell, Colin L., with Joseph E. Persico. *My American Journey*. New York: Random House, 1995.

Preston, Michael B., Lenneal J. Henderson, Jr., and Paul Puryear, eds. *The New Black Politics: The Search for Political Power*. 2nd ed. New York: Longman, 1987.

Record, Wilson. *The Negro and the Communist Party*. Chapel Hill: University of North Carolina Press, 1951.

———. *Race and Radicalism: The NAACP and the Communist Party in Conflict.* Ithaca, NY: Cornell University Press, 1964.

Reed, Adolph L., Jr. *The Jesse Jackson Phenomenon: The Crisis of Purpose in Afro-American Politics.* New Haven: Yale University Press, 1986.

Reid, Willie. *Black Women's Struggle for Equality.* New York: Pathfinder Press, 1976.

Remmick, David. "The Joshua Generation: Race and the Campaign of Barack Obama." *The New Yorker* (November 17, 2008): 1–13.

Rogers, J. A. *The Five Negro Presidents.* St. Petersburg, FL: Helga M. Rogers, 1965.

Romero, Patricia W., ed. *In Black America 1968: The Year of Awakening.* Washington, DC: United Publishing, 1969.

Shaw, Lisa, ed. *In His Own Words: Colin Powell.* New York: Berkeley Publishing, 1995.

Singh, Nikhil Pal. *Black is a Country: Race and the Unfinished Struggle for Democracy.* Cambridge, MA: Harvard University Press, 2004.

Singh, Robert. *The Congressional Black Caucus: Racial Politics in the U.S. Congress.* Thousand Oaks, CA: Sage, 1998.

Stone, Chuck. *Black Political Power in America.* Indianapolis: Bobbs-Merrill, 1968.

———. "Black Politics: Third Force, Third Party, or Third Class Influence?" *The Black Scholar* 1 (December 1969): 11.

Swain, Carol M. *Black Faces, Black Interests: The Representation of African Americans in Congress.* Cambridge, MA: Harvard University Press, 1993.

Tate, Katherine. *From Protest to Politics: The New Black Voters in American Elections.* Cambridge, MA: Harvard University Press, 1993.

Taylor, George E. "The National Liberty Party." *Voice of the Negro* 1 (October 1904): 479–481.

Vincent, Theodore G. *The Legacy of Vicente Guerrero, Mexico's First Black Indian President.* Gainesville: University Press of Florida, 2001.

Walters, Ronald W. "Black Presidential Politics in 1980: Bargaining or Begging?" *The Black Scholar* 11 (March/April 1980): 22–31.

———. *Black Presidential Politics in America: A Strategic Approach.* Albany: State University of New York Press, 1988.

———. *White Nationalism, Black Interests.* Detroit: Wayne State University Press, 2003.

———. *Freedom Is Not Enough: Black Voters, Black Candidates, and American Presidential Politics.* Lanham, MD: Rowman & Littlefield, 2005.

Walters, Ronald W., and Lucius J. Barker, eds. *Jesse Jackson's 1984 Presidential Campaign: Challenge and Change in American Politics.* Urbana: University of Illinois Press, 1989.

Walters, Ronald W., and Robert C. Smith. *African American Leadership.* Albany: State University of New York Press, 1999.

Walton, Hanes Jr. "The Negro in the Early Third Party Movements." *Negro Educational Review* 19 (April 1968): 73–82.

———. *The Negro in Third Party Politics.* Philadelphia: Dorrance, 1969.

———. "Blacks and the 1968 Third Parties." *Negro Educational Review* 21 (January 1970): 19–23.

———. *Black Political Parties: A Historical and Political Analysis.* New York: The Free Press, 1972.

———. *Black Politics: A Theoretical and Structural Analysis.* Philadelphia: J. B. Lippincott, 1972.

——. *Black Republicans: The Politics of the Black and Tans.* Metuchen, NJ: Scarecrow Press, 1975.

——. *Invisible Politics: Black Political Behavior.* Albany: State University of New York Press, 1985.

——, ed. *Black Politics and Black Political Behavior: A Linkage Analysis.* Westport, CT: Praeger, 1994.

——. *African American Power and Politics: The Political Context Variable.* New York: Columbia University Press, 1997.

Walton, Hanes, Jr., and William H. Boone. "Black Political Parties: A Demographic Analysis." *Journal of Black Studies* 5.1 (1974): 86–95.

Walton, Hanes, Jr., and Ronald Clark. "Black Presidential Candidates: Past and Present." *New South* (Spring 1970): 6–10.

Walton, Hanes, Jr., and Vernon Gray. "Black Politics at the Democratic and Republican Conventions, 1868–1972." *Phylon* 36 (1975): 269–278.

Walton, Hanes, Jr., and Robert C. Smith. *American Politics and the African American Quest for Universal Freedom.* New York: Longman, 2000.

Walton, Hanes, Jr., Sharon Wright, and Frank Pryor. "Texas African American Republicans: The Electoral Revolt in the 1920 Presidential and Gubernatorial Election." *National Conference of Black Political Scientists Newsletter* 16 (Spring 2002): 1–6.

Walton, Hanes, Jr., Josephine Allen, Sherman Puckett, and Donald R. Deskins, eds. *Letters to President Obama: Americans Share Their Hopes and Dreams with the First African American President.* New York: Skyhorse Publishing, 2009.

Walton, Hanes, Jr., Josephine A. V. Allen, Sherman Puckett, Donald R. Deskins, Jr., and Billie Dee Tate. "The Literature on African-American Presidential Candidates." *Journal of Race & Policy* (Spring/Summer 2008): 103–124.

Warren, Mac, ed. *Independent Black Political Action, 1954–78.* New York: Pathfinder Press, 1982.

Wesley, Charles H. "The Participation of Negroes in Anti-Slavery Political Parties." *Journal of Negro History* 29.1 (January 1941): 32–76.

Wilson, James Q. *Negro Politics: The Search for Leadership.* New York: Free Press, 1960.

Wittner, Lawrence S. "The National Negro Congress: A Reassessment." *American Quarterly* 22 (1968): 883–901.

Wright, George C. "Black Political Insurgency in Louisville, Kentucky: The Lincoln Independent Party of 1921." *Journal of Negro History* 50 (October 1965): 239–258.

Wright, Nathan, Jr., ed. *What Black Politicians Are Saying.* New York: Hawthorn Books, 1972.

Yancey, Dwayne. *When Hell Froze Over: The Untold Story of Doug Wilder, A Black Politician's Rise to Power in the South.* Dallas: Taylor Pub, 1989.

Contributors

Omar H. Ali is on the faculty of the History Department at Towson University in Maryland; a graduate of the London School of Economics and Political Science, he received his Ph.D. from Columbia University. Ali published *In the Balance of Power: Independent Black Politics and Third-Party Movements in the United States* (2008), and has served as a guest editor of *Souls: A Critical Journal of Black Politics, Culture, and Society*. He is working on a book entitled *Black Populism in the New South*.

Josephine A. V. Allen is Professor Emerita of Policy Analysis and Management in the College of Human Ecology at Cornell University where she became the first African American to be tenured. She earned her Ph.D. at the University of Michigan, and has a life commitment to social justice. Among her publications is a co-edited study *Youth in Transition: A Comparative Study of Adolescent Girls in Community-based and Residential Programs*.

Charles Orson Cook teaches American History in the Honors College at the University of Houston; he earned his Ph.D. in History at the University of Houston. Cook has special interests in nineteenth-century popular culture and American race relations. Among his publications are *The Battle of Cape Esperance: Encounter at Guadalcanal* and *Horatio Alger: Gender and Success in the Gilded Age*.

David Cullen is Professor of History at Collin College. Among his most recent publications are, "Back to the Future: Eugenics, A Bibliographic Essay" in *The Public Historian: Journal of Public Policy* (Summer 2007) and "Populism" in the *Encyclopedia of American Social Movements* (2004); he is co-editor of the forthcoming collection of essays, *The Texas Left: The First Century, 1865–1965* (Texas A&M University Press, 2010).

Donald R. Deskins, Jr. is Professor Emeritus of Urban Geography and Sociology at the University of Michigan. He holds a Ph.D. in Geography from the University of Michigan.

Paul Finkelman is President William McKinley Distinguished Professor of Law and Senior Fellow, Government Law Center at Albany Law School. A specialist in American legal history, race, and the law, Finkelman is the author of more than a hundred scholarly articles and more than twenty books. Among his books are *An Imperfect Union: Slavery, Federalism, and Comity*, *Slavery and the Founders: Race and Liberty in the Age of Jefferson*; he is editor in chief of the eight-volume Oxford University Press *Encyclopedia of African American History*, and editor of *Encyclopedia of the United States in the Nineteenth Century* and *The Encyclopedia of American Political History*.

Bruce A. Glasrud, an independent historian residing in Seguin, Texas, is Professor Emeritus of History, California State University, East Bay, retired Dean, School of Arts and Sciences, Sul Ross State University, and a Fellow of the Texas State Historical Association. A specialist in the history of blacks in the West, Glasrud has authored or co-authored more than thirteen books including *Black Women in Texas History*, *The African American West: A Century of Short Stories*, and *Buffalo Soldiers in the West*.

Dwonna Naomi Goldstone is an Associate Professor in the Department of Languages and Literature, Coordinator of the African American Studies Minor, and Associate Dean in the College of Arts and Letters at Austin Peay State University in Clarksville, Tennessee. Goldstone received her doctorate in American Civilization from the University of Texas at Austin. She is the author of *Integrating the Forty Acres: The Fifty-year Struggle for Racial Equality at the University of Texas*, which won the 2006 Coral H. Tullis Memorial Prize for best book on Texas history. She lives in Nashville, Tennessee, with her three dogs: Satchel Paige, Butterfly McQueen, and Charlie Parker.

Maxine D. Jones is Professor of History at the Florida State University. She is the co-author with Joe M. Richardson of *Talladega College: The First Century* and *African Americans in Florida*. Jones is also co-author with Joe

M. Richardson of *Education for Liberation: The American Missionary Association and African Americans, 1890 to the Civil Rights Movement* (2009). Professor Jones served as Principal Investigator for the Rosewood Academic Study commissioned by the Florida legislature and is currently researching blacks in twentieth-century Florida.

Sherman C. Puckett works with the Wayne County Department of Public Services. He holds a Ph.D. in Urban and Regional Planning from the University of Michigan. He lives in Detroit, Michigan.

James M. Smallwood is Professor Emeritus at Oklahoma State University where he taught Black History for twenty-six years. Smallwood is the author or editor of thirty-five books and more than forty-five articles. His *Time of Hope, Time of Despair: Black Texans During Reconstruction* won the Texas Historical Association's Coral Tullis Award in 1982 for best book of the year on Texas history. He became the first scholar to win the Tullis Award twice for his 2008 book *The Feud that Wasn't,* a story of violence in Reconstruction Texas. He is a Fellow of the East Texas Historical Association and the Texas State Historical Association.

Jean Van Delinder is Associate Professor of Sociology, with affiliated appointments in American Studies, Africana-African American Studies and Women's Studies, at Oklahoma State University. She received her Ph.D. in Sociology from the University of Kansas. Her book, *Struggles before Brown: Early Civil Rights Protests and their Significance Today* (2008) examines the early years of the civil rights movement in the Midwest. Van Delinder also published several articles in leading journals.

Hanes Walton, Jr. is Professor of Political Science at the University of Michigan and Senior Research Scientist at the Center for Political Studies in the Institute for Social Research. He received a Ph.D. in Political Science from Howard University. Among his numerous publications are *Black Politics and Black Political Behavior, African American Power and Politics: The Political Context Variable,* and *Invisible Politics: Black Political Behavior.*

Carolyn Wedin is Professor Emeritus of English at the University of Wisconsin, Whitewater. A frequent lecturer and speaker, Wedin's publications include *Inheritors of the Spirit: Mary White Ovington and the Founding of the NAACP* and *Jessie Redmon Fauset, Black American Writer.*

Kyle G. Wilkison, Professor of History at Collin College, Plano, Texas, earned his Ph.D. in History from Vanderbilt University in 1995. He writes about working people and radical movements. His book, *Yeomen, Share-*

croppers and Socialists: Plain Folk Protest in Texas, 1870–1914 (2008), won a Fehrenbach Book Award.

Cary D. Wintz is a Professor of History at Texas Southern University and is a specialist in black political history and the Harlem Renaissance. Wintz is the author of numerous books including *Harlem Speaks, Black Culture and the Harlem Renaissance,* and *African American Political Thought, 1890–1930.* He also served as an editor of the Oxford University Press five-volume *Encyclopedia of African American History, 1896 to the Present.*

Index

Page numbers in italics indicate photographs. Page numbers followed by "t" indicate tables.

239

Kwanzaa:
Black Power and the Making of the African-American Holiday Tradition

By
Keith Mayes

"A groundbreaking, thorough, and illuminating discourse on Kwanzaa by one of the new leaders in the field. *Kwanzaa: Black Power and the Making of the African-American Holiday Tradition* is a vital resource that will enrich and enhance the discipline of African-American Studies. A pioneering work about a deeply important holiday."
—M.K. Asante, Jr., director of *The Black Candle: A Kwanzaa Celebration*

"Keith Mayes situates Kwanzaa's invention within the black holiday tradition while demonstrating how embedded it was in the cultural nationalism of Black Power. Those wishing to further their understanding of African American holidays and their place in American culture would do well to read this book."
—Ellen M. Litwicki, Professor of History, State University of New York at Fredonia—author of *America's Public Holidays, 1865–1920*

"*Kwanzaa* is an important contribution to our understanding of the Black Power movement, cultural nationalism and the history of Kwanzaa ... it is certain to be the leading text surveying the history of Kwanzaa and its place in the history of African American cultural politics."
—Scot Brown, author of *Fighting for US: Maulana Karenga, the US Organization, and Black Cultural Nationalism*

Since 1966, Kwanzaa has been celebrated as a black holiday tradition—an annual recognition of cultural pride in the African American community. But how did this holiday originate, and what is its broader cultural significance?

Kwanzaa: Black Power and the Making of the African-American Holiday Tradition explores the political beginning and later expansion of Kwanzaa, from its start as a Black Power holiday, to its current place as one of the most mainstream of the black holiday traditions. For those wanting to learn more about this alternative observance practiced by countless African Americans and how Kwanzaa fits into the larger black holiday tradition, Keith A. Mayes gives an accessible and definitive account of the movements and individuals that pushed to make this annual celebration a reality, and shows how African-Americans brought the black freedom struggle to the American calendar.

Clear and thoughtful, *Kwanzaa* is the perfect introduction to what is now the quintessential African American holiday.

ISBN 10: 0–415–99854–9 (hbk)
ISBN 10: 0–415–99855–7 (pbk)
ISBN 10: 0–203–87486–2 (ebk)

ISBN 13: 978–0–415–99854–3 (hbk)
ISBN 13: 978–0–415–99855–0 (pbk)
ISBN 13: 978–0–203–87486–8 (ebk)

Available at all good bookshops
For ordering and further information please visit:
www.routledge.com

The Black Power Movement:
Rethinking the Civil Rights Black Power Era
Edited By
Peniel E. Joseph

"In *The Black Power Movement*, Peniel Joseph has assembled a formidable collection of essays by scholars who are rewriting the history of Black Power in America. Too long neglected or dismissed, Black Power is finally receiving the attention it deserves, and Joseph's collection captures the influences, breadth, and complexity of the movement with extraordinary sophistication."

—Robert Self, author of *American Babylon: Race and the Struggle for Postwar Oakland*

"These fresh interpretations of the Black Power movement are eye-opening. This provocative work is core reading for anyone interested in the history and culture of African Americans and of the United States."

—Brenda Gayle Plummer, author of *Window on Freedom: Race, Civil Rights, and Foreign Affairs, 1945–1988*

"*The Black Power Movement* provides compelling reinterpretations of not just the past, but also the present by providing detailed and illuminating case studies of local community struggles, recovering unsung pioneering Black feminists, and the inauguration of cultural practices. This is the most significant collection of work on Black Power since the Black Power Movement."

—Sundiata Keita Cha-Jua, author of *America's First Black Town: Brooklyn, Illinois, 1830–1915*

The Black Power Movement remains an enigma. Often misunderstood and ill-defined, this radical movement is now beginning to receive sustained and serious scholarly attention.

Peniel Joseph has collected the freshest and most impressive list of contributors around to write original essays on the Black Power Movement. Taken together they provide a critical and much needed historical overview of the Black Power era. Offering important examples of undocumented histories of black liberation, this volume offers both powerful and poignant examples of "Black Power Studies" scholarship.

ISBN 10: 0–415–94595–X (hbk)
ISBN 10: 0–415–94596–8 (pbk)

ISBN 13: 978–0–415–94595–0 (hbk)
ISBN 13: 978–0–415–94596–7 (pbk)

Available at all good bookshops
For ordering and further information please visit:
www.routledge.com

Yes We Can?: White Racial Framing and the 2008 Presidential Campaign

By
Adia Wingfield Harvey
and
Joe Feagin

In *Yes We Can?: White Racial Framing and the 2008 Presidential Campaign*, Adia Harvey Wingfield and Joe Feagin offer one of the first sociological analyses of Barack Obama's historic 2008 campaign for the presidency of the United States. Using many events from this unprecedented political campaign as case study data, Harvey Wingfield and Feagin extensively explore its many and striking racial dimensions. To do this, they further develop the concept of the white racial frame, the term for the old and broad white-created worldview that enables people to make sense of and interpret various racial issues, events, and circumstances. Harvey Wingfield and Feagin argue that, far from being a monolithic reality, this white racial framing includes distinctive hard and soft versions, which are periodically met by important counterframes stemming mostly from Americans of color. Both the hard and soft versions of the dominant racial frame, and the important counterframes, are regularly used by people to understand issues and shape everyday actions in U.S. society. In this interesting and provocative book, Harvey Wingfield and Feagin show the many ways that these significant racial frames shaped the reality of this historic presidential campaign and thus of U.S. society.

ISBN 10: 0–415–99986–3 (hbk)
ISBN 10: 0–415–9987–1 (pbk)

ISBN 13: 978–0–415–99986–1 (hbk)
ISBN 13: 978–0–415–99987–8 (pbk)

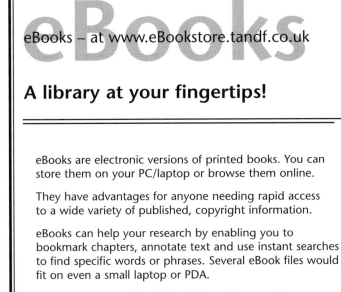